Talbot Baines Reed

Sir Ludar

A story of the days of the Great Queen Bess

Talbot Baines Reed

Sir Ludar
A story of the days of the Great Queen Bess

ISBN/EAN: 9783337321710

Printed in Europe, USA, Canada, Australia, Japan

Cover: Foto ©ninafisch / pixelio.de

More available books at **www.hansebooks.com**

SIR LUDAR

A STORY OF THE DAYS OF THE GREAT QUEEN BESS

BY

TALBOT BAINES REED

Author of
"The Fifth Form at St. Dominic's," "My Friend Smith,"
"Tom, Dick, and Harry," etc., etc.

LONDON
THE OFFICE OF "THE BOY'S OWN PAPER"
4 Bouverie Street and 65 St. Paul's Churchyard

CONTENTS

CHAPTER		PAGE
I.	How I saw my Queen	9
II.	How I served a Disorderly Printer	20
III.	How I rode post-haste to Oxford	29
IV.	How I met a Runaway Scholar	39
V.	How I parted with my Cloak	49
VI.	How I walked with a Rebel	59
VII.	How I found Trouble on my Return	69
VIII.	How I was Cast Adrift	77
IX.	How I caught the *Miséricorde*	87
X.	How we sailed with a Poet of the First Water	98
XI.	How the *Miséricorde* changed her Crew	108
XII.	How we sailed into Leith	119
XIII.	How we brought the Maiden to her Father's House	129
XIV.	How Ludar fired the Beacon on Knocklayd	139
XV.	How Ludar took Dunluce	149
XVI.	How Sorley Boy M'Donnell came home to his Own	159

CONTENTS

CHAPTER		PAGE
XVII.	How a Dog's Head was set on Dublin Gate	170
XVIII.	How I found Myself again in London	180
XIX.	How I was concerned in Treason and Love	190
XX.	How there came Visitors to Master Walgrave's House	199
XXI.	How a certain Man was hanged at Tyburn	209
XXII.	How Master Walgrave fell short of Type	218
XXIII.	How the *Miséricorde* sailed for Rochelle	228
XXIV.	How the Invincible Armada came into British Waters	236
XXV.	How the Dons sailed Up Channel	245
XXVI.	How Ludar brought back the Duke's Letter	255
XXVII.	How Ludar sailed North and I South	264
XXVIII.	How I enlisted on a new Service	274
XXIX.	How Captain Merriman came and went betwixt me and the Light	284
XXX.	How the Sun went down behind Malin	296
XXXI.	How we came into Calm Water after all	304

SIR LUDAR

A STORY OF THE DAYS OF THE GREAT QUEEN BESS

CHAPTER I

How I saw my Queen

EVERY story, whether wise or foolish, grave or gay, must needs have a beginning. How it comes to pass that my story begins on a certain day in May, in the year of our Lord 1585, I can never, although I am far on in life now, properly explain.

For that was not the day on which I was born. That adventure had befallen me eighteen years before, at the parson's little house in Felton Regis. Most people who write their histories have a pride in dragging their readers back to the moment when they first hallooed defiance to this wicked world ; but I, since I have clean forgotten the event, must e'en confess that my story does not begin there. A like adventure chanced often at the parsonage, and, at nine years of age, I reigned king absolute over a nursery full of her Majesty's subjects who called me brother, and quailed before my nod like Helots before the crest of a Spartan. But, as I say, all that is neither here nor there in my story.

Nor, in truth, is that grey September day, when, on the tail of a country hay-cart, I rode tremulously at my dear father's side into London ; where, with much pomp and taking of oaths, I was bound apprentice, body and soul, to Master Robert Walgrave, the printer, in the presence of the worshipful Master, Wardens, and Assistants of the Company of Stationers, who enriched themselves by 2s. 6d. at my father's cost, and looked upon me in a hungry way that made me

SIR LUDAR

tremble in my bones, and long to be out of their sight before they should order the bill of fare for their next feast. That was a day in my life truly, but it was ancient history when my story begins. I had grown a big lad since then, and was the king of Clubs without Temple Bar, and the terror of all young 'prentices for a mile round, who looked up with white cheeks when I swaggered by, and ran with their tails between their legs to hide behind counters and doorposts till I was out of sight.

No ; nor yet does my story begin even at that sad day—alack !—when I stood by my widowed mother at the open grave of him who had been the pillar of our house and the pride of our lives. " Humphrey, my boy," she had said as she placed her hand on my arm and led me, like one in a dream, from the place, " it is God who has taken—He will surely also give. Shall I count all lost, with a stalwart arm like this to lean upon ? " Then she kissed me, and I, for very shame, dried my eyes and held up my head. Ah me ! that was but a year before ; the world had still moved on, the grass covered his grave, and still my story lacked a beginning.

How comes it, then, that this day in May, of all others, should stand up like a wall, as I look back over my life, and seem to me the beginning of all things ? Perhaps this history may show—or, perhaps, he who reads it may come to see that I was right when I said I could not explain it.

It was a great day in London, within and without Temple Bar ; and for me, if for no other reason, it was famous, because on that day, for the first and last time, I saw the great Queen Elizabeth. About eight o'clock, while I stood, as was my wont, setting types in my master's shop, I looked from the window (as was also my wont), and spied two falconers in their green coats, with a trumpeter riding in the midst, ambling citywards. In a moment I dropped my stick (and with it, alack ! a pieful of my master's types), and was out, cap and club, in the Strand, shouting till I was hoarse, " God save her Majesty ! "

On the instant, from every shop far and near, darted 'prentices and journeymen, shouting and waving caps—some because they saw me do so, some because they guessed what was afoot, some because they saw, even now, the flutter of

"GOD SAVE HER MAJESTY"

approaching pennons, and caught the winding of the royal huntsmen's horns along the Strand.

The Queen was coming!

I went mad that day with loyalty. I kicked my fellows for not shouting louder, and such as shouted not at all, I made to shout in a way they least expected. Through the open door of Master Straw's, the horologer's, I spied his two 'prentices, deaf to all the clamour, basely gorging a hasty pudding behind the bench.

"What!" shouted I, bursting in upon them, and seizing each by his cropped head, "what, ye gluttonous pair of porkers, is this the way you welcome her Majesty into our duchy? Is this a time for greasy pudding and smacking of lips? Come outside and shout, or I'll brain you with your own spoons."

Whereupon, forgetting what I did, I dipped the white face of each in his own mess, and dragged them forth, where, to do them justice, they shouted and howled as loud as any one.

And now the Strand overflowed from end to end with loyal citizens. From the windows above, the faces of the city madams beamed, and the white necks of their daughters craned; while behind, with half an eye on us clubs below, peeped, on tiptoe, the maids. At each shop-door stood the grave forms of our masters, thinking, perhaps, of a lost day's profits, and setting the cost thereof against the blessings of her Majesty's happy reign. At the roadside, beggar, scholar, yokel, knight, and noble jostled in a motley throng. But the sight of all that crowd was the 'prentices, who swarmed out into the road, and raised our shouts above the clanging of St. Clement's bells and the trumpets of the Royal servants. 'Twas no pageant we had come out to see. Giants, and whales, and bottomless pits, and salvage men, and the like we could see to our hearts' content on Lord Mayor's Day; and the gilded barges and smoking cannon on the river's side. But it was not every day her Majesty ambled through the city on her hunting horse, and passed our way with her gallants for a day's sport in Epping woods.

As for me, I had no eyes or throat for any but that queenly woman, as she cantered boldly on her white palfrey, a pace or more ahead of her glittering courtiers. Had any one said

SIR LUDAR

to me that Elizabeth was that day neither young nor lovely —had anyone even dared to whisper that she was not divine —I would have brained him with my club where he stood. For a moment her head turned my way, she waved her hand —it had a little whip in it—and her lips moved to some words. Then as I rent the air with a " God save your Majesty ! " she was past.

At Temple Bar, the Lord Mayor and Sheriffs, arrayed for the hunt, with buglers and dogs attending, stood across the way, and with mighty ceremony and palaver admitted her to the City. Woe betide them, for all their gold collars and maces, had they kept her out !

But the halt, short as it was, served our purpose. For there was no more going back to work on a day like this.

" To the front, clubs, and lead the way," shouted I, with what voice was left me.

It was enough for the lads without Temple Bar. They closed on me with a cheer, and followed me at the run, past the gaping Court ushers, past the royal jockeys, past the Queen herself (Heaven bless her !), past Lord Mayor, Sheriffs, and yapping beagles, through the echoing gates of Temple Bar, till we stood at the head of the procession, and longed, with a mighty longing, that someone might dispute the way with us.

But we had no work for our clubs that morning. As we moved forward, our body, like a growing snowball, was swelled by the 'prentices of each ward, shouting as lustily as we, " Make way ! " and hurling defiance, like us, on all the Queen's foes by land and by sea. Even the gay sparks of the Temple gave us no handle for a sally, for they shouted with the best of us.

And so, down Fleet Street and in at the Ludgate, past the square tower of St. Paul's, and along merry Cheap, we passed ; our numbers swelling at every step, till it seemed as if all London was out escorting her Majesty through the city. As you passed below Bow Church you could scarcely hear the clanging of the bells for the shouting of the people.

At the New Exchange there was like to be a battle at last. For the 'prentices of the Bridge had heard the uproar from afar, and swarmed down upon us in a flood, so that had we

WE ARE NOT TO BE PUT ASIDE

not held our own stoutly, we should have been driven back upon the royal huntress herself.

"Stand, if you be men, and fall in after us!" I shouted.

"Ho! ho!" answered they; "since when was the printer's devil outside the Bar made mayor of our town? Follow you us."

It was not a time for bandying words. "From behind us came a shout, "Pass on, pass on; room for the Queen!" And at the word we charged forward, shoulder to shoulder, and brushed those unmannerly mercers and barber-surgeons aside as a torrent the nettles that grow on its bank. Let them follow as they list. The Queen went hunting to-day, and was not to be kept standing for a score of London Bridges, if we knew it.

After that we passed shouting up the Cornhill, and so on to the Bishop's Gate, where at length we halted and made a lane in our midst for her Majesty to ride through.

Never, I think, did monarch ride down a prouder road than that, walled four-deep for the length of two furlongs by youths who would fain have spilt their blood twice over to do her service, and who, since that was denied them, flung their shouts to heaven as she passed, and waved their caps club-high. I think, in truth, she needed no telling what kind of road it was, for as she cantered by her face was flushed and joyous, her head was erect, and the hand she waved clenched on the little whip, as though she grasped her people's hand. Then in a moment she was gone.

Thus for the first and only time did I set eyes on the great maiden Queen; and when all was over, and the clattering hoofs and yelping hounds and winding horns were lost in the distance, I came to myself and found I was both hungry and athirst.

The crowd melted away. Some returned the way they had come: some slunk back to their deserted shops: I to Finsbury Fields. For I accounted it a crime that day to work—I would as soon have set up types on Lord Mayor's Day. This day belonged to her Majesty, and I would e'en spend it in her service, wrestling and leaping in the meadows, and training my body to deeds of valour against her foes.

So I called on my clubs to follow me, and they came, and many besides; for those who might not see the Queen hunt

SIR LUDAR

might see her loyal citizens jump; and on a day like this it was odds if the nimblest 'prentices in all London were not there to make good sport.

Therefore we straggled in a long crowd to Moorgate—man and maid, noble and 'prentice, alderman and oyster-woman, jesting and scolding as we jostled one another in the narrow way, and rejoicing when at length we broke free into the pleasant meadows and smelt the sweetness of the early hay.

Already I spied sport, for there before us swaggered the mercers' 'prentices of London Bridge, ready to settle scores for the affront they had received at the New Exchange.

"Ho! ho!" quoth I, with vast content, "'tis time we had dinner, my lads, if it comes to that."

So we besieged the booths, and fortified ourselves with beef and ale, and felt ready for anything that might happen.

'Twas no battle after all; for, as ill-luck would have it, just as we faced them and bade them come on, the alderman of the Bridge Ward rode up.

"What! a shame on you to mar a day like this with your boyish wrangles! Is there no wrestling-ring, or shooting-butts, or leaping-fence where you can vent your rivalry, without flying at one another's throats like curs? Call you that loyalty? Have we no enemies better worth our mettle than fellow-Englishmen?"

This speech abashed us a little, and the captain of the Bridge 'prentices said, sulkily:

"I care not to break their heads, worship; there's little to be got out of that. Come, lads, we can find better sport in the juggler's booth."

"His worship came in a good hour for you," cried we. "Thank him you can slink away on your own legs this time, and need no one to drag you feet foremost off the Fields."

"Come, come," said the good alderman, "away with such foolish talk. Let's see a match struck up. I myself will give a new long-bow and a sheaf of arrows to the best jumper of you all. What say you? The highest leap and the broadest? Ho, there!" added he, calling a servant to him; "bid them clear a space for a match 'twixt the gallant 'prentices of the Bridge and the gallant 'prentices without Temple Bar. Come, boys; were I forty years younger I'd

THE GOOD OLD ALDERMAN

put you to it to distance me. But my jumping days are gone by, and I am but a judge."

Then we gave him a cheer, the bluff old boy; and, forgetting all our quarrel in the thought of the long-bow and arrows, we trooped at his horse's tail to the open space, and doffed our coats in readiness for the contest.

A great crowd stood round to see us jump. The scene remains in my mind's eye even now. 'Prentices, bare-headed, squatted cross-legged on the grass, bandying their noisy jests, and finding a laugh for everybody and everything. Behind them stood a motley throng of sightseers, men, women, and children, for the most part citizens, but interspersed here and there with gay groups of gentlefolk, and even some who wore the bright trappings of the Court. Behind them the beggars and pickpockets plied their arduous calling; and in the rear of all, at a little distance, wandered the horses of the gentles, cropping the fresh grass, with no eye to the achievements of Temple Bar or London Bridge. Beyond them soared the windmills and the hills of Isledon and Hoxton.

It was a scene familiar to me, for I had often taken it in before; and yet for a while to-day it seemed new, and my eye, as I waited at the post, wandered here and there to detect what it could be which made all seem so strange. After a while I discovered that, wherever else they roamed, my glances returned always to one bright spot, close by where stood a maiden.

It seemed to me I had never known what beauty meant till I looked on her. She was tall, and dressed more simply than many a citizen's wife, and yet her air was that of a goddess. Every movement of her head bore the signs of queenliness; and yet in every feature of her face lurked a sweetness irresistible. At first sight, as you saw her, tall, erect, with her short clustering hair and fearless eyes of blue, you would have been tempted to suppose her a boy in disguise. Yet if you looked a moment longer, the woman in her shone out in every step and gesture. Her cheeks glowed with health and maidenly modesty; and her eyes, that flashed on you one moment almost defiantly, dropped the next in coyness and delicious confusion.

She stood there, conspicuous and radiant amid the jostling crowd, yet wholly heedless of the glances and whispers and

SIR LUDAR

perplexity she drew forth. As for me, I scarcely knew where I was, and when the alderman cried, "Make ready, now," I obeyed him as a man in a dream.

But I recovered myself of a sudden when presently I saw the captain of the Bridge 'prentices, who was a shorter man than I, leap over the bar as high as his own shoulders, and heard the triumphal shouts of his fellows. After him, one by one, came the picked men of either side, but at each leap the bar sprung into the air, and the champions retired worsted from the contest.

Then came my turn. I dared to dart a hurried glance where stood the only onlooker whose applause I coveted. And she turned her head towards me.

So I took my run and cleared the bar.

"A match! a match!" cried the crowd, closing in a step; "a match between Will Peake and Humphrey Dexter."

"And take my sword and cloak," shouted a Bridge boy, who owned neither, "if Will Peake do not overjump the printer's devil's head."

This made me angry. Not that I cared for the gibe; but because I disliked that one there should hear me called by so graceless a name.

Well, we jumped once more; but this time I dared not look anywhere, but straight before me. Yet I cleared the bar.

Whereupon the Bridge boys vaunted themselves more soberly, and he who had offered his cloak and sword now offered only his belt.

"Set the bar two points higher," I cried, "and clear me that, Will Peake, if you can."

At that our lads rent the air with shouts, and Will Peake pulled a long face. For the bar now stood level with his eyes, though it only reached my chin.

It fell out as I hoped. He jumped, and the bar sprang six yards into the air as he missed it.

Then our 'prentices made up for the silence of those of the Bridge; and this time the gamester offered not so much as a shoe lace.

For all that, I must clear the bar, if I was to make good my challenge; and I drew a long breath as I stood a moment and glanced round.

A FAIR ON-LOOKER

Yes. Her eyes of blue were on me, her lips were the least bit parted, and a glow of expectation was in her cheeks.

So I took my run and cleared the bar, with an inch to spare.

Then, as I heard nothing of the shouts which yet deafened me, and durst not so much as raise my eyes, the cheery alderman's voice cried :

"So Master Dexter hath won the high jump. See if he also win the broad. Clear away there, and stand back, good people, to give our brave lads fair play."

When I took courage at last to look up, I saw a sight which made the blood in my veins tingle.

She stood still where she was ; but next to her had squeezed himself a smirking gallant, bravely bedizened, who looked round impudently into her face, and whispered something in her ear.

To me it seemed as if at first she was heedless of his presence, then, hearing him, she turned upon him a startled gaze, and, flushing angrily, moved a scornful pace away.

This I saw, while the alderman was saying—

"The first leap is yours, Master Dexter. See you set us a good lead."

I leapt, scarcely thinking what I did, and leapt badly ; for though one by one the others failed to reach it, Will Peake reached it, and lit in my very footprints.

"A match again!" cried everyone, "and a close match, too!"

The gallant had made up to her again, and was tormenting her sweet ear once more with his whispers. She stood rigid like a statue with her eyes before her, showing only by the heaving of her bosom that she was aware of his unwelcome presence.

"You keep us waiting, lad," cried the alderman. "Jump, unless you mean to yield the victory to your adversary."

I jumped, listlessly again, and again alighted within an inch of my former distance. And once again, Will Peake landed in my very hoof-marks.

"A mortal match!" cried the crowd.

"One leap more," said the alderman, "and if that does not decide——"

He was there still, and, worse than before, had caught the little hand that hung at her side in his. The colour had gone from her face. I saw that she bit her lips, and for one moment her eyes looked up appealingly and, so it seemed to me, met mine.

Then with my heart swelling big within me, I walked to the starting-point, and ran for my last leap.

It was with all my might that I jumped now, and I cleared two good feet beyond my former distance; so that the onlookers could scarcely shout for amazement.

But I waited neither for their shouts nor for Will's jump, for I knew he could not reach me. With beating heart, and fingers digging into the palms of my hands, I walked straight to where she stood, pale and trembling. Her right hand was still his prisoner, and his cursed lips were still at her ear. But not for long.

Before he was aware, I had seized him with a grip which made him howl; and next moment he was reeling and staggering a dozen yards away in the midst of the enclosure. It all happened so quickly that even she seemed scarcely to know of her deliverance, till she saw him draw his sword and look round for me.

Then, to draw the combat away from her, I went on to meet him with my club; and before his first onset was done, his sword flew over his head in two pieces. It was an old trick, and cost nothing to a 'prentice outside Temple Bar. And while he looked round, bewildered, after his weapon, I took him by the nape of his neck and the cloth of his breeches, and walked with him to the pond hard by, where I left him, and so was well rid of him.

By this time the Fields were in an uproar. So intent had all been on the leaping, to see if Will Peake would equal my jump (which, Heaven help him! he could not do), that the gallant was swinging over the pond before anyone understood what was afoot. Then they broke up the ring and closed in on us, so that I, having dropped my burden amidst the duck-weed, was fain to lose myself among the crowd and give one and all the slip.

I thought I had done so, for while all stood gaping and jeering as they fished out the sputtering hero from his pea-green bath, I sauntered back unheeded to the place where last I had seen her for whose sake all the pother arose. At first I feared she had fled, but on looking I spied her in company

CLUBS TO THE RESCUE

with an elderly woman, who soothed and chid her in turn, and began to hurry her from the place.

But when she saw me, she brushed the old servant aside, and with a blush beckoned me to her. Shall I ever forget the vision of her, as she stood there, stately and beautiful, with hand outstretched, smiling on me with mingled pity for my shyness and gratitude for my service?

"My brave friend," said she, and her voice fell like music on my ears, "I have nothing but my poor thanks to give thee, but they are thine."

The crimson now came to my cheeks, for it hurt me to hear her talk of payment.

"I would gladly do it all again," said I.

"Nay," she laughed, "once is enough surely, at least for me."

Then I wished the ground might swallow me, for I deemed she thought me a fool.

"She would come," put in the old servant in an accent which, though I had never heard it before, I took to be Scotch or Irish; "I told her myself what to expect among a crowd of rude, rascally City sparks, that don't know a lady when they see her, and when they do, don't know how to behave themselves. It serves her right, say I, and it's myself will see she frolics no more, I warrant you—a low, unmannerly pack of curs, with a plague on all of you."

"Never heed my old nurse," said the young lady, sweetly; "she and I were parted in the crowd, and but for you, brave lad, I might have rued my folly in coming hither more than I do. Thanks once more, and farewell. Come, Judy—thank good Master Dexter for taking better care of me than ever you did, and then come away."

I stood like a mule gaping after them as they went, unable to stir or say a word till they were lost to view. Then as I turned came a shout at my ears: "There he stands!—there stands the villain! Seize him and hold him fast. He shall learn what it is to assault a captain of the Queen's guard."

Ho! ho! There were a round dozen of them, and one on horseback. But I knew of two dozen better than they within call.

So I shouted, "Clubs, clubs, to the rescue!" and began to lay about me.

CHAPTER II

How I served a Disorderly Printer

MY assailants were a mixed crew, some being lackeys of the half-drowned gallant, some constables of the watch, others idle swashbucklers ready to lend a hand to any cause and against any man for a pot of ale. But they took no advantage from hiring themselves against a poor 'prentice from without Temple Bar, for they got sore heads for their pains.

I myself could not do overmuch till my comrades arrived, for I was in an open place and could not see all sides of me at once. So, after three of them had gone down, I was wellnigh being mastered by the rest, but for the timely help of my honest club-fellows.

Foremost among these who should come but honest Will Peake, my late enemy, who, when it was a matter between 'prentices and Court bullies, forgot all old sores, and laid about him like a man. Behind him came a score or two of honest lads, some of my ward, some of others; and between us all you may judge if the numskulls who set upon me had a merry time of it. We left them mostly on the ground in a sorry plight, and the rest we sent packing back to them that owned them, with a message to send a few of better mettle than they if they wanted to catch us.

Then, as the messengers did not return, we gave loud cheers for the Queen, and went each our several ways.

As for me, I was in no humour for the noisy company even of my own fellows, and excused myself from a march home through the wards. I made a pretext to go and find my coat and cap, and let them depart without me.

For I was haunted yet by the memory of that fair face and the sweet music of her voice, and I wished to be alone.

I GREET MY ENEMY

Moreover, it vexed me grievously that any servant of so gracious a Queen as ours could be base enough to offer a helpless maiden a discourtesy, and that in chastising him I must needs put an affront on the dignity of her Majesty's Court. But that weighed less when I remembered what I had seen, and I would fain have had the doing of it all again, despite her gentle protest.

So I waited till the crowd was gone, and then paced, moodily enough, citywards.

But, at the entrance to the Fields, there overtook me a handful of horsemen, bravely equipped; amongst whom, as I looked round, I saw the author of all this mischief himself. His gay cloak hid the stains of the duck-weed, and as for his sword, he had borrowed another from one of his men. Mounted as he was, it was not likely he should notice a common 'prentice lad like me, yet I resolved notice me he should, even if I went to the pillory for it.

So I stood across the way, and said:

"Farewell, brave captain. The pond will be deeper next time, and Humphrey Dexter will be there to put you in it."

He turned about, crimson in face, and cursed savagely as he saw me—for he knew (or guessed, shrewdly enough) who I was. Then calling loudly to his servants:

"An angel to the man who catches the knave!" cried he. "Seize him, and bring him to me."

Whereat, being only one footman to a dozen horse, I gave a clean pair of heels.

I soon shook off my pursuers, who liked not the narrow alleys and winding lanes of our city, where their horses stumbled and they themselves missed their way. One only, whether from stubbornness or the hope of the angel, kept up the hue and cry, and, being mounted on a nimble pony, followed me close. At length it seemed shame to be running from a single man; so at the next corner I turned and waited for him. He ran at me with his weapon, and called loudly on the watch to help him, but I pulled him from his horse and had him up against the wall before he could cry again —yet not before he had pricked me in the arm with his blade.

He was a stout little man, and a brave one; but, by no fault of his, he was powerless in my grip. I wrenched the sword from his hand, and held him by the throat till he signalled a surrender.

"Tell me first your master's name. On your knees, and with an oath, lest I find you lie," said I, in none too sweet a mood.

He had naught else he could do; so, falling on his knees, took Heaven to witness that his master's name was David Merriman, a captain in her Majesty's service; lodging now at the Court, but presently about to join the Queen's forces in Ireland.

That was enough for me.

"Tell Master David Merriman I shall remember his name, and bid him remember mine against we meet next—and so farewell."

I left him puffing for breath against the wall, and departed. But hearing the watch raise a new hue and cry at my heels, I quickened my steps, and so after many a tedious circuit, ran into my master's shop just as he was about to bolt the door for the night.

He received me sourly, as indeed I expected.

"So," said he, "this is your faithful service which you swore to render me; and you a parson's son, that should know what an oath is."

He was for ever taunting me with my dear father's holy calling, and it vexed me to hear it.

"I am also under oath to serve my Queen," said I, "and I put that before all."

"And you serve her by drunkenness, and rioting, and breaking the heads of her loyal subjects! I have heard of you this day. How comes it that your fellow-'prentice Peter Stoupe——"

"A plague on Peter Stoupe!" said I, for I disliked him. "And as for drunkenness, I was never drunk in my life; nor, by my own leave, a rioter."

"By whose leave, then?" asked Master Walgrave.

"By the leave of them who behave themselves as knaves," said I, getting hot as I thought of Captain Merriman; "and had they twenty skulls, and a crown on each, I'd crack 'em."

"Had they no crowns, they would not be worth the cracking," said a cheerful voice behind us; and there stood Mistress Walgrave herself. "Come, husband," said she, soothingly, "be not too hard on Humphrey, he is but a lad.

PETER STOUPE GIVETH THANKS

He serves us well most days, when the Queen is not to the front. I warrant thee, Robert, thou wast a merry 'prentice once thyself."

"That I never was," said Master Walgrave, with an acid face; "but get in with you, sirrah, and to bed. I had a mind to leave you on the other side of the door this night, to cool your hot blood." And he bolted the door, whilst I slunk up to my garret.

Peter Stoupe was already asleep and snoring; and as he lay clean across the bed, I must needs arouse him to take his own side and make room for me.

"What, Humphrey!—I give God thanks to see thee back," said he, drowsily; "I feared something was amiss. There was a rumour that you lodged this night in Newgate."

"You listened to a lie, then," said I.

"And it is not true, is it, that you naughtily assaulted a gentleman of the Court?"

"And what if I did?" I demanded.

"Alas! Humphrey, think of the trouble it is like to bring on our good master and mistress. Have you no thought for anyone but yourself? Yet, I give thanks thou art safe, so—far—my—good—Hump——" and here he rolled off to sleep and left me in quiet.

Yet not in peace, for I could not sleep that night for many an hour. For my life seemed to have taken a strange turn round since morning. Before to-day I had thought the 'prentice's life the merriest life in the world. I had cared for nobody, and it had troubled me little if nobody cared for me. Strange that now I felt like a greyhound in the leash, longing to be anywhere but where I was.

Besides, I had more solid grounds for wakefulness. However well to-day I had given my pursuers the slip, I guessed I had not heard the last of Captain Merriman and his merry men. They would find me out; and I might yet become, as Peter had said, a lodger in Newgate, and, worse than that, a cause of trouble and distress to good Master Walgrave and his lady.

For, however poorly I esteemed my master, I could ill afford to bring harm on his family. For my mistress was ever my champion and my friend, and her children I was wont to love as my own brothers and sisters.

So I spent half the night kicking in my bed—of which

SIR LUDAR

kicks Master Peter received his full share—and rose very early, resolved to try what hard work could do to cure my unrest.

No one was stirring that I could hear, and I went down the stairs silently and took up my labour at the case. My stick lay on the floor, where I had dropped it the morning before, and, alack! the squabbled type lay there too, a sight to make a man sad. Slowly and painfully I saved what I could, and was setting myself to make good the rest, when my ears caught a strange sound below my feet. It was a beating sound, followed by the dull fall of something, and, on listening, it came and went every two or three minutes.

I had guessed more than once before now that under the house was a cellar, although I had never been there, nor, indeed, knew how to approach it. For there was no opening, front or back, to the outer world that I knew of, and, if there at all, it must be pitch-dark and hard to breathe in. And yet the noise I now heard, if it came from anywhere, came from below. I looked about carefully, hoping for a crack in the floor through which to solve the mystery. But crack there was none. Only as I looked further I saw that the reams of paper, which lay usually near the press, were moved somewhat to one side. Now, as my master was always particular that the paper should lie always in the same place, it seemed strange to me they should be so disturbed. But on going nearer I perceived the reason. For there, usually hidden to view, was now exposed a cunning trap-door, opened by a hinge and sunken ring in the boards.

Now, having found so much, it would have been out of all nature had I gone back to my work and thought no more of the matter; besides, the strange noise still continued. I lifted the door cautiously about an inch and peeped below.

The cellar—for cellar it was—was bright with the light of a lamp, by which I could plainly discern my master (or, as I believed for a moment, my master's ghost), with coat off, and sweating with the heat of the place, working like any journeyman at a printing-press, on which lay a forme of type, which he inked with his balls and struck off in print with the noises which had perplexed me above.

Then I pulled up the trap and called out:

"Master Walgrave, spare yourself so much toil, I pray you, and let me help you."

MY MASTER IS MODEST

He turned round, with a face the colour of dough, like a man who had just received an arrow in his vitals; then he rushed as if to put out the lamp. But his presence of mind returned before he got that length, and he demanded of me angrily enough how I dared to play the spy on him and come where I was not bidden.

I replied I was no spy, and, as for coming where I was not bidden, had I known who it was down there I would have stayed where I was. But, being there, might I help him, I asked, at the work? He answered angrily, "No," and bade me begone. Whereupon I returned to my case, and waited till he should come up to the earth's surface.

Meanwhile I recalled not a few rumours I had heard about Master Walgrave. One was, that, though he was only licensed to have one press, and seemed to have no more, yet (it was whispered of some) he had another in hiding, which now I found to be true. Moreover, as I was in Stationers' Hall one day, a month or more ago, to pay the fee for a register, I overheard Timothy Ryder the beadle and another talking about my master.

"He prints more than he registers," said one.

"And he should have his ears cropped for his pains," said Timothy, "did I but know where to have him."

Then seeing that I waited (for they had forgot to give me my acquittance), they dropped talking suddenly.

By all this I guessed that my master was no favourite with them of Stationers' Hall, and, moreover, that he was addicted to disorderly practices contrary to the Acts binding printers. But so well did he keep his own secret, and so busy was I with my own affairs, that it all passed from my mind, and now only returned when I saw that what had been said of him was true.

He came up from below presently, and I was ready for him. "Master," said I, "I have displeased you against my will, and I have seen what you would fain have kept a secret. You shall find it remains safe with me, for I am your 'prentice and bound to you. Therefore cheer up."

He brightened at this.

"You are a good lad," said he. "It concerns no one what I do below. 'Tis an amusement of my own, no more."

As he stood there, pale and anxious, with weary eyes, it

seemed to me an amusement which yielded him but little sport. However, I did not dispute the matter, and we said no more about it.

But after that day I observed that my master, although he seemed to like me less, was more sparing of his bitter words than heretofore. Whereby I guessed plainly enough that the amusement he spoke of, were it to come to the ears of the Master and Wardens of the Company, would get him into no little trouble.

Mistress Walgrave, his wife, as I said, was ever my good friend. She was no common woman, and how those two made a match of it always puzzled me. Before she came to England (so she had told me often) she lived at Rochelle, in France, where her first husband was a merchant in lace. Then, when he died of the plague ten years ago, she came with her two young children (the elder being but five years) to her mother's home in Kent, where Robert Walgrave, being on a visit to Canterbury, met her, and offered her marriage. And in truth she had been the brightness of his house ever since, and her two French children, Jeannette and Prosper, now tall girl and boy, lived with her, as did some three other urchins who called Master Walgrave father. Sweet Jeannette was my favourite; for she was lame, and had her mother's cheery smile, and thought ill of no one, least of all of me whom she called her big crutch, and tormented by talking French.

Many a summer afternoon, when work was slack, I carried her to the water-side, where she might sit and watch the river flowing past. And to reward me she made me read her about King Arthur and his knights, and stories from Mr. Chaucer's book; much of which I understood not, though (being a printer's 'prentice) I knew the words.

One still evening as we sat thus, not a week after my adventure in Finsbury Fields, she broke in on my reading with—

"*Voilà*, see there, Master Humphrey; *mais, comme elle est jolie!*"

"I don't know what you say, when you talk like that, mistress," said I; for I liked not the French jargon, although by dint of long suffering it I had a better guess at the meaning of it often than I cared to own.

A PICTURE FIT FOR MR. CHAUCER

"Look, I say," said she, "would not she be a queen of beauty for the knights of old to fight for?"

I looked where she pointed; and there, gliding within a few yards of us, passed a boat, and in it, drinking in the beauty of the evening, sat a maiden, at sight of whom I felt the blood desert my cheeks, and the hand that held the book tremble. Her old companion was beside her dozing, and the waterman lugged lazily at his oars, humming an air to himself.

Jeannette, happily, was looking not at me but at her, and so my troubled looks escaped her.

"I never saw a face more fair," said she. "'Tis like a picture out of Mr. Chaucer's book. And now that she is past, the day seems darker. Go on reading, please, kind Master Humphrey."

I tried to go on, but I blundered and lost my place, while my eyes tried to follow the boat.

Would she but have looked round! Could she but have known who it was that watched her! Could I myself have dared even to shout or call!

Alas! the boat glided by, and her form, stately, erect, fearless, lost itself in the distance. What dreamed she—a queen—of an uncouth London 'prentice?

"Master Dexter," said Jeannette's soft voice presently, "for five whole minutes you have been trying to read one little sentence, and it still lacks an ending. What ails you?"

"Nothing, mistress; but I am a bad scholar and the words are hard; I pray you forgive me. Besides it grows late. 'Tis time we went in."

So I carried her in to her mother, and then ran wildly back to the river's edge, if by good hap I might see that lady return, or at least catch sight of her boat in the far distance. But I did neither. The tide still ran out, and amongst the many boats that dotted the water citywards who was to say which was hers?

As I returned by way of the Temple to my master's house, I met Peter Stoupe, my fellow 'prentice.

"I am glad I met thee," he said. "A man came to me just now in the shop and said, 'Be you Humphrey Dexter?' I told him no, and asked him what he wanted. He told me that was his business. I bade him wait where he was and I would fetch you, for I had seen you go out; but he went away grumbling, saying he would choose his own time, not mine. Alas! Humphrey, you have brought us all into sad trouble by your naughty ways."

"What trouble are you in, sirrah?" said I, wrathfully. "It matters little to you what comrade is laid by the heels, so that you get your platter full, morning and evening."

"But our good master and mistress——" he began.

But I waited not for him and went quickly home.

That night my master called me as I was going to my bed, and said, "Humphrey, there is like to be sad trouble here on your account. A warrant, I am told, is out to seize you, you know best for what; but, if it be true, you struck a gentleman of the Queen's household——"

"I struck a dog who affronted a defenceless maiden," said I, "and I put him in the pond, to boot, and I care not if I go to the cage for it."

"But I care. If I harbour you here I am like to receive the punishment which belongs to you. And if I give you up I lose a good 'prentice. I can say thus much for you."

"Then," said I, not heeding his flattery, "I had better go away myself."

I never guessed he would take to this; but, to my surprise, he did.

"I and your mistress think so, too, Humphrey. Whilst the hue and cry lasts you are better anywhere than here. When it has ceased, you may safely return. Meanwhile, as fortune will have it, I can employ you still in my service."

Then he told me how he desired to send a letter to a friend of his at Oxford, which, being of the gravest importance, he wished delivered by a trusty messenger—as he took me to be. Therefore, if I was ready to forward him in the matter, I might avoid my pursuers, and do him a service to boot.

I hailed the offer with joy and thankfulness. I longed for a change somewhere, I cared not where, and, if skulk I must, an errand like this would please me vastly more than hiding for a week in my master's cellar.

"Be secret," said he (meaning, I suppose, Stoupe). "To-morrow early be ready to start to Kingston, where you may get a horse. Meanwhile your mistress is herself making you a cloak which shall be proof against all weathers. So good-night, Humphrey, and see you rouse yourself betimes in the morning."

CHAPTER III

How I rode post-haste to Oxford

THE summer sun had not been up long before I too was out of bed. Early as the hour was, my master and mistress were both astir, and bade me make a hearty meal in view of my journey.

While I ate, my master said:

"As the tide runs now, Humphrey, you may make a good part of your journey by water, and 'twill do you no harm to be your own waterman."

"Indeed no," said I; for I hated to sit idle in a boat.

"Should you reach Brentford on the flood, there are many who will ease you of your craft, and bring her back. Meanwhile 'tis an easy road by the river's bank to Kingston. We have a good friend there, one Master Udal, the minister, with whom this letter will procure you a welcome, and at his house you are to lie to-night. He will lend you a horse and put you on the way to Oxford."

"And see here, Humphrey," said my mistress, holding up a brave cloak of dark red cloth, as long as to my knee, "here is what will comfort you against the cold morning air, and change you into a veritable highwayman on the road."

It was a brave cloak indeed, so weighty and well padded, that had my journey been not to Oxford, but to the Poles, it would not have been amiss.

"See you take care of it," continued my good mistress.

"It is your gift and your making," said I, "so I can readily promise that."

"I can lend you a hat to match it," said my master, "and a sword."

"I have a sword of my own," said I, proudly, for I had taken one from Mr. Merriman's bully, a week ago.

SIR LUDAR

"Well, well. The weather promises fair for your journey. Do whatever the minister bids you, and return speedily when your business is over. Here is a purse which will cover all your needs, with something to bring back to me at the end. And so, farewell, Humphrey. Be secret, and talk to no one on the way without necessity."

My mistress also bade me farewell, and between them they hurried me off to the wherry. In my haste I was near leaving behind me my brave new cloak. But my master, seizing it, came with it angrily, and said :

"Is this your care, sirrah! If you end your journey no better than you begin it, 'twill be little enough to boast of."

Which I considered fuss enough about a matter which concerned only my own person, and not his errand. For what was my cloak to him? Yet I felt ashamed to have neglected my mistress' kindness, and I told him so, whereat he was pacified.

The tide served me some three hours and more, in which time, by dint of hard rowing, I reached Brentford, where I left the boat. Being weary and hot (for the sun was now high and fierce), I resolved to dine before I went farther, and sought the nearest tavern for that purpose. It was an ill-looking place, and kept by an ill-looking host; but hunger is no respecter of persons; and, as he called me "your worship," and set before me a brave leg of pork, with ale to keep it in countenance, I forgave him his ugly face, and fell to without more ado. When I came to pay him, and pulled out the purse my master had given me, he grew monstrous civil, and offered to take me across the ferry himself.

Which he did, with one of his men. And, half-way across, the two set upon me with one accord, and thought to rob me. But I, being new to travel, and so suspecting everybody, was ready for them, and knocked their heads soundly together for their pains. I also lightened the boat of my host's servant, bidding him get to shore some other way. So my host, fearing a like ducking for himself, took me over quietly enough, and never asked a fare.

From there I floundered through the swamps, with the river on my right hand, till I came to Kingston, where it was not long till I found Master Udal's house.

He was a little grave man, whom I might have swallowed

MASTER UDAL QUESTIONS ME

at a gulp, and yet he had an air about him I durst not disobey, and an eye which, when I caught it, made me think of my sins. He asked me many questions about Master Walgrave and his manner of life, which I answered plainly, all except one or more that concerned the secret press in the cellar.

"Your master keepeth one press out of sight?" said he.

"If that be so," said I, "'tis no wonder if I know nothing of it."

He smiled.

"Then, he labours at it himself, without your aid?"

"If you say so, sir, no doubt but he does."

Master Udal smiled again.

"Thou'rt good at a secret, lad, and I'll tempt thee no more."

Whereupon he did what was worse, and began to question me about my own ways, and that searchingly, so that I was fain to plead weariness, and asked for my bed. This was even worse; for, being a lonely man, he had but one bed in the house, and that was his own. And that he might have the more of my company, he came to bed too.

He was a good man—this Master Udal—for he prayed long with me at the bedside, and talked comfortingly to me about my home, and the snares of my city life. But with his grave talk he would not let me rest. Even when we lay in bed, and it was too dark to see his face, I felt his eye upon me still, and was fain to confess myself to him, like a Papist to his priest. But when I told him tremblingly that I loved a maiden, he gave a grunt of displeasure and turned over on his side, and left me in peace.

And so that fair maiden, little as she knew it, rescued me that night from a great tribulation; and it were strange if, in gratitude, I did not dream of her.

Master Udal roused me betimes, and after reading again my master's letter, asked me, was I a horseman? I said I could sit a horse with any 'prentice in Finsbury Fields, even at the water leap. Then he asked, had I a cloak? I said, proudly, yes, my dear mistress had given me one, with which I would not part for two others as good. He said that was right, unless Master Penry wished it.

"Who is Master Penry, then?" I demanded.

"Him you go to see at Oxford—and you are to do

SIR LUDAR

everything he tells you, even if it be to part with your cloak. Here is a letter to him, at St. Alban Hall. You are to go to him privately, and submit to him in all things."

It all seemed strange enough to me, but I said I would do as I was bidden. For all that, I resolved that if it came to parting with my brave cloak to a stranger, I would be hard put to it before I suffered so much wrong to my mistress' goodness.

Then Master Udal instructed me carefully as to the way, showing me by what roads I should ride, and where I should halt for the night. He also cautioned me about speaking to strangers by the way, and bade me beware lest I fell among thieves.

Then he went to the stable and fetched his horse—a sorry nag, and ill accustomed to my heavy weight. Then he fetched me some food to carry in the saddle-bag; and, after a prayer that God would protect me and further the business on hand, he let me go.

I was glad to be alone in the sweet summer morning air, with the lark carolling high above my head, and the new-mown hay scenting the meadows, and the early sun slanting through the lime trees, and the half-awakened cattle standing to watch me as I passed. It was enough to make any heart glad, and if I myself sang in tune with the birds as I ambled on, it was because I could not help it.

The road was hard to find betwixt Kingston and Hounslow, for it was across country, and the narrow lanes twisted and twined so that, had it not been for the sun, I should soon not have known if I was going north, south, east, or west. Except a few yokels trudging to their work, and now and then a blithe milkmaid calling to her cows, I met no one. These looked hard at me, and wondered what such a one as I, in cloak and sword and hat, wanted there at that hour. But I let them guess, and pushed on, along the river's bank, to Twickenham, and then over the wild heath, and through the woods, till at last I came to Hounslow, where I halted to rest my beast.

As I was leaving that place, there overtook me an important-looking man with two men-servants, mounted, following him. He seemed friendly disposed and talkative, and as he too was going to Oxford, we agreed to join company, and

THE BISHOP OF LONDON'S MAN

fell into conversation. He asked me my errand and I replied, truly enough, I went to visit a gentleman at Oxford. He told me, with not a little bluster, he too went to wait upon a gentleman at Oxford, but he guessed the varlet would get little joy out of his visit.

"Why," said I, "are you an officer of the courts of law, or a bailiff?"

"Yes and no," said he. "I serve a great master, and go to catch a great rogue."

Then, being warmed by the ale he had had at Hounslow and my questions, he told me he was no other than the Bishop of London's man; and that wind had come to his Grace that some evil-disposed persons had been issuing a wicked and scandalous libel against the Queen and her bishops and clergy, and that the arch offender in this bad business was known to be a certain—he would not say who—at Oxford. He told me how he would give a finger off his hand to have the rascal laid by the heels, ay, and the printer too, who had vilely lent himself to the business. He waxed so fierce and eloquent in defence of the good bishops, that I promised him, should my urgent errand in any way permit it, he might count on me to assist him in his righteous hue and cry. For I loathed all that set itself up to vex our gracious Queen and the peaceful order of her kingdom. The man commended my loyalty, and we talked of other matters—he doing the most of it—till we came to Colnbrook, where, finding my nag slow, and his business being very urgent, he left me and rode forward; appointing to meet me two days hence at the inn at Iffley, should I still be of a mind to do him and the bishop a service.

All this talk had made me uneasy, for he had hinted broadly that a close watch was being kept on all disorderly printers; and I, remembering my master's press in the cellar, hoped no suspicion might attach to him, and resolved to warn him when I returned home.

From Colnbrook I rode solitary in the heat of the day. So hot was it that I was tempted to take off my cloak and lay it across the saddle in front of me. It was my vanity and the pride of being seen in so brave a garment that hindered me; and it fell out well that it was so. For just over the heath, as you come upon Topley, there sprang out upon me a rider, who without any parley let fly at me with a pistol; and but that the ball, badly aimed, glanced off from the stiff padding of my cloak, I had not been here to tell this tale.

Before he could load again I spurred my horse, hoping to close with him. But the wretched jade was no match in pace for his, and he got away. But not before I had let fly my club at him, from twelve yards away, and dealt him a crack on the cheek that should have caused him to bear me in mind for a week. I expected him back after that, but being dazed by the blow, and seeing that I was not the gentleman he took me for, he spurred off; and I, waiting only to pick up my club and make sure that the bullet had done me no harm, did the same, and rode on to Maidenhead.

Here an odd adventure befel me; for, going to the inn of the place where I meant to lie that night, I found it in possession of a roystering crew of gallants, who sat and quaffed their sack and sang lustily, roaring and quarrelling enough to deafen a man. When, by dint of hard pushing, I had made myself a seat at the table and called for my supper—for I was hungry—they gave over their wrangling and began to look hard at me. There was much whispering among them, and one said:

"I know the rogue in spite of his cloak. Call me an ass if there be not a shaven crown under that hat of his."

"If you mean by that," said another cavalier, "that he's a Jesuit——"

Here the company took up the word. "A Jesuit!—a Jesuit!" they cried, and at the sudden accusation I turned crimson and blushed like a girl.

"Smelt out?" cried the company. "To the gallows with him!" Then it seemed to me to be time to go.

"Who called Jesuit?" said I, pulling out my sword.

They laughed at this, and one of them cried:

"If you be not, drink to the Queen, where you stand, and confound her enemies!"

I took off my hat, that they might see I wore no monkish tonsure, and drank.

"That shows nothing," cried another. "They might curse the Pope himself, and yet be all the better Jesuits."

"A crew of cowards," said another, "who never dare be what they seem or seem what they are."

HANGING TOO GOOD FOR 'PRENTICE

"Then," said I, "if that be so, I can easily prove I am a true and loyal subject of the Queen. Let who will come on, two at a time, and take back his lie at the point of my sword." And I put my back up to the wall and cast my cloak back over my shoulder.

Whereat they laughed again, and he who had spoken first said:

"If I doubted it before, I am sure of it now, for no one but a Jesuit could feign a swagger like that. Come, let's hang him and have done with him."

"Come on," said I. "I tell you I'm no Jesuit, but a loyal London 'prentice, on a message for my master to Oxford. If you hold it English that twenty men should set upon one, then——"

"What! a plague on you!" cried my opponent, before I could finish. "Why did you not say what you were before? We have something better to do than hang 'prentices. Get you gone—a stick to your back is what you want, unmannerly dog."

"Fetch it then," said I, "for before I leave here I shall finish my supper, and if you like not my company, you may go elsewhere."

I think they were abashed at that, for they tried to laugh it off, and go on with their carouse. Indeed I think they meant only to frighten me all the while, so perhaps I was a fool to take it all in earnest. However that be, I finished my supper and bade them all good-night; whereat they laughed again. Then, as an hour of daylight remained, I called for my horse and resolved to ride to the next inn and lie there for the night.

I had no cause to complain of the company here (it was the house midway betwixt Maidenhead and Henley, as you come to Bisham), for I had the place to myself. Nor did I wonder at that when I saw the pig-sty of an inn which it was. The landlord, a villanous-looking rogue, demanded to finger my money before he would admit me; and as for my horse, I had to see to him myself, for there was no one about the place to do it for me. However, a night's lodging was all I wanted, and, having brought away the stable key in my pocket, I pulled my bed across the chamber floor, wrapped myself up in my cloak, and slept like the seven sleepers.

SIR LUDAR

The man eyed me surlily enough in the morning, and told me, if I doubted his honesty, I might go and lie somewhere else next time; which I promised to do, for I guessed when he talked of honesty that he had tried to steal my horse in the night, and being baulked of that, had had it in his mind to rob me. We parted in dudgeon; but I felt well out of that place with my purse in my pocket and my horse under me.

As I rode through Henley, who should overtake me but a troop of horsemen, among whom I recognised not a few of the roysterers who had used me so scurvily at Maidenhead the night before. I drew aside to let them pass, for I wanted none of their company. But one—he who had voted to hang me—came up in a friendly way.

"Come, lad," said he, "look not glum; our gallants will have their jest."

"'Tis no jest to call a loyal subject of the Queen a Jesuit, still less to hang him," said I.

"Well, well," said he, "next time we'll call thee Puritan and burn thee—that will make the balance straight. Meanwhile join us, and scour that frown off thy visage," and he clapped me on the back with a whack which made my nag prick up her ears and jump a foot off the ground.

It took me some time to follow his last advice; but as the fellow seemed honest, though a fool, and he and his comrades made little more pace than I did, I made the best of what I could not help, and ambled beside him at the tail of the troop.

Then he told me that they were going to Wales to get together provisions for an expedition to Ireland, and offered me good pay and plenty of knocks if I would only join them.

"We shall have a merry time of it," said he, "with a merry man for captain."

At this I pricked my ears.

"What is his name?" asked I.

"What I say: Captain Merriman, a gallant officer, and a desperate man of war."

"I know he is that," said I, with the blood rushing to my temples.

"You know him, then?" said the man, "and you will

NEWS OF CAPTAIN MERRIMAN

join us. Ho! ho! Who would thought I could find him such a recruit?"

"Before I serve under your Captain Merriman," said I, losing temper, "you may do what you promised last night, and hang me up on the nearest tree."

He stared at me when I said that.

"Why, what mean you?"

"That is my business," said I, shortly; "but if you would take him a message, you may tell him there is as good duck-weed in Ireland as ever there is in Finsbury Fields, and that Humphrey Dexter says so."

The man burst into a laugh.

"Did ever I see such blustering roarers as you city 'prentices? I warrant you Captain Merriman will shake in his shoes when I tell him. I do not know if I should not run you through the body for talking thus of a gallant gentleman; but I'll spare thee, Humphrey, this time: 'tis too hot to fight."

"Not for me," said I, "if that is what you mean."

He laughed again at that.

"Come along," said he, clapping me again on the back, "join us, and you shall tell Captain Merriman all about the duck-weed yourself; and a proud man he will be, I warrant you."

I was sorry now I had bragged, for nothing but contempt came from it, as indeed, had I been a little wiser, I might have known. So I said no more about the matter, and let my comrade talk, which he did to his heart's content, telling me of the battles he had fought in, and the spoils he had taken, and the triumphs he had seen.

Thus talking, we beguiled the time till we came to where we had to part company; for the troop went by way of Abingdon, whereas I, following Master Udal's directions, continued on the east bank of the river to Oxford. He bade me think over what he had said about joining the wars, and told me where he might be found during the next week or two.

"Ask for Tom Price," said he; "they all know me. And on the day you're Lord Mayor of London, which I take it is not far hence, find me a humble seat below the salt at your lordship's table; and so farewell."

SIR LUDAR

I felt it lonely enough after my company had left; besides which, I clean lost my way, and was forced at last to seek the river and guide myself by that. Heavy work it was; for the river's bank was swampy and often impassable with bushes and woods, so that I had to go miles out of my way to circumvent them, leading my horse by the hand. At last, when I hardly knew where I was, night fell; and worn out with weariness and hunger, I made for the first house I could see—which chanced to be an inn—and resolved to go no farther that night.

Had I gone on, I am certain of one thing, which is, that this veritable history would never have been written. For I should not then have met the wild person who, just as I stood unharnessing my nag at the door, dashed past me and flung himself into the house.

CHAPTER IV

How I met a Runaway Scholar

AS I entered the poor kitchen of the inn—for it was a sorry shed altogether—there rose to meet me a figure which, if I live to Methuselah's age, I shall not easily forget. He was tall and had the limbs of a giant. His hair was tawny and inclined to red, and hung in disorderly waves on his shoulders. His raiment—for he had flung his scholar's cap and robe to a corner of the room—was poor and ragged, and seemed scarcely to hang together on his brawny back. His arms were long and nervous, and the hands at the end of them twitched uneasily even while the rest of his body was motionless. His carriage was erect and martial, and you knew not whether to admire most the weight and solidity of the man as he stood still, or the tiger-like spring in every limb when he moved.

Yet it was not one of these things which made me stand almost in awe as I saw him. It was his face, which, if ever a man's face deserved the name, was beautiful. I cannot explain why; for I have seen features more finely carved and better proportioned in faces which never seemed to me so beautiful as his. I have seen more strength of mouth, more light of eyes, many a time, and yet never looked twice; I have seen faces as noble which never struck me as his did. I know not how it was. I think it was the expression which moulded all his face into a look, partly wild, partly noble, partly sad, and wholly gentle. For as you watched it, it changed like an April day from cloud to fair, from thunder to lightning, from night to day; yet whatever came or went, the look of a gentle man remained.

Man, did I say? He was scarcely my senior, even if he was my equal in years; and his beardless chin and the boyish glow on his cheek made him seem younger than he was.

SIR LUDAR

But why all this picture-drawing of a stray Oxford student, whom, while I talk about him, I keep standing in front of me on the floor of that poor kitchen? You shall hear.

It was not to do me obeisance that he rose as I entered. His dirk was drawn and his face was thunderous as he took a step forward and spoke.

"I want you not! So leave me."

My Lord Burleigh himself could not have spoken the words more royally, although he would have spoken them with less music and more of an English accent in his voice.

Now, moved as I was by the look of my companion, it offended me to hear a loyal London 'prentice talked to thus like a dog, or, worse, like the drawer of the inn.

"By your leave," said I, and it was not often I said as much to any man, "unless you be the landlord of the place, I have as good a right to be here as you."

"Then," said he, solemnly and, as I thought, sadly, "guard yourself." I whipped out my sword. In my boastfulness, I thought I had too great an advantage with my long weapon against his short and not too highly-tempered blade, and I resolved with myself not to run him through if I could otherwise satisfy him. But my tune changed as soon as we closed. I could do nothing. My fine thrusts and parries wherewith I was wont to set Finsbury Fields a-gaping all went for nothing. He got in at me over my guard, under my guard, beside my guard, and through my guard. Nor could I even do myself justice. For while I fenced, I was fascinated by the flashing of his eyes and the noble gracefulness of his every motion. In two minutes he had me disarmed, pinned up against the wall, as helpless as a silly ox in the grip of a tiger.

It mortified me as much as anything to find that when he had me thus at his mercy he dropped me half disdainfully, half pitifully, and put his dirk back into its sheath.

"Will you go now?"

"No," said I, doggedly. For so chapfallen was I that I wished nothing better than that he should do his worst with me.

At that he looked at me in solemn perplexity, and I expected to see his hand back at his girdle. But, to my confusion, he only shrugged his shoulders and turned away.

This completed my humbling; for no man had ever

I MEET MY MATCH FOR ONCE

disdained me thus before. I might easily have reached my sword, which lay at my feet, and run him through before he could face round; yet he did not even deign to notice me, and walked slowly to the fire, where he sat with his back to me.

I could stand it no longer, and crossed the room to face him.

"You have beaten me," said I—and the words were hard to say—"take my sword, for, by heaven, I will never wear it again, and fare you well."

The cloud on his face broke into sunlight as he sprang to his feet, and, taking my arm, said—

"No. Stay here and let us be friends. I am too poor to offer thee supper, but here's my hand."

I took his hand like one in a dream. I could not help it, strange as it seemed.

"Sir," said I, "whoever you be, I strike hands on one condition only, that is, that you sup to-night with me. I'm a London 'prentice, but I know when I meet my match."

What that had to do with his supping with me, I know not; but I was so flurried with my late defeat and my enemy's sudden friendliness, that I scarcely knew what I said.

"If that be the price, I must even pay it," said he, solemnly, "so long as we be friends."

So I called to the man of the house to bring us food quickly, and, while it was coming, set myself to know more of my new comrade.

Yet when I came to question him I felt abashed. For he looked so grave and noble that, despite his ragged clothes, it seemed presumptuous to ask him who he was. While I doubted how to begin, he spared me the trouble.

"Are you going to Oxford?" said he.

"I am," said I. "I was to reach there this night, but lost my way; and even yet do not know how near I am."

"Not an hour from the cursed place," said he, giving his student's cap, which lay on the floor at his feet, a little kick.

"Then it agrees not with you?" said I.

"Agrees!" said he, and then dropped silent, far more eloquently than if he had spoken a volume.

"Pray, sir," said I, after an awkward pause, "do you know one Master Penry of St. Alban Hall?"

He laughed at that.

SIR LUDAR

"The Welshman? Verily, I know him. What do you want with him?"

"I am to deliver him a letter from my master. Can you take me to him?"

"No," said my companion, "for I shall never enter Oxford again."

"Is your term done, then?" I asked.

"For me it is," said he. "I have been here two months, and will have no more of it."

"But are you free to leave?" I asked—for my curiosity was roused.

"Free!" said he: "I am here, that is enough. If my tutor come after me, there will be two men who will never see Oxford again."

I pitied his tutor, whoever he was, when he said that.

"But where are you going then?" I asked.

"To-night I shall lie here. The man of the place is my friend, and will shelter me, though I have nothing to pay him. To-morrow I shall take the road."

Here our supper came in: a fine big trout from the river, and a dish which mine host called mutton, but which I smelt to be venison.

It smote me to the heart to mark the struggle in my comrade's face to keep down the ravenous joy which for a moment hailed the coming in of these good things. But the ecstasy lasted only a moment, and when I bade him fall to, he said indifferently he had no appetite and wanted nothing.

"But it was a bargain," said I.

So he took a small helping. It plainly cut him to the quick to receive hospitality from a 'prentice, and he would, I think, as soon have starved, but for his promise.

I feigned not to notice what he took; yet I could not help marking the hungry way in which he devoured what was on his platter. Then when it was done, he rose and went to his seat at the fireplace, while I finished my supper at the table.

Before I had done, I filled my cup, as was my wont, and drank to Her Majesty, bidding my guest do the same.

He came gravely to the table at that, and filled a mug of ale to the brim. "Here's to my Queen," said he.

This struck me as odd, for his tone and manner were as

I CHANGE MY HABITS

if he were drinking to another toast than mine. Yet I did not dare to question him about it, and only hoped so noble a youth was one of Her Majesty's loyal servants.

Our host had but one small room with a single bed in it to offer us, which accordingly we shared for the night. Nor was it long before we were each sound asleep, forgetful of our troubles and quarrels and weariness.

Before we fell over, however, my comrade said:

" When go you into Oxford ? "

" To-morrow, betimes," said I, " for my message is urgent."

" You will have trouble enough," said he. " There is little love between town and gown there, and unless you like knocks, you had better send your letter by the hand of one who does."

" I mind no knocks," said I, groaning a little at the memory of some I had received that very evening ; " besides, I am bound to give my letter by my own hand."

" Then," said he, " take my cap and gown : they are no use to me and may be a passport to you. Lend me your cloak in exchange. It will serve to hide me, while it would but betray you as an intruder inside Oxford."

" This cloak," said I, " is the gift of my dear mistress in London. But perhaps your advice is good. I will go into Oxford in a scholar's garb, and you meanwhile shall shelter here in my cloak till I return about noon. Is it a bargain ? "

" As you please," said he, and fell asleep.

I was the more pleased with this exchange, as I remembered what Master Udal had said concerning the fancy Master Penry might take for my brave cloak. It would be safer here, protecting my comrade, than flaunting in the eyes of the ravenous youth of Oxford.

When I arose next morning with the sun, my bedfellow still slept heavily. I could not forbear taking a look at him as he lay there. His face in sleep, with all the care and unrest out of it, looked like that of some boyish, resolute Greek divinity. His arm was flung carelessly behind his head, and the tawny hair which strayed over the pillow served as a setting for his fine-cut features.

But I had no time for admiring Greek divinities just then ; and slipping on the scholar's robe and cap, which, to my thinking, made me a monstrous fine fellow, I left my own

SIR LUDAR

cloak at his bedside, and, taking my letter, started on my errand, afoot.

In the clear morning I could plainly see the towers of the city ahead of me before I had been long on the road. But it is one thing to see and another to touch. The inn where I had lain was at the river's bank, and yet no road seemed to lead to it or from it. As for mounting the river bank, that was impossible, by reason of the thickets which crowded down to the water's edge. I had to tramp inland, through marsh and quagmire, in which more than once I thought to end my days, till, after much searching, I hit upon the road which led to the city. Before I entered it the bells were clanging from a score of steeples, and many a hurrying form, clad like myself, crossed my path.

As I gained the east bridge, there was no small tumult in progress. For a handful of scholars, on their way to morning lecture, had fallen foul of a handful of yeomen bound for the fields, and were stoutly disputing the passage. When I appeared, I was claimed at once by the scholars as one of them, and willy-nilly, had to throw in my lot with them. The fight was a sharp one, for the yeomen had their sticks and shares and sickles, and laid stoutly about, whereas the scholars were unarmed, all except a few. At last, when two of our side had been pitched head first over the bridge, our leaders seemed inclined to parley; but the countrymen, puffed up with success, and calling to mind, perhaps, some old grievance, called, "No quarter! To the river with them, everyone," and closed in.

Then the scholars had to fight for their lives; and I, forgetting I was not really one of them, girt my gown about me, and, shouting to them to follow me, charged the varlets. They were sorry then they had not ended the matter sooner. Two or three of them went over the bridge to look for our comrades beneath, others were soundly cudgelled with their own sticks, while our fists slowly did the rest. All of a sudden up rode two or three horsemen, at whose coming our men showed signs of panic, while the townsmen cheered loudly and made a fresh stand. This vexed me sorely, for I had supposed the battle at an end. Wherefore, I made for the chief horseman, and, putting out all my strength, pulled him off his horse. Scarcely had I done so when my comrades

A GREAT FALL FOR THE MAYOR

behind raised a shout of " 'Tis the Mayor !—'tis the Mayor ! Fly !—fly ! " and off they made, dragging me with them. To think that I, a loyal London apprentice, should have lived to assault a mayor ! But there was no time for excuses or reproaches. The citizens were at our heels shouting and threatening, and as they followed, the whole town turned out in hue and cry. One by one the gownsmen dodged like rabbits into their holes, leaving me, who knew nothing of the city, almost alone. At last the enemy were almost up to me, and I was expecting every moment to be taken and perhaps hanged, when, as good luck would have it, just as I turned a corner, there faced me a wall not so high but that a good leaper might get over it. Over I scrambled just as the pack in full cry rushed round the corner.

Then I laughed as I heard their yapping, and grumbling, and questioning what had become of me. But I gave them no time to find out, for, crossing the garden into which I had fallen, I quickly slipped out at the gate into a fair cloistered square where, adjusting my battle-stained gown, I marched boldly up to the house at the gate and knocked.

A porter came at my summons and demanded, surlily enough, what I wanted.

"I am a fresh man here," said I, "and have lost my way. I pray you direct me to St. Alban Hall."

"St. Alban Hall?" said he. "Art thou a scholar of St. Alban Hall?"

"No," said I, "but I bear a message to one there, Master Penry by name."

"How comes it," demanded the porter, who, by the tone of him, might have been the chancellor himself, "that you wear that gown, sirrah?"

"That is my business," said I, seeing it was no profit to talk civilly to him, "and if you want not to see your neck wrung, give over questions, and tell me where is St. Alban Hall."

He grew red in the face as I gripped his arm, which he could by no means get free till I let him.

"This is St. Alban Hall," said he, "and Master Penry lives over my lodging."

Then I thought it better to be civil to the fellow, as he guessed I had no business there in a college gown. So I gave him a groat, and bad him take me up forthwith.

SIR LUDAR

Master Penry was a lean, wrathful-visaged Welshman, with deep grey eyes, and a large forehead, and a mass of straight black hair down his neck. As I entered his room, which was disordered and dirty, he was pacing to and fro, talking or praying aloud in his native tongue. He let me stand there a minute or two, amazed at his jargon, and scarcely knowing whether I had lit upon a sane man or not. Then he stopped suddenly in front of me and scanned me.

"Well?" said he, in good English.

"Are you Master Penry?" I asked.

"I am. You have a message for me?"

"I have; from Master Walgrave. Here it is," said I, putting the letter into his hand.

He tore it open and read it eagerly, and, as he did so, his face relaxed into a grim smile.

"That is well, so far," said he. Then, looking hard at me, he added, "Have you ridden from London in that disguise?"

"No," said I, "this gown was lent me by a friend to protect me against annoyance from the wild men of the town."

His face suddenly turned pale and passionate.

"Then where is the cloak your master speaks of in this letter?"

"The cloak!" I knew from the very first there would be trouble about that, and I was glad now I had left it behind in the safe keeping of my comrade at the inn.

"What is my cloak to you?" said I, not relishing the tone of his voice, "I have given it away to my friend."

"Fool and jackass!" said he, gnashing his teeth, "do you know you have ruined me and your master by this?"

"No, I do not," said I, "and as for the foul names you call me, take them back on the instant, or I swear I will ram them down your mouth!"

He took no notice whatever of my wrath, but went on, breaking in on his speech every now and then with Welsh words which I took to be curses.

"You must get it back at any price," said he. "Lose not a moment! Where is this friend? Who is he? If he resist you, you must slay him, so as you get it back. If it fall into the hands of an enemy, you and I, aye and your master, and all that belongs to you will perish. Ah, the folly of the man to trust such a missive to this thick-headed

MY CLOAK IS IN REQUEST

blunderer! What time lost, what labour wasted, what peril run, what ruin on our holy cause!"

I was well out of temper by this time, and, but that he looked so miserable and ill fed, I would have rattled his bones a bit. At last:

"That cloak," said he, coming up to me, "contained papers sent by your master to me; which, if they be found on any one's person, mean Tyburn. Do you understand that?"

"Yes," said I, beginning to see the drift of his coil, "and if you had told me so at first, I had been halfway back to get it by this time. Heaven is my witness, you are welcome to the cloak if that is what it contains; and I doubt not my friend will give it up to do you a pleasure."

"Hasten!" cried he, with tears of vexation in his eyes, "there is not a moment to be lost—nay, I will go with you. where did you leave it? Come!"

"Nay," said I, remembering it for the first time, "I am not very sure where it was. 'Twas at a river-side inn, about four miles from here."

"And who is your friend? Is he a true man?"

"I know not that either," said I. "He is a valiant man, and hath a dirk at his girdle; and I pity the man who tries to take the cloak from him by force."

Master Penry made another speech to himself in Welsh.

"Fool!" exclaimed he, half blubbering. "This precious missive you leave at an inn you know not where; with a man you know not whom; and yet your master speaks of you as a trusty lad. Bah! Lead on!"

I swallowed my wrath and obeyed him. He stalked impatiently at my side, saying nothing, but urging me forward so that I could scarcely keep pace with him. I was in luck, in one way, to have his escort; for as I came near the East Bridge, there lurked not a few of the townsmen who had been in the fight when I assaulted the Mayor. Seeing me with Master Penry, who, I suppose, was a man of some standing, they did not look twice at me; else I might have been caught, and put to rest my limbs in the cage. When we had crossed the bridge, and were in the country, my companion suddenly stopped.

"This friend of yours," said he, "with the dirk in his girdle. Was he a scholar?"

"He lent me this gown," said I.

SIR LUDAR

" An Irishman ? "

" I know not. He spoke good English, with a foreign trip of the tongue."

" A great big boy, with wild fair hair, and hands that never are still ? "

" The very man. You know him ? "

" Do I know him ? For two months I have endured the pains of the lost through him. A wild, untamable savage, subject to no laws, a heathen, a butcher, a scoffer at things holy, an idler, a highwayman, a traitor, a rebel, an Irish Papist wolf-hound ! Do I know my own pupil ? And—oh my God !—is it he who has the coat ? Oh, we are doubly lost ! Knaves, fools, all conspire to ruin us ! "

I let him run on, for he was like one demented. But you may suppose I opened my eyes as I heard this brave character of my new friend.

" Your pupil, is he ? " said I at last ; " then I counsel you to stay where you are ; for he will assuredly eat you alive if he gets you."

The Welshman paid no head to this warning, but rushed on, jabbering in Welsh to himself, and groaning, aye, and even sobbing now and then in his excitement.

At last, after an hour's hard work, we came to where I had found the road that morning. Then, for another hour, I dragged him through the swamps and marshes. His strength had begun to fail him long ere we reached the river's bank ; and he was fain, when at last we felt solid earth under our feet, to cry a halt.

" I must rest for one moment," said he, puffing and panting and clutching at his side in a way that made me sorry for him. Then he fell on his knees and prayed in his own tongue, and before he was done, sunk half-fainting on a tree-trunk.

" Master Penry," said I, helping him from the ground, " you are not fit to go on. I pray you, let me go alone. This pupil of yours is my friend, and will give me the cloak. Stay here, unless you would spoil all ; for assuredly if he see you, he will turn at bay and yield nothing. The inn is but a mile from here. In less than an hour I will be back with the cloak, that I vow."

He had no strength in him to protest. So I left him there and ran on towards the inn.

CHAPTER V

How I parted with my Cloak

MY mind was all in confusion as I hurried forward to the river-side inn. Everything seemed to be going wrong with me, and I wished heartily I was back in London with my fellow 'prentices, and my kind mistress, and the sweet Jeannette. They, at least, believed in me; but here, everyone with one consent conspired to tell me I was but a fool. I had made myself a laughing-stock at Maidenhead; I had been pinned up against the wall, by a boy my own age, in this place; I had assaulted a Mayor at Oxford; I had parted with my cloak, which contained life and death in the lining of it, to a stranger; and more than all, I had given my love to a fellow who, if the Welshman was right, was a horrible traitor and Papist! A fine piece of work, verily; and little wonder if my conceit was somewhat abated after it all!

Yet, as I ran on, I thought more about my wild friend at the inn, than about any one else. I could hardly believe him to be a rogue; although all that the Welshman said of him tallied with my own observation. Nay, more, to my dismay, I found by my heart that even were he all the rogue he was painted, I could scarcely bring myself to like him the less.

"At least," thought I, "if he be a knave, he is an honest one; and my cloak will be safe with him."

As I came to the inn, which I had scarcely yet seen by daylight, it seemed gayer and more bustling that I had found it last night. Three brave horses stood saddled and bridled at the door, and voices of good cheer from within showed me that mine host was having some little custom for his sack. I wondered if my solemn scholar was of the party, or whether, the better to avoid detection, he still lay abed.

SIR LUDAR

As I entered, I recognised the chief of the four men who sat at the table as my friend the Bishop's man, whom I had met on the road two days ago, but whom, as well as my promise to meet him to-day, I had since clean forgotten. He hailed me gaily, as if he expected me.

"Welcome, lad; you are a man of your word. I knew you would come. Come and join us, there is brave sport afoot."

I coloured up, to be thus commended for what I did not merit.

"Indeed," said I, "I—I am glad to meet you again, but —but (how I stammered) just now I am looking for my friend."

"What! Have you not done your errand?" said he. "You told me it was in Oxford."

"It was. I have done it—but I left a friend here. Mine host," said I, turning to the man of the place, "is my comrade astir yet?"

The host crammed his apron in his mouth to keep in a laugh.

"Astir! Sir Ludar astir! I warrant thee half the bucks in Shotover Wood are astir too before now."

"What!" said I, my face falling suddenly, "is he gone then?"

"An hour since; and by your leave, young sir," added mine host, "I would take leave to remind your grandeur that the score of last night's supper, and a trifle my lord took for his breakfast, with the shoeing and meat of the horse, and the price of your night's lodging, awaits your noble acquittance."

"Gone!" cried I, not heeding all the rest. "And did he leave aught for me?"

"I doubt not he left his blessing, but nothing else."

"But my cloak, he had my cloak."

"If he have it not still, aye, and the nag too, it will be because he has met a stronger man than ever I saw yet on earth," said mine host.

"But the cloak!" roared I, "that cloak had papers in it; it was——"

Here the Bishop's man put down his mug and pricked up his ears.

"Which way did he go?" cried I. "Saddle me my horse. I must overtake him or all is lost."

THE BISHOP'S MAN AGAIN

"Papers?" said the Bishop's man. "What sort of papers, prithee?"

"I know not," said I. "Oh, that cursed cloak!"

"Harkee, my lad," said the man sternly, "answer me two questions, if you will."

He laid hold of my arm, and looked so menacing that I was fairly taken aback.

"And if I do not," said I, as I began suddenly to see what it all led to.

"Then in the Queen's name I shall know what to do with you," said he, beckoning to his three men, who rose and approached me.

I was fairly in a corner now, for a man who held the Queen's warrant was not one lightly to be resisted. Yet what could I tell him?

"Let me hear your questions," said I, as civilly as I could, and edging a little towards the door, "perhaps I can answer them."

"That's a wise lad," said he, mollified, "I know you are but a tool—men, stand back there—I blame you not for doing your duty, but you must tell me here, the name of the man, your master, who sent you this errand, and the name of him to whom you bore it."

"I can tell you neither," said I.

He turned to his men, but before they could rise, I had rushed to the door and was outside. A key stood in the outside of the lock, which mine host used to turn and take with him when business called him to leave his inn empty. I had just time to turn this and vault on one of the three horses, when the window was flung open and the leader of the band sprang on to the casement.

But he was too late; for before he could level his musket at me, I was twenty yards away at a gallop, leading by the bridle the two spare horses which had stood at the door beside the one I rode.

The shot, badly aimed, whistled past my ear, and served to urge on the horses to a wilder pace, so that, before even the party was outside, hallooing after me, I was a furlong off, plunging deep into the wood.

I had no time to think if I had done well or ill, or what the upshot of it all was like to be. Time enough for that

SIR LUDAR

when I had won clear. The led horses, after their first fright, jibbed at the reins and struggled to get free. So, as they checked my speed, I let them go, and saw them plunge away among the trees, no easy capture for their lawful owners. Meanwhile, I dashed forward whithersoever the horse took me. I remember, even amid my panic, what a delight it was to sit astride of so noble a beast, who seemed to scorn my weight, and skim the earth as lightly as if he carried a child. Had it been my own sorry nag I should long since have been by the heels.

Once clear of the wood I suddenly sighted Oxford towers to my left, and found myself on the road by which I had passed but an hour ago with the angry Welshman. I had forgotten him, and 'twas well for him that I had.

I had no mind to put myself again within reach of his worship, the Mayor of Oxford, and his merry men; so I tugged my right rein and kept my horse's head turned to the wooded hills northward. There, thought I, I can at least find time to draw breath and determine what must be done next. To the forest I sped, then, marvelling at the pace of my brave horse, and wondering if the Bishop's man was yet on the road at my heels.

On the steeper ground my horse slackened a bit, but I urged him forward till we were deep in the wood, with a choice of four or five paths, any of which led, heaven knows where. Here I let him stand and get his wind, while I turned over in my mind what should be my best course.

While I was debating, to my surprise, my horse pricked up his ears and gave a loud neigh, which was answered from no great distance by another. At first I supposed his companions had followed us, or that our pursuers were nearer than I reckoned for. But, on listening, I perceived that the strange horse was ahead of us, not behind. I therefore moved slowly forward in the direction of the sound. What was my surprise when I saw my own poor nag tethered to a tree, with my cloak—the cause of all this trouble—laid carelessly over his back.

Master Penry's wild pupil was nowhere near, yet I scarce gave him a thought at the time, so overjoyed was I to recover my long-lost prize. I sprang from my borrowed horse, letting him stray where he would, and fell upon the garment like a

A BURIED LIBEL

mother on her lost child, except that I, having taken it to my arms, whipped out my knife and proceeded to rip it up from top to bottom.

Master Penry had been right! The cloak was stoutly padded with printed sheets, of which I took out fully three score. They were all the same, a short tractate of twelve pages duodecimo, set in my master's type (for I recognised the letter and the flowered initials), and printed, there was no doubt now, at his secret press.

The title of the tractate was "A Whip for the Bishops," and to my wrath and confusion as I read, I found it contained wicked and scandalous abuse of their Graces of Canterbury and London, whom it called wolves in sheep's clothing, antichrists, and I know not what horrid names besides! And it was to carry this wicked libel I had been sped on this journey, decked with my brave cloak, and commended to that Welsh varlet, who, no doubt, was the author, and counted on me as the tool to help him to disseminate his blasphemous treason!

He little knew Humphrey Dexter. Although I had put a queen's officer in the duck pond; although I had assaulted a mayor; although I had defied a bishop's warrant, and made off on a bishop's horse, I yet was a loyal subject of Her Majesty, and hated schismatics as I hated the Pope himself. They had played me a trick among them; I would play them one back.

So I gathered up the libels, and dropped them one and all, together with the false lining of the coat, into the hollow of a rotten tree; where, for all I know, they may be to this day. And if, years hence, some lover of the curious should seek to add to the treasures of his library a true copy of that famous lost tract, "A Whip for the Bishops," let me tell him in his ear, the book is to be had cheap, midway across Shotover wood, somewhere to the left of the lower path which leads to Heddendon. Nowhere else was it ever published, to that I can vouch.

I had scarcely finished my task when I heard a whoop from among the trees, followed immediately by the whiz of an arrow which glanced betwixt my cheek and my shoulder, and buried its head deep in the trunk of a near tree.

I had scarcely time to face round and draw my sword, when I perceived coming down the glade my wild scholar

SIR LUDAR

with a bow in his hand, and a dead fox on his back. He had plainly not seen who I was at first, but recognised me as soon as I turned. He marched gravely towards me, equally heedless of my drawn sword, and of the shaft which a moment ago had all but taken my life.

"Is it you?" said he; "I took you, in your cap and gown, for my tutor."

"You all but killed me, too," said I, wrathfully.

"Aye, it was a bad shot. Yet, had you not moved your head, it would have spiked you by the ear to that tree. What brings you here?"

I was taken aback by the coolness of the fellow, who talked about spiking me by the ear as if I had been the fox he carried on his back.

"Marry," said I, "you should know what brings me here. My horse and my cloak, they brought me here, sirrah."

"Nay, they brought me here; but I am not sorry to see you. I was about to return to the inn, to look for you."

I flushed to the roots of my hair, to think how readily I had set this man down as a runaway thief. Never was a face less deceitful, or a manner less suspicious; and I, if I had not been a fool, might have known as much.

"I did you an injustice," said I, returning my sword, "I believed you had given me the slip, and were——"

"A thief," said he, with a scornful curl on his lips. "I thank you, master 'prentice."

I would sooner he had cut at me with his dirk. But further parley was ended by a sudden noise of horns and a tramp of horses close by.

I sprang to the alert in an instant.

"The bishop's men!" cried I, "we are pursued. Fly!"

"Too late for that," said my comrade, as a party of huntsmen, some mounted, some on foot, broke through the glade at the very spot where we stood.

It was not the bishop's men; but to my horror I recognised in the leading horseman, his worship the Mayor.

At sight of me in my cap and gown, and of my comrade with his bow and the dead fox, and of the horse tethered to the tree—(the bishop's horse had strayed, I know not whither) —the hunters raised a loud cry, and closed upon us.

"Seize the varlets," cried the mayor, "they are caught

THE MAYOR GOES A-HUNTING

at last. By my life, a scholar, too. If he smart not for this, and something else, call me a dullard."

I saw by that he did not recognise me, although he cherished a lively memory of that morning's adventure.

My comrade, somewhat to my surprise, submitted quietly to superior numbers, and I was fain to do the like. It were better to be punished for poaching, than to be arraigned before the High Court of Star Chamber for publishing seditious libels.

"Bring them away, bring them away," cried the mayor, who was in no amiable mood. "I warrant they shall learn one lesson well, for once in their lives. Scholars indeed! a parcel of lewd, blood-thirsty, poaching scoundrels, with no more conscience than a London apprentice. Come, away with them to the city."

At this a gay young stripling rode up.

"Father," he said, "is our day's sport to be spoiled for a brace of rogues like these? Surely they will keep an hour or two, while we have our chase. Let some one guard them in the ranger's house, and we can take them up with us as we return at evening."

His young companions seconded his request. So the Mayor, who would have enjoyed more to clap us in the pillory than to win half the antlers in Shotover woods, consented, and bade three of his men conduct us to the ranger's lodge hard by, and keep us there till the party returned.

I saw my comrade's eye light up at this, but he said nothing; and looking very crestfallen and abashed we followed our guard, with hands tied, and heard the huntsmen's horns tantivy merrily away for their day's sport.

The ranger's lodge was a hut of but a single room, into which our keepers thrust us with little ceremony, and made-to the door. They were stout men, all of them, and carried cross bows, besides the daggers at their girdles. We heard them grumble angrily to be baulked of their day's sport by a couple of college boys like us, and to be shut up here all day long with neither drink nor food nor anything with which to make good cheer.

Whereat one of the party pulled out a box of dice, and for lack of better sport they began to play.

Meanwhile, I watched my comrade, who, on entering,

had thrown himself on the floor, and composed himself as if to sleep. But though he lay with his head on his hands, it was plain to see he was not dreaming; for the muscles of his face were working, and his body once or twice seemed exercised as with some effort. What this was, I guessed soon enough. He was gnawing the cord which bound his wrists; whereupon I set to do the same, and, in a quarter of an hour I was free. Already my comrade had signalled to me that he was rid of his bonds, but warned me to give no sign, but wait the signal from him. So we both lay still, and I, the better to keep up the part, snored long and loud.

Our keepers, meanwhile, gave us no heed, but played deep and eagerly. We could hear by the growls and oaths that kept company with the rattle of the dice, that the luck was not going even. One of the three won the throw, time after time, and crowed so loud at each success, that the others (as was only natural) turned first surly, then angry. But the winner heeded not their wrath, but continued to cackle insultingly, until their patience being all spent, they knocked over the table, and fell to blows. Now, surely, thought I, is the time for us. But my comrade still lay low, and signed to me to do the same. For we were unarmed, and had we been too soon, all had been spoiled.

The fight that followed was short and sharp. The single man held his own for a few minutes, but fell at last, borne down by superior numbers and a stab in the thigh from one of his assailants. Then, when in dismay, the two dropped their daggers and knelt to see if he were dead or alive, my comrade gave the signal, and we sprang at one bound to our feet. In a moment the two men were in our grip, and at our mercy, and so taken aback were they by our sudden attack, that they cried quarter, even without a struggle, and let themselves be bound with the cords of which we just now rid.

As for the third, he was wounded, though not badly, and we left him unfettered. Then arming ourselves with a cross bow apiece (the spoils of war) and our own blades, we locked the door on our keepers, and bade them farewell. One thing troubled me in our escape, which was this, that my nag (or rather, Master Udal's) and my cloak were both gone a hunting with the mayor. However, we could not both have ridden the one, or worn the other, and we might perchance run less

A TREATY OF ALLIANCE

risk without them than with them. As for the college cap and gown, my comrade nailed them with our keeper's two daggers on the outside of the door when we left, in token that here he bade farewell for ever to the life of a scholar.

It was scarcely three o'clock in the afternoon when we made good our escape. Before sundown, thanks to my comrade's knowledge of the country (which was all the more wonderful that he had been only two months at Oxford), we had fetched a wide circuit round the north of the city, and were safe on the Berkshire side of the river beyond Wightham, on the road to Abingdon.

For four hours my comrade had paced at my side without a word, and I, finding nothing to say, had been silent too. When, however, all danger from our pursuers was past, and night invited us to halt at the first convenient shelter, he stopped in the road and broke silence.

"Friend," said he, "what is your name?"

"Humphrey Dexter, at your service," said I. "May I ask yours?"

"You may call me Sir Ludar," said he, gravely. "And since we two have been comrades in peril, give me your hand, and let heaven witness that we are friends from this day."

I gripped his hand in silence, for I knew not what to say. My heart went out to this wild, odd comrade of mine, of whom I knew nothing; and had he bidden me follow him to the world's end, I should yet have thought twice before I refused him.

That night, as we lay in a wayside barn (for my purse was run too low to afford us an inn), Sir Ludar told me something of his history: and what he omitted to tell, I was able to guess. He was the youngest son, he said, of an Irish rebel chieftain, Sorley Boy M'Donnell by name; who, desiring at one time to cement a truce with the English, had given his child in charge of a Sir William Carleton, an English soldier to whom he owed a service, to be brought up by him in his household, and educated as an English scholar and gentleman. The boy had never seen his father since; for though his guardian began by treating him well, yet when M'Donnell turned against the English, as he had done, Sir William's manner changed. He kept hold of the boy, not so much as a ward but as a hostage, and ruled him with an

SIR LUDAR

iron rod. The lad had been handed over from governor to governor, from school to school, but they could do nothing with him. Some of his masters he had defied, others he had scorned, one he had nearly slain. His guardian had flogged him times without number, and threatened him still oftener. His guardian's lady had tried to tame him with gentleness and coaxing. He had been admonished by clergy, and arraigned before magistrates. But all to no purpose. He snapped his fingers at them all, and went his own way, consorting with desperate men, breaking laws and heads, flinging his books to the four winds, making raids on her Majesty's deer, flouting the clergy, denying the Queen, and daring all the Sir William Charletons on this earth to make an English gentleman of him. At last his guardian (who really, I think, meant well by the lad, rebel as he was) sent him to Oxford, to the care of Master Penry, the Welshman, who, by all signs, must have had a merry two months of it. At least, I could understand now why he had been more anxious to get back my cloak than his truant pupil. Nor could I blame him if he sighed with relief when Ludar, having fallen foul of every one and everything at Oxford, and learned nothing save a smattering of Spanish from a Jesuit priest, took up his cap and gown and shook the dust of the University from his feet.

"And so," said my comrade, who, as I say, left me to guess the half of what I have written down, "I am rid of them all; and, thank the saints, I am no gentleman yet."

Whereupon he dropped asleep.

CHAPTER VI

How I walked with a Rebel

"WHERE do we go next?" asked I in the morning as we shook ourselves free of the hay which had been our bed, and sallied out into the air.

He looked at me with a smile, as though the question were a jest.

"To my guardian's," said he.

"Why!" said I, "he will flog you for running away from Oxford."

"What of that?" said Sir Ludar. "He is my governor."

It seemed odd to me for a man to put himself thus in the lion's maw, but I durst not question my new chief.

"You shall come too, and see him," said he. "It passes me to guess what he will do with me next, unless he make a lawyer or a priest of me."

"I must back to my master in London," said I.

"The printer!" said he, scornfully. "He is thy master no more; thou hast entered my service."

This staggered me. For much as I loved him, it had never occurred to me to bind myself to a penniless runaway.

"Pardon me, sir," said I. "I am bound to the printer by an oath. Besides, I know not yet what your service is."

"My service," said he, "is to be free, and to put wrong right."

"'Tis a noble service," said I, "but it fills no stomachs."

"You 'prentices are all stomach," said he, sadly. "But 'tis always so. No man that ever I met believed in me yet. I must fight my battles alone."

This cut me to the quick.

"Not so," said I. "Last night I swore to be your friend. It was a mad oath, I know; but you shall see if I do not observe it. But till two years are past, I am bound by an oath to my master the printer, and him I must serve. Then, I am with you."

This I thought softened him.

"Well," said he, "who knows where we may be two years hence?"

"God knows, and we are in his hands."

"So be it," said Sir Ludar, crossing himself, to my grief. "Meanwhile, Humphrey, we are friends. I may claim your heart if not your hand?"

"You may—or," here I blushed, "a share of it."

"What mean you by that?" asked he, sharply. "What man holds the rest?"

"No man," said I.

He laughed pleasantly at that.

"A woman? I have heard of that distemper before. It comes and goes, I'm told. Had it been a man, I should have been jealous."

There was little sympathy in that for my sore heart, so I said no more.

"Come," said he presently, "you shall come to my guardian's. He lives at Richmond, and it is on our way to London. If he turn me off, you shall take me to London, and make a printer of me, if you please."

I agreed to this, and we stepped out on our journey.

A strange journey it was. My comrade, for the most part, stalked silently half a pace in front of me, sometimes, it seemed to me, heedless of my presence, and sometimes as if troubled by it. Yet often enough he brightened up, and began carolling some wild song; or else darted off the road after a hare or other game which he rarely failed to bring down with his arrow; or else rallied me for my silence, and bade me talk to him.

At these times I asked him about his own country, and his father, and then his face lit up. For though he had not seen either since he was a child, it was clear he longed to be back.

"What prevents your returning now?" said I.

He looked at me in his strange wondering way.

"Know you not that M'Donnell is an exile, and that the hated Sassenach holds his castle?" demanded he.

TOKENS OF BROTHERLY LOVE

I confessed I did not; for a London 'prentice hears little of the news outside. Besides, though I durst not tell him as much, I did not know who M'Donnell, his father, might be; or what he meant by Sassenach.

"But he will feast in Dunluce once more," cried he, "and I shall be there too. And the usurper woman Elizabeth shall—— "

Here I sprang at him, and felled him to the ground!

The blood left my heart as I saw what I had done. As he lay there, I could hardly believe it was I who had done it; for I loved him as my own brother, and never more so than when he leapt to his feet, and with white lips and heaving chest stood and faced me.

I was so sure he would fly at me, that I did not even wait for him to begin, but flung myself blindly on him. But he only caught me by the arm and shoulder, and flung me off with such strength that I reeled and staggered for a dozen yards before I finally fell headlong with my face in the dust.

Then he turned on his heel and walked on slowly.

It was no light thing, after that, to pick myself up and, spitting the dust from my mouth, go after him. But I did. He never turned as I came up behind, or heeded me till I stood before him and said:

"Sir Ludar, I smote you just now for speaking ill of my Queen. A man who is disloyal to her is no friend of mine; therefore farewell."

He glanced me over, and his face had lost all its anger.

"She is no Queen of mine," said he. "I was born her enemy. For all that, you did well to strike when I spoke ill of her. I would do as much to you were you to speak evil of my Queen." And here he raised his cap.

"Your Queen?" said I. "And who may she be? There is but one Queen in these realms."

"I know it," said he. "Her I serve."

"Do you mean," said I, "that you serve—— "

"Hush!" said he, with his hand at his belt. "I serve Queen Mary, and all the saints in Heaven preserve her! Now, Humphrey Dexter, is it peace or war?"

"I pray every day for the confusion of her Majesty's enemies."

SIR LUDAR

"Why not?" said he, "so you pray not aloud. I do the same."

"Not so," said I, "or I should not have struck you. Nor shall it be peace if you dare to breathe her Majesty's name again in my hearing."

"Heaven is my witness I have no wish to breathe it," said he, with a curl of his lips. "Nor, if you breathe the name of mine, need you look for so gentle a tumble as I dealt you just now. Come, your hand on it."

So we struck hands for the third time and went on.

My conscience troubled me sore the rest of that day. What had I come to, to assort thus with a declared enemy of our gracious Queen, and, more than that, to love him more every mile we walked? I could not help it, as I said before. He was so unlike a common rebel, and so big in his heart to every one and everything that claimed his aid.

Once that day, as we toiled along the hot road, we overtook a poor woman carrying a bundle in one arm, while with the other she strove to help along a little, footsore child, who whimpered and stumbled at every step. Without a word, Sir Ludar took the child and bundle both from the scared mother, who gave herself up for lost, until he asked her gently whither she went, and might he help her so far with her burdens? Then she wept, and led us a clean four miles off our road to her cottage, where Sir Ludar put down the bundle and the now sleeping urchin and bade her adieu before she could thank him.

Another time, as we were mounting a hill, we came up with a hay cart which the patient horse could scarcely drag. Whereupon he set to to push the cart behind, calling on me and the bewildered carter to do the same, till we had fairly hoisted it to the crown of the hill.

Another time he fell foul of a parcel of gipsies who were ill-using an old man of their tribe, and a lively fight we had of it, we two against six of them, amongst whom was the old man himself. When at last we had got rid of them I hoped that our adventures for the day were done, for I was tired and wanted to rest my bones in a bed.

But as we passed through Reading the righteous soul of my comrade was vexed by the sight of a boy sitting howling in the stocks.

TO THE STOCKS WITH THE BEADLE

"No doubt he deserves punishment," said I.

"Deserve or not, he has had enough, for me," said Ludar, and began kicking away at the boards.

Of course there was a commotion at that, and the constable came to see what the noise was about. Ludar desired nothing better, for he made the fellow disgorge his key, which saved a vast power of kicking. Then, when the boy was free and had darted off to the woods, Sir Ludar, with a grim smile, locked up the beadle in his place, and flung the key into the pond. Then as the watch and a posse of the townsfolk turned out to see what the uproar was, we ran for it and got clear.

This last proceeding did not please me. For it was defying the Queen's law, and as I said to my comrade, it was not for us to set ourselves up against authority.

But Sir Ludar would listen to no reason.

"The lad was miserable where he was," said he.

"So is the beadle now," said I.

"The better the lesson for him," said Ludar.

There was no use arguing, so we trudged on some miles further till night fell, and we took shelter again in a barn.

The next day, guiding ourselves chiefly by the river, we came to Windsor, where I had much ado to hinder my comrade from going a-hunting in her Majesty's forest. Had it not been that I persuaded him we might almost reach Richmond that night, I think, for mere spite of the law, he would have stayed.

As it fell out, we were far from reaching Richmond that night. For the way was difficult with swamps and thickets, so that we were glad enough to reach Chertsey by sundown. I was for spending what little remained of my money at the inn, but this he would not hear of; so we took our supper, and then, as the night was fine, slept in a field of hay. Sweet lying it was too, and when early next day we plunged into the clear river and refreshed out travel-stained limbs, we felt men again.

It was well on in the afternoon when we arrived at Richmond. We should have been there sooner, but that my comrade was for ever calling a halt or turning aside on some errand of chivalry. Mad enough I thought some of them, but then he never asked me what I thought; and if ever I hung back, he did what he needed without me. Yet whatever he did, it was to help some one weaker than himself, and if my patience now and then failed me, the honour I had for him grew, as I said, with every mile we went.

I say it was afternoon when we reached Richmond. As we approached the place my comrade's desire to see his guardian waxed cool, and he cast about him for an excuse, if not to avoid going to the house, at least to put it off till night. I proposed that we should rest ourselves under the trees in the park, to which he agreed. But it was an unlucky move. For we had not lain half an hour, enjoying the shade, and I half asleep, when he started up with a "hist," and slipped an arrow into his bow.

At that moment a fine buck went by. He had not spied us while we lay still, but the moment my comrade moved, he threw up his head and bounded off. Yet not before a quick twang from Sir Ludar's bowstring had sent an arrow into his quarter

"Are you mad?" cried I, in terror, "it is the Queen's deer!"

"Follow! follow!" shouted Sir Ludar, who was every inch a sportsman.

I tried to hold him back, but he heeded me no more than had I been a fly. With a loud whoop, he dashed away in pursuit. He had not gone twenty yards from me, when there was a great shout and clatter of horsemen, and before I well knew what had happened, I saw Sir Ludar disarmed in the clutches of half a dozen men. I rushed to his help, but could do nothing except share his fate. For they were too many for us, and we had no time even to hit out.

"Where is the captain?" cried one of the men.

Just then up rode a man at sight of whom the blood tingled in all my veins. I mean Captain Merriman.

I do not know if he recognised me at first, for he scarcely gave us a look.

"Away with them to your master," said he, riding on, "and see they give you not the slip."

So we were marched off, a pretty end to our jaunt. And to make our plight worse, Sir Ludar whispered to me as we went along, "Unless I mistake, the master of these men is my guardian, Sir William Carleton."

Sure enough it was.

AN OMINOUS ARREST

The house we were conducted to stood in a large park with a view far over the river, perhaps the fairest view in England. Yet I had no mind just then to admire it; for the presence of that hated horseman made me forget all except one fair face, which I seemed to see as I had seen it that day at Finsbury Fields. He rode forward as we entered the park and bade the men bring us safely in.

"Come, step out," said one of the men, giving me a flick with his riding-whip, "we have been waiting for you these three weeks, my gentlemen; and I promise you a warm welcome from his worship. The captain, his visitor, will be in high favour, now that he has run the vermin to earth—what say you, Hugh?"

"I warrant you that," said Hugh. "For our master had set his heart on catching the vagabonds, and nothing could please him better."

"Heigho! It is we have had all the watching these weeks past; but this gay spark will have all the glory now. Well, so the world goes. I shall be glad to see him started on his Irish wars, for I like him not."

"Nor I—and yet we are not like to see the last of him soon, if the rumour which my lady's maid hath whispered me, that some fair company is expected shortly at the hall, be true."

The other laughed.

"No, truly, he is no proof against the flutter of a skirt, as some here know. Did I tell you what befel him not long since in London town, at the place where the 'prentice boys' sport? I had it from one of his own men. But here we are at his worship's. You shall hear the story another time, and I warrant you will crack your sides over it."

Sir William, being an old man and gouty to boot, saw his prisoners in his own room, whither we were accordingly conducted. I had no chance to get a word with my comrade, who, I noticed, kept his hand to his mouth, and pulled his cap over his eyes—I suppose, to conceal himself from those about the place who might know him. As for me, I had no desire to hide myself from the only man there who knew me.

Sir William was a fine, red-faced, white-headed old gentleman, with something of the old soldier in his air, and (when he came to speak) a good deal of him in his words. He sat

SIR LUDAR

in a great chair, with one foot swaddled on a stool before him; and the oaths with which he greeted each twinge as it came, boded ill for us his prisoners.

He kept us waiting a long time at the dimly lit end of the hall, while he spoke to his guest. At last he ordered us to be led forward. As we advanced, and their eyes fell on us, each uttered an exclamation. I kept my eye on Captain Merriman, and watched the storm that gathered on his brow, and the crimson flush that sprung to his cheeks. It was plain he knew me again, and I was content.

As for Sir Ludar, he stared listlessly at his guardian till it should please his worship to speak.

His worship began with a string of oaths.

"Why, what means this, sirrah! How came *you* here, you vagabond Irish whelp, in this company? Speak, or by my beard, I'll—I'll—— "

He did not say what he would do, for his foot gave him a twinge which demanded of him every word he could spare.

"I have left Oxford, Sir Guardian," said Ludar, "I liked not the place, or the ways of the place, or the Welshman, my keeper; and as for my present company," said he, turning to me, " 'tis good enough for me. It was I shot the deer, not he; and so pray bid these fellows loose him."

At this the angry old soldier nearly went off in a fit. He flourished his stick towards the offender, and even tried to rise from his chair, a proceeding which brought on fresh pangs, and set him swearing hard for a minute or more.

"How now! what, a murrain on you, puppy! Am I to be told my duty by a raw-boned, ill-conditioned Irish gallowglass that I have fed at my table and spent half my life in making a gentleman of? What do you think of that, Sir Captain? How would you like to be saddled with a young wolf-hound cub like that—Sorley Boy's son he is, no other, on my life—that I was fool enough to take wardship of when he was a puling puppy and his father an honest man? What do you think of that? Curse the whole tribe of them, say I."

"By your leave, Sir William," said the captain in a smooth soft voice, that made every hair on my body bristle, "good deeds have always their reward; but as for the deer that was shot, your ward is generous enough to shield the real offender

ALL THE WORLD IS AGAINST ME

at his own cost. I should be sorry indeed had it been otherwise."

I could see the veins in my comrade's neck swell while this talk went on. But he remained silent, while Sir William said :

" By my soul, it wants but to look at the varlet to see poacher written in his face ! And the Queen's deer too ! Come, you men, which of you was it caught the rogue ? "

Here one of the men, seeing how the wind lay, swore before heaven that he saw me shoot the deer, and took me red-handed, with my bow in my hand. And when one sheep leads the way, the others follow. They all swore it was I ; while some added that my comrade lay asleep under a tree, and knew nothing of the matter till I was captured.

Then Sir William grunted, and turned to his ward.

" 'Tis well for you, sir puppy, these honest fellows give you the lie. Had they done otherwise, I could have believed them ; and I promise you, ward and all as you are, I would have hanged thee for slaying the Queen's deer, as surely as I will hang this cunning rogue here. Let the boy go, men ; and now you," said he, turning to me, " you ill-looking hang-dog, you, say your prayers, for to-morrow you ride to the Assizes, and then the Lord have mercy on thy black soul ! "

It surprised me that Sir Ludar took his release quietly, and now stood by with thunderous face, but apparently heedless of my sentence.

" Take him away there," said his worship, " and make him fast in the cellar. These dogs are slippery vermin, so take care. When the rope is round his neck he may wriggle to his heart's content. Come, be off with him."

I looked at Ludar, but his back was turned. I looked at Captain Merriman, and he was smiling to himself. I looked at his worship, and he was swearing at his foot. So as all seemed against me, I turned sadly enough and followed my guard to the dungeon. I cared little enough what came to me. Ever since I set foot out of London things had gone against me. I was steeped breast-high in disloyalty and lawlessness ; I had staked my peace of mind on a rebel, and now it seemed even he had done with me. Yet I could not believe that. Had I done so, I think I should have beaten out my brains upon the wall of that damp cellar. As it was,

SIR LUDAR

I sat there, too bewildered to think. And so, for lack of anything else to do, I fell asleep.

I know not how long I had slept, when I was aroused by a hand on my arm. As I might have known, it was Ludar. He had a dish of venison pasty and a flagon of wine in his hands, which he set before me, and in dumb show bade me eat. I obeyed heartily, for I had not tasted food since the morning. Then he took me by the hand, and led me in the darkness up the steps and into the open air. Once clear of the house he broke silence.

"Farewell," said he, "I may stay here. My guardian threatens to send me back to Oxford in charge of a troop, but I think I shall stay here a while."

"But," said I, "will you not get yourself into trouble over this?"

"Over what? your release?" said he, laughing, "I think not. The old gentleman will rave somewhat at first, but when it comes to hanging me or nobody, he will hold his peace. He cannot afford to see a ward of his swing with his feet off the ground. Moreover, as soon as I can hear news from the north, I shall go to find my father. So, farewell, Humphrey. Expect me in London ere long, and forget not our oath."

I gave him my hand in answer, and with a heavy heart started on my way.

I had not gone many paces when he came after me.

"Who and what sort of man is this Captain?" said he.

"He is the Devil," said I. And I told him what had passed between us. He laughed loud when I spoke of the duck-pond—so loud that I feared we should be heard.

"Oh," said he, when the tale was done, "that settles it."

"Settles what?" I asked.

"I mean," said he, "that I think I shall slay him."

And with that we parted, he back to the house, I, dismally enough, to London.

CHAPTER VII

How I found Trouble on my Return

IT surprised me to find how desolate I felt as I set out alone on the last stage of my journey. For when I started from London not two weeks ago I was blithe enough, and well content with my own company. But since Ludar came across my path, I was conscious that there was some man better and nobler in the world than Humphrey Dexter ; and to be left now to my own sweet society seemed a poor exchange for the companionship I had had the last few days.

My first thought was to find my way to Master Udal's at Kingston, so as to be near my friend and my enemy both at Richmond. But when I remembered I had lost the minister's horse and failed to carry out his errand, it seemed to me wiser not to go near him at present, but push on to my master's house and make a clean breast of all to him.

The dawn was breaking as I got clear of the park and found the road to Brentford Ferry. I cared not much if Sir William's men came after me, nor was the prospect before me at my journey's end enough to urge me forward with much eagerness. So I dawdled the morning away on the river's bank, bathing and lying disconsolately in the shade, so that it was well nigh midday before I reached the ferry.

Here the strangest adventure befel me. For as I sat watching the boat come over towards me, I perceived that it contained three persons, of whom one was a serving man, and two were women. What was it which made me tremble and catch my breath as my eyes lit on the upright, fearless figure of the maiden who sat in the stern ? I knew her a hundred yards off. I stood irresolute, not knowing whether to fly or wait. If I waited and she knew me not, 'twould

SIR LUDAR

be more than I could bear. Yet, if I fled, I were a paltroon and a boor.

I waited, and the minutes seemed hours while the boat came over. There were four horses also in the boat, one laden with baggage, as for a journey. Were they then leaving London for some distant home where I should never see her more ? Yet if so, why came they this way ?

As they came to shore, I summoned up courage to advance. She knew me in a moment, despite my travel-stained garb and unkempt look ; and held out her hand with a smile of mingled surprise and welcome.

" My kind protector," she said. " To think of meeting you in a place like this."

" I am returning from a long journey," said I.

" And we are starting on a longer," said she.

" And a pretty prey we be," said the old nurse, " to all the bandits, and man slayers, and women eaters with which you English line your high roads. In Ireland, my pretty lady might walk alone from Bengore to the Head of Kinsale, and not a body would hurt her ; but here, we durst not turn a corner, for fear of one of ye."

" Nay, Judy, talk not to our friend here as if he were one of them we fear. Besides," added she, seeing, I suppose, the trouble in my face, " we are like to have a brave enough escort, if what Sir William promises come true."

Sir William ! A great terror came over me when I heard that name.

" Are you then going to Sir William Carleton's ? " said I.

" Yes, and how came you to know it ? " said the maiden.

" Madam," said I, " pardon my boldness. Do you know who is there ? "

I thought she looked offended at this, for she said, gravely :

" Sir William is my mother's kinsman. Is his house far from here ? "

" Not far. I pray you let me take you so far."

" By no means," said she, " our ways lie in different directions. I have a conductor, as you see. Will you inform him as to the way ? "

I obeyed, and, further, bade the fellow look well to his mistress, and keep his eye on a certain captain, who might be at the place to which they went.

BRENTFORD FERRY AGAIN

Then, as I assisted the maiden to mount her horse, I summoned up courage, cost what it would, to say:

"Sir William hath a guest whom you and I saw last at Finsbury Fields. I beseech you, maiden, let me go thither as your servant."

She bridled up proudly, yet, not unkindly.

"No," said she, "if I needed a protector, I could have none better than you. But I need none. Farewell, and thanks, good Master Dexter. The O'Neill's daughter will not forget that one Englishman at least never did her harm. Adieu."

And without waiting for more, she rode forward, followed by her attendants.

Then it seemed as if the sun had gone out of heaven. What was I, a mean London 'prentice, to such as she? Nay, what right had I to suppose she needed either my warning or my protection?

One thing only comforted me. Sir Ludar was still at his guardian's house, and with him there, no harm could well befall any distressed maiden. In my vanity I even wished he could know that in serving her he would be serving me, his friend. Yet, I fancied, if it came to the point, he might as soon wring the captain's neck for the maiden's sake, as for mine.

The one thing this meeting had gained for me, was that it assured me, however little she cared for me, she yet remembered me; and, further, now I knew her name, and that to one in my plight was no small prize.

"If your worship be not pressed for time," said a voice, "I am; so good-day to you."

I looked round, and there was my old acquaintance the ferryman, making ready to put off.

This roused me, and I jumped into the boat.

This time the ill-looking Charon made no venture for my purse. Little enough he would have found in it, had he got it. He demanded his fare as if he had never before seen me; nor was it till I demanded if his rascally mate, whom I pitched into the river, had ever reached the shore, that he condescended to recall what happened ten days before.

But I was in no humour to heed his bluster; and I let him swear on. Had he been civil I should have had to pay

SIR LUDAR

him; as it was, he spared me that, and was lucky that I did not crack his skull with his own oar, into the bargain. I spent the twopence on bread and meat at his inn, and he durst not refuse it; then, with light purse and heavy heart, I set out to reach London that night. It mattered little to me that the way was beset with robbers and bullies. I had neither horse nor cloak; my homely apparel was rent and dirty; my boots were in holes, and my belt was empty. I was not worth robbing, and the few who set on me in mistake, did not stay long when they found the temper I was in. So late that night—it must have been towards midnight—I brought my journey to an end, and stood at my master's door.

Here a sore rebuff met me. For a long time I knocked and called in vain, and woke the echoes of the sleeping Strand. Then from an upper window a voice descended:

"Who goes there? Hold your peace, with a plague on you, or I'll call the watch."

"It is I, Humphrey Dexter. Is that you Master Walgrave?"

"Walgrave! Master Walgrave! you will find him where he has a right to be, in the White Lion; and if you be the apprentice that he spoke of, harkee, the less you are seen about here the better for you; for they say you are as great a knave as your master."

"The White Lion! My master in gaol!" cried I, amazed. "How comes that? Is it true or a lie? By whose order?"

"Make less noise at this hour," said the voice, "and if you doubt me, go and ask. But take my warning and be not seen too near here. Your indentures are ended for long enough. Go and seek a new master and a better; and leave me to sleep in peace."

With that, the window closed, and there was no more to be said.

I could scarcely believe the news the man told me. And yet, when I remembered my master's disorderly ways, and the secret press in the cellar, it was easier understood. Yet it must be for some other business than that which took me to Oxford. For the Bishop's man I had met certainly never had Mr. Walgrave's name from me, nor had a single copy of that scandalous libel, "A Whip for the Bishops," escaped from the hollow tree in Shotover wood.

MASTER WALGRAVE HAS VISITORS

If Master Walgrave were in durance vile, where was my mistress and her family? It was vain, I knew, to attempt to learn more from the sleepy caretaker, at least till morning; nor was there anyone else, that I knew of, from whom I could get satisfaction. So I had e'en to tramp the streets like a watchman till daybreak; and weary enough I was at the end of it.

Then I remembered that Mistress Walgrave had a constant gossip in Mistress Straw, the horologer's wife, three doors off. Perhaps Mistress Straw could give me news. So I waited till the 'prentices (the same two who had shamefully eaten hasty pudding that day the Queen came into London) came to open the door and set out their ware. With them, to my surprise, I saw Peter Stoupe, my fellow-'prentice. He looked sheepish when I hailed him.

"What, Humphrey," said he, in his doleful drawl, "thou hast returned at last. In what misfortune dost thou find us! Our good master in prison, you and I homeless, my dear mistress and her poor babes——"

"Aye, what of them?" demanded I, in no humour to hear him out.

"My dear mistress and her poor babes," continued he, heedless of my tone, "dependent on the goodness of others. Oh! Humphrey, hadst thou stayed at thy post, instead of——"

"A pox on your canting tongue!" cried I. "Tell me where my mistress is, or, by my soul, I'll shake every tooth out of your head."

And I put my hand, not lightly, on his shoulder.

This brought him to reason; it generally did. Peter Stoupe could never remember how to talk till he was reminded.

"She is here, in this house; and I am here to take care of her, by my master's orders," said he, "and there is no room for thee too."

"And Master Walgrave, when was he arrested, and why?" I asked.

"Only yesterday—pray, unhand me, good Humphrey, thy hand is irksome—a pursuivant of his Grace's, with Timothy Ryder from Stationers' Hall, and a handful of the Company at their backs, made a sudden visitation, and searched us up and down, till they lit on—you know what."

SIR LUDAR

"The secret press," cried I, like a fool, letting him see that I knew of it.

"Alack! Humphrey," said he, "there is nothing secret that shall not be made manifest. Without more ado, my poor master was seized and hauled away to the White Lion. 'Woe is me,' said he, as he departed, 'an enemy hath done this, Peter—a viper whom I have nourished at my hearth. Look to my poor wife and little ones, my faithful friend '— these were his words—' and Heaven will reward thy faithful service.' It seemed to me, Humphrey, that when he spoke of the viper, he meant thee. Pray Heaven I may be wrong."

Fancy if I felt merry at this speech! But that I knew by the blink of his eyes the rogue was lying, I could have saved the gallows a job. As it was, I flung him aside and went into the house.

No one but the 'prentices were stirring; so I sat in the shop and waited. It cost me a pang to see the gourmands devour their breakfast, with never a bite for myself; yet, since Peter Stoupe was of the company, it would have cost me a greater pang to eat, had any been offered me—which it was not. For a round hour I sat there, like a hungry bear, neither speaking nor spoken to, when at last there came the sound of a halting footstep on the stairs.

It was my sweet little mistress, and at sight of me she broke forth into crying and laughing.

"Oh, he has come! *Maman! voici notre bon Humphrey.* Why did you stay so long? Why were you not there to save our *pauvre père?* Oh, I am glad to have you back. We shall be happy again."

And she put up her face to be kissed, which I did with beating heart; for she had never looked to me so sweet, nor had her voice sounded so like music to my ears.

"They said you had deserted us," said she, "but I knew it was a bad lie. Peter, *méchant,* what think you now, he has come back, our Humphrey? Go and tell *maman,* and Prosper and the little ones."

You would have been sorry for Peter at that! His face was glum enough when I kissed my little mistress; but it looked fairly ugly when she sent him on this errand. What cared I? There were some yet who thought not ill of Humphrey Dexter.

MY DEAR MISTRESS

Mistress Walgrave, my dear mistress, received me sadly yet kindly. Whether she had believed the false tales of my fellow-'prentice or not, I know not. But she had nothing but welcome for me when she heard my story. And when it was done she told me how she wished I had been home when all the trouble happened.

" 'Tis as well this journey of yours failed," said she. " It might have brought us even greater peril. Your master is too busy a man ; one press was not enough for him, nor one libel. What they took was I know not what, some lamentable complaint, far less harmful than that we sewed in your cloak. How they knew of it, we know not."

" And what is to be done now ? " I asked.

" We cannot stay here," said she, " Mistress Straw, kind as she is, hath not the room nor the means to keep us. Besides, my husband bade me, when this happened, seek shelter from Master Udal, the minister, at Kingston. To him we must go, anon. As for you and poor Peter—who means well, I think—I grieve for you. For I can give you neither work nor board."

"Nay," said I, "you are not done with me, mistress. I will at least see you and the little ones safe to Kingston. But first I would see my master, if I may."

"You may try," said she, brightening up, "but before that, you must have food, for you look weary and half-starved. Come, Jeannette, make ready something for breakfast, and do you, Peter, help us."

After much ado, I was admitted to see Master Walgrave, in the White Lion. He was in a sour mood and well disposed to look on me as the author of his troubles. When I showed him how that could not be, he softened a little.

"I make no complaint for myself," said he. " 'Tis a good cause on which I am embarked, and I shall see it through yet. As for my wife and little ones, let your last service to me be to see them safe to Master Udal's. Had it been possible, I would have had them safe at Rochelle, where even their Graces have no jurisdiction. But for the present I have a claim on the minister for this shelter. Peter Stoupe I mistrust, the more so that he bade me mistrust you. When I am released, you may still claim me as master, though I can no longer claim you as apprentice."

SIR LUDAR

I assured him I wanted no better master, and hoped I might yet serve him. Meanwhile, I promised, that same day, to conduct his family to Kingston.

I had some trouble to persuade Peter Stoupe that his service was neither expected nor desired. Nay, he claimed so stoutly his master's authority to be the guardian of the family, that I had to shake his obstinacy out of him a bit before he would be still. My mistress and the pretty Jeannette were, I think, glad to be rid of him ; and after many thanks to Mistress Straw, we embarked on a fair tide, by which, Prosper and I plying the oars diligently, we reached Mortlach ; whence in a cart we drove as night fell to Kingston. Little enough baggage we had, for the Company's men had forbidden aught to be removed from the house till such time as a further search should be made. So all had to be left until then.

You may fancy Master Udal's amazement, when we landed at his door. He had gone to bed, and had our cart come to take him off to Tyburn, he could scarcely have shown himself more alarmed. However, he was a good man, and owed much to Master Walgrave. So, after praying for strength, he took us all in and bade us lie as we could till morning, when he would make better provision. His own chamber he gave to my mistress and her little ones, while Prosper and he and I lay on the hard floor of the kitchen. Many were the religious exercises in which he led us before he let us sleep ; and even when they were done, he fell on me, and drew from me a full and penitent account of my journey to Oxford and my follies there, for the which he called me many hard names, and bade me take shame to myself, and pray God I might not one day become a knave as well as a fool. Which prayer I humbly uttered then and there, and many a time since.

CHAPTER VIII

How I was cast adrift

MASTER UDAL, the minister, was not a man to bandy compliments. He told me, as we rose next morning, that he had neither the means nor the desire to keep me at Kingston. There was nothing to make my stay of any service to him; nor did the thickness of my skull encourage him to keep me there for my soul's sake.

"In short," said he, "what is to prevent you from going at once? You can find breakfast for yourself on the road as soon as I could find it for you here, and it beseems a body of your size"—heavens! what a name to call me—"better to be serving your calling in London than dangling here at the skirts of a parcel of women. So away with you, Humphrey Dexter, and if you should visit us a week hence, come at an hour when you can return by the road you came the self-same evening."

I should have been angry, but that I knew I had lost him his nag at Oxford, and that the good man (how, I could not guess) was going to board and lodge my poor mistress and her little ones while their distress lasted. I had nothing for it but to obey him meekly. Only I was glad he hinted that I might presently come back to see them.

And now, what was to become of me? My master was in the White Lion, my mistress was at Kingston, the house without Temple Bar was in the custody of Timothy Ryder; there was warrant against me for assaulting a Queen's officer; if I went to Richmond there was a dungeon for me there; if I went home my mother could ill afford to keep me; if I went to the Stationers' Company I was too old now to apprentice to anybody. I was in a bad plight, and what was worst of all, it seemed as if no one cared much what I did or what became of me.

SIR LUDAR

"At any rate," said I to myself as I jogged Londonwards, " I can go to the wars and fight for my Queen—Heaven bless her!"

It was a sore temptation as I passed near Richmond to climb the hill and see what was going forward at the Hall. That house harboured the two people I held dearest in the world, and the one I hated most. Yet I was afraid to go, not because of Captain Merriman or the cellar, but lest I should not read a welcome on Ludar's brow, or should be scorned by that fair lady. No; I must wait till Ludar came to me in London. Meanwhile, forward thither.

I took the boat we had left last night at Mortlach, and went down on the tide. The hard labour of rowing did me good, and made me forget all but the biggest of my troubles. I resolved first to go to my master's house, and see more closely how the land lay there. To my surprise, as I entered, unexpected, I found great noise and revelry afoot; and there sat in my mistress' snug little parlour Timothy Ryder himself making merry with no other than my fellow-apprentice, Peter Stoupe. And if I mistook not, the good cheer on the table came out of Mistress Walgrave's own larder.

"Oh, ho!" thought I. "You are a pretty pair. Now there is like to be a pretty three of us."

So I walked in, and just as Master Peter was lifting the tankard to his hypocritical face, I caught him a whack on the back which sent him off his chair, choking, and groaning aloud that the end of the world was come.

When they saw who it was, their jaws fell a bit, and Timothy Ryder began to bluster.

"Come, come," said he. "What do you here? Who bade you here, pray? Know you not this place is in the Company's keeping? Come, make off with you, rascal, or some of us will see you go keep your rogue of a master company."

"Hold your peace, beadle," said I, "or you shall swing on the beam over your head. Here, Peter, get up."

Peter rose, purple in face, and not very steady in the knees.

"Now," said I, "tell me, where got you that ale?"

"Indeed, Humphrey, I was invited to it. I never——"

"Where got you that beef and bread?"

"I—oh, dost thou think so ill of me as to suppose——"

"That when your master is in gaol, and your mistress and her little ones are homeless, you would come here and

ASSAULTING A CONSTABLE

gorge your vile paunch with the food that belongs to them ? yes, I suppose every word of it, Peter Stoupe."

" But," said he, " I have a right as a 'prentice—— "

" 'Prentice ! " shouted I, " you a 'prentice ! a mean, chicken-livered, gluttonous sneak like you, a 'prentice ! 'fore heaven, you do the craft honour ! Come, bustle away with you, and God save my master from such dirty thieves as you."

Here Timothy Ryder was foolish enough to laugh ; which enraged me past all enduring.

So, beadle and all as he was, I took him by the nape of his neck like a puppy, and flung him into the Strand, bidding him, as he valued his bones, not come within arm's length of me or my master's house till I asked him. As for Peter, he made off without my help ; and here I was with the house to myself.

Then I knew I was in a scrape beside which all the troubles of the past few weeks were as nothing. I had shamefully outraged the beadle of the Worshipful Company of Stationers, acting under the authority of his Grace the Bishop of London ! Nothing I could say or do could undo that. Even if I fled now—which I was not in the humour of doing, since my blood was up—it was too late. For already a crowd was in the Strand, some led by curiosity and Peter's lamentations, others by Timothy's halloos ; and before I knew where I stood, I was besieged.

I had barely time to bolt the door and heap up reams of paper across the passage, before such a battering began as you never heard. I ran upstairs and surveyed the enemy from a window. There were half the men of the Watch there—they wanted me for assaulting a beadle. There were Timothy and a body of Company's men—they wanted me for defying the authority of the Master and Wardens. There were my old friends the Court bullies—they wanted me for the trouble that had happened in Finsbury Fields. There were a crowd of idle townboys—they wanted their fling against a 'prentice. Take it altogether, I seemed to be in request.

It was not much use hurling types at them from the window ; there was nothing bigger than Brevier to give them, and that was too small to break any bones. Nor had I any other weapon. So I put out my head and shouted " Clubs ! Clubs ! " with all my voice, and then went down to be ready for the first man that should break in.

SIR LUDAR

'Twas not long before the door came down; but then they had to pass the barrier I had put up in the passage. I had at a few of them across that, and sent them sprawling; but the enemy was too many for me. And the clubs outside, although they rose to my call, kept themselves to the town-boys and court bullies, and were hands-off to the Watch and the Company. At last one slippery rogue scrambled over the barrier and dodged past me. And while I was engaging him, three or four more did the same; till presently it seemed the game was up. I had to yield the outer passage and retreat to the printing room, where three of the besiegers got in with me before I could make to the door. There was no time to lose, for the door was a weak one, and in five minutes would be down. So I laid about me with the printer's balls, and stunned one of my men and upset another. Then I put the third down the trap-door, which stood open, just as the door began to totter inwards. It was time to go. No good could be got by staying, and whatever came of it, no one would be the better for my capture. So I darted out by the back way that I knew of, where nobody looked for me; and running down the garden, and over my Lord's ground to the river's edge, I took a wherry and made for the other bank.

I could see the crowd presently break through my master's house into the garden, and stand disappointed when they saw I had given them the slip. But I was beyond pursuit; and they trooped back angrily, I suppose to make fast the place against my further intrusion.

Much good I had done by my silly riot! My master's house was wrecked, where it need only have been robbed. My mistress' goods and chattels were no nearer being handed over than they were before; and, since some one must suffer for it all, and I had escaped, it was likely enough my master's lot would be all the worse for him by what had happened. I had no cause to be proud of myself; and to be just, I was not proud.

Now, I knew enough of Peter Stoupe to be sure he would guess I had fled to Kingston. So to disappoint him and the watch both, I turned my boat's head down stream, and resolved to lie hid a week in the city before I showed myself again there. By that time the hue and cry would have ceased, and, further, the time named by Master Udal for my visit would be come.

A FOOL FOR MY PAINS

As luck would have it, I was hailed, as I rowed under London Bridge, by a man from a vessel which had just dropped anchor in the pool. She was a French craft, full of merchandise, part for London and part for Leith, in Scotland; and being under-manned, the captain, seeing me idle, offered me and a few others plying about three days' work in helping to unload. The offer suited me well; and if ever a free man worked like a galley slave, I did for that week. Yet the French fellow was kindly enough, and hearing I was a fugitive from the law, he suffered me to lie on his boat at nights, and even let me feed with his men. Finding, too, that I could talk a smattering of his tongue he tempted me sorely to take service northward with him, and become a sailor. I would have done it but for two things—I must see how my mistress and Jeannette and the little ones fared; and, further, I knew not when I might receive a summons from Ludar to fulfil my pledge to him. So I refused, to his regret, yet we parted friends; and, as you may hear later on, not for the last time.

At the week's end, I found myself once more knocking at Master's Udal door at Kingston. The place looked pleasanter already for the presence of my gentle mistress and her daughter. The little garden was trim and well kept, the windows were brighter, and the children's voices near made the air gladder. As for Master Udal himself, when he opened the door, I could have laughed to see the change in him. His hair was kempt, and the rents in his garments were mended; there was a peep of ruffle at his wrists, and his stockings, which had ever lagged down at his heels, now held up bravely by the buckle at his knee. More than that, he looked scared and jaded, like a man undergoing some penance, and doubtful what will be wanted of him next.

But when he saw me his face grew black, and without a word he flung-to the door in my face. I was so taken aback, that I was minded to laugh and suppose the good man to have lost his wits. But when I came to knock again, and no answer, then the jest went out of the business. What had happened? I walked round the house, hoping to meet someone, but not a soul could I see. Then I tried the door again, but with the same luck as before. At last, quite dazed by the mystery, I gave it up and wandered off anywhere. In the village I met an old man, carrying wood; him I accosted, and asked how the minister fared.

He cackled and laid down his faggots.

"Grammercy, the poor lad's head is turned, neighbour. The Frenchwoman who has come has looked over him. Why—he! he!—he's been to the barber's, and—ho! ho!— he preached an hour short on Sunday, and, forgive us! he hath gotten him a new shirt. She's a witch, I tell'ee; and mark me if the next bundle of sticks I carry up be not for her burning. Ha! ha!"

I told him he was a fool; but the idea was firm stuck in his head, and more I could not get out of him. No doubt but the presence of two sweet women in his house had sorely exercised the minister, but that was not enough to make him shut the door just now in my face and vouchsafe me not a word after my journey.

I wandered on towards the river, wondering what I was to do, when I came upon a sight which explained everything in a twinkling. Down on the bank sat, side by side, Peter Stoupe and the boy Prosper, fishing amicably in the stream. It needed no conjurer to say now who had come betwixt me and my master's family. Peter, no doubt, had brought down a pretty story of me from London; and if, as I feared, my riot with the Company had made matters only worse for my master in the White Lion, it would be easy for my mistress to believe any evil that was told of me. And as for Master Udal, Peter Stoupe was just the lad to pay dutiful heed to his exhortations, and so find admittance where I, a fool and reprobate, was not allowed.

I came on them so suddenly that I had not time to retire before they saw me. Peter seemed taken aback at the sight of me, but the boy Prosper, being a gallant lad, and greatly emboldened by the presence of his protector, rose up with a red face, and shouting, "There goes the villain! Have at you!" flung a stone my way, and would have followed it up had not Peter taken his arm and forcibly held him back.

That was quite enough for me. Had I been guilty of the villainy they suspected, I could not have turned tail more miserably. Had Peter been there alone, I might perhaps have solaced myself by pitching him out into the river. As it was, I could find nothing to say or do except to sneak away

A CRISIS WITH ME

and leave them—one smiling, the other storming at my retreat.

That was not the worst. As I passed once more near the minister's house on my way to reach the London road, I came upon my mistress and Jeannette, walking slowly beneath the willows. At sight of them, my heart thumped hard within me, and I resolved at least to say a word for myself. But as I doffed my cap and crossed the way to meet them, I saw that my mistress looked hurt and distant, and, turning her head from me, drew the maid's arm in hers, and walked forward without heeding me. It stunned me, so that I could not even put one foot before the other, but stood there in the road, cap in hand, gasping for breath, and gazing after them like a man in a trance. Once, when they had gone a step or two, Jeannette glanced round with tears in her eyes, and a look that seemed not all reproach. But her mother drew her forward, and she turned; after which, for long enough, I saw her face no more.

That moment, as I stood there, was a crisis with me. My old life seemed suddenly to have drifted from me. One after another the bonds that held me to it had snapped and sundered. The pleasant 'prentice days were over. My master was in gaol, my occupation was gone, the Company from which I hoped promotion were out against me—London was no place for me now. Even my mistress frowned on me, and my sweet Jeannette, who was wont to believe in me through thick and thin, had turned away.

Was it a wonder, then, if my mind turned with a swing to the only friend that was left me, or if I vowed with myself that, if Sir Ludar would have me, I would follow him wherever he should lead?

My spirits rose—such is the buoyancy of youth—even as I turned and walked towards Richmond. Ten days ago I had not been my own master to follow him when he bade me. To-day, save my Queen, no man but he had a claim on me—aye, and what use had her Majesty for a villain like me who had assaulted a beadle!

It was late at night when I came near Richmond. I durst not show myself in the village, but hid that night in a hut near the river, wondering how I should apprise Ludar of my presence; and ever and anon, in my weakness, asking

SIR LUDAR

myself how it would fare with me were I to find that he too had deserted me?

All the next day I wandered about, hoping for news, but getting none. One man whom I accosted looked so hard at me when I questioned him about the Hall, that I gave him no time to answer, but slunk away to avoid him. At night, my patience came well-nigh to an end, and I resolved, come what would of it, to go to the park, if by chance I might meet Ludar there or at least send him a message.

It was dark when I climbed the palings. There was little chance, unless I marched boldly to the door of the Hall, of seeing him that night, so I resolved to bide my time, and lying somewhere within view of the house, watch till he came out in the morning. I found a thick clump of bushes separated from the house by the width of a lawn. Behind these I ensconced myself, and composed my limbs as best I might to await daybreak.

I was almost dozing, when I started suddenly to hear footsteps and voices not far away. Could it be he? It was too dark to distinguish anything, and as yet their voices were not near enough to detect the words. But they were coming nearer, and in a moment my suspense was at an end. It was not Ludar.

"That is well," said a voice which I knew to be Captain Merriman's. "You say he knows to expect you?"

"Yes, sir; I sent him word that a week hence we should join him at Milford."

"Good. Then we must start to-morrow."

"The men have orders to be at Maidenhead to-morrow night."

"Well, now, Laker; you understand our plan. I am called hence suddenly to-morrow, to London, by the Queen's order."

"Yes, sir."

"To-morrow night, an express comes to you that I am detained at the Court, and ordering you, my second in command, to haste forward to join our men in Wales. Sir William shall also receive a letter telling him that my heart is broken that I cannot take charge of the young lady to Ireland, but that you, an honest elderly dullard, will give her safe escort."

THE VOICE OF THE NIGHT BIRDS

" I thank you, sir."
" That will pacify our young wolf-hound. He counts you a friend."
" Then, Laker, two days hence, at the—— "
" Hush, I know the place. She shall be there, sir."

That was what I heard ; and fool as I may have been, I had wits enough to guess what it all meant.

It was no time for marvelling by what strange chance I had been brought there to hear what I did. How to prevent the villainy was more to the purpose. At daybreak the captain would depart, and a day after, unless we could hinder it, the dove would be in the hawk's clutches. Yet for five hours that night had I to lie still and do nothing! If I showed myself and was caught, all might be lost. Yet if I missed my chance of warning Ludar betimes of the peril impending, it might be too late. So I sat there chafing, through the brief summer night, and at dawn was on the watch.

True to his plan, an hour after daybreak, Captain Merriman mounted his horse and sped briskly away from the Hall. Let him go! We should meet perchance again. But after that I watched the door for hours, and never a sign of Ludar. Should I have to fight for the maiden single handed after all ? At last when I was well-nigh desperate, he sallied out, cross-bow over shoulder, with solemn face, and walked towards the woods. Hiding myself well by the trees and shrubs, I made across to meet him.

His countenance lit up as he saw me ; but otherwise, I might have parted from him but an hour ago.

" I expected you," said he. " Come along. This is no place for talking."

So I followed him in silence deep into the wood, where presently he flung down his bow and put his great hand on my shoulder.

" Humphrey," said he, and I could see that something big was on his mind. " Am I the same Ludar you parted with a week ago ? "

" No," said I, for I had never seen him thus before.

" Humphrey, my lad," said he, " I am undone. I have lived ill and the saints have found me out. My arm hangs feeble at my side. I am turned back from being a man into a boy. I am unworthy of you—and a shame to myself—Humphrey," said he, clutching my arm till every vein in it tingled. "I am bewitched for my sins. Dost thou hear—I am——"

"In love," said I, with sinking heart. I had known what it would come to the moment I parted with the maiden at the Ferry that day. I had prayed against it; I had laughed myself out of the terror that was on me; I had called to mind his scornful jests at love. But all the while I knew what was to come of it. And I knew that what he had won I had lost.

So I finished his sentence for him; and in reply he took my hand and looked at me with an almost humble gaze.

"And you do not scorn me?" said he.

"I love myself," said I.

"Ah! yes," said he, "you told me so; and I scorned you for it. Now—— But what brings you here, Humphrey?"

The change in his voice was so sudden and resolute that it forbade me to say another word about the matter our hearts were fullest of. Who knows but that, had I spoken then, he might have guessed the truth; and so our lives might have broken asunder at that point? Now the chance was past.

But the chance was come to tell him my news, which I did, then and there, and marvellously it moved him. Not that he spoke much, still less raved. But his face grew thunderous and his eyes flashed; and the few questions he asked me he put in a voice which half startled me by its smothered passion.

He took in the whole peril in a moment; and if once I had been fool enough to imagine I should direct the enterprise which was to thwart the villainy, I was soon undeceived.

"Humphrey," said he, "are you free to stand by me in this?"

I told him that now I owned no master but him.

His face cleared up joyously for a moment at that.

"Good; I claim you, then, not as a master, but as a comrade. Be here to-night as the sun sets. Take this bow and dirk; and farewell, my friend, till we meet again."

And he left me.

CHAPTER IX

How I caught the *Miséricorde*

SO restless and anxious was I as the day passed that I hastened back to my hiding-place in the wood early in the afternoon, determined rather to lie there than run the risk of being seen in the village. It was well I did so, for I had not been there half-an-hour when I heard Ludar's heavy tramp crashing through the underwood.

He threw himself beside me, haggard and dejected.

" How is she to know of this ? " said he.

" Tell her," I answered.

He smiled scornfully.

" Had you ever seen the maiden," said he, " you would know that it is no light task. She has me at arm's length. If I tell her of her peril and offer my protection she will perhaps say she needs not my protection, or that, if I like not the peril, I need not face it. Or she may suspect me of serving myself while I denounce my enemy. Or she may take the case to Sir William, whom I believe to be the Captain's friend. To speak plain, Humphrey, I am afraid to speak to her, and for that reason I have come to you."

" Indeed," said I ; " if she would not hear you, how would she be like to heed a plain London 'prentice like me ? "

" At least she would not suspect you of any motive but that of serving her."

Little he knew ! Yet I never saw him less courageous or more humble than now. He was a rude, uncouth outlaw, he said, and knew none of the arts and speeches of a fine gentleman. She laughed at his clumsy ways and despised his ignorance. She would as soon think of trusting her safety to him as to this elderly rascal Laker.

I did my best to reason with him, but in vain. At length,

SIR LUDAR

by sheer compulsion, he dragged me with him towards the park, reminding me of my vow, and bidding me, as I loved him, be his deputy in this matter.

By a lucky fortune, as we approached the gate, who should ride up on her palfrey but our maiden herself. She was alone and without attendant. Ludar told me afterwards that such was her wont. Once he had offered his escort, and she had replied he might come if he could promise her merrier company than her own. "Whereat," said Ludar, "I stayed behind."

She reined up as she saw us in the path before her, and a flush of surprise and pleasure sprang to her cheeks. How much may a man see in a moment! As she sat there, glowing with her rapid ride, and glancing from one to the other of us, I read a long history in her eyes. They were frank and fearless as ever; but as ever and anon they lit on Ludar, where he stood uneasy and blushing, they seemed to me to soften for a moment into a gentleness in which I had no share. If before I had only guessed my fate, something in her air made me sure of it now. And yet, had you seen her there, you would have said the maiden thinks no better of one of these lads than the other; nor does she think over much of either.

"Humphrey, my friend," said she, "I am glad to see you, and in this brave company. Have you taken service under our Knight of the Rueful Countenance, or does he follow you?"

"May it please you," said I, gallantly, "Sir Ludar and I know no service but yours."

"I knew not that you knew one another," said she, ignoring my speech. "Have you been hunting the English Queen's deer again, Sir Knight?"

"No, maiden," said Ludar, gravely. "But Humphrey here hath news for you if you will hear it."

Thus put forward, I related as shortly as possible what I had overheard in the park. She listened calmly; but I could tell by the paling of her cheeks and the heaving of her bosom that my story was a shock to her.

"If this be true," said she presently, "as I suppose it is, why stand we idly here?"

"The Captain quitted the Hall at daybreak," said I. "I saw him go. To-night the letter should reach Sir William

MARCHING ORDERS

announcing his detention at Court, and committing you to the charge of this man Laker."

"Before which time," said the maiden, resolutely, "I shall be far enough away, and with a better escort. What say you, Sir Ludar? When shall we set out?"

So she had accepted our protection before ever we offered it! It would have done you good to mark the joyous smile on Ludar's face as he saw all his difficulties vanish at a word, and found that she took him after all for her champion.

"In an hour's time," said he, "if it be not too speedy a making ready."

"'Tis a long journey," said she. "Which way do we go? and are we to gallop from here to Ireland all the way with the enemy at our heels?"

Then I spoke.

"By your leave," said I, "I know of an easier and safer way than the road. There is a trading ship sails to-morrow from London Bridge to Leith. I know the captain, a Frenchman. If the lady will trust herself by sea——"

"Trust the sea!" cried she, with a laugh. "Why Humphrey, my heart bounds at the thought of it. I was born on the sea. I played by it as a child. It is the only thing free under heaven. Of course we will go by sea. And while our pursuers play hide and seek by road, we shall be drinking the salt breezes, listening to the music of the waves, and watching the happy gulls as they wheel round our heads or speed forward to those we love with tidings of our coming."

And she laughed like a child to whom a holiday is offered, so that we, had there been a thousand roads, could have chosen no other for her or ourselves.

Two hours later, as it grew dusk, I lay in a boat beneath the willows, where the Park sloped down to the river's edge. Thanks to Sir William's gout, and the absence of the Captain, his guest, no one had taken the trouble to recognise me and ask me my business. And any one who may have seen me there would certainly have set me down as waterman to some visitor at the Hall, waiting my orders.

So indeed I was; and as the moments passed, I grew impatient and anxious. The tide would scarcely serve us all the way; and should the Frenchman haul his anchor too early on the morrow, we might find him gone. Besides, every moment they delayed, the man Laker might perchance suspect what was afoot and take measures to spoil our escape.

At length they came, Ludar supporting the old nurse, the serving man carrying a box, the maiden walking quietly in front, as calmly as if she were taking an evening walk to hear the nightingale sing. Not a word was spoken as they embarked, or until the boat, with Ludar and me at the oars, was dropping swiftly down the stream. Then the old woman broke out in a torrent.

"A plague on all these schoolboy antics!" cried she. "Here be we, at an hour when honest folk should be abed, slinking down the river like pirates, with ne'er a pillow to our backs or a covering to our bones—and for why? What am I to say to my master your father, child, when he knows of your running thus from your lawful guardian, and committing yourself to a brace of rawboned gallowglasses that ye scarce know the names of, and for all we know, are bringing us into worse plight than ever they pretend to save us from? Ochone? glad I shall be to see ye safe under O'Neill's roof; for since the day I had charge of ye, I never knew a moment's peace. Are ye not ashamed, hussy? Had ye not lesson enough among the low 'prentices, that day in the fields, and among the gallants here at Richmond, that ye trust yourself now, aye and me to, poor body that deserve better of you, to a parcel of loons on a wild voyage like this? Are ye fool enough to expect any good of such as they? Was not I myself served thus when I was a fresh young maid like you? Innocent indeed! I fancy I can see the ship they talk of, and the hills of old Tirconnell! Take my word, 'tis a trap to lead ye back to London, girl, and no more. And then, you had better have gone west with the Captain, than east with these smooth-faced schemers."

Thus she complained, and the maiden soothed her as best she could, and composed her gently to rest. Amongst us, we made the poor body a bed on the floor of the boat, where she might at least lay her limbs at ease.

For an hour or more she broke fitfully into murmurs and complaints, but presently, as we neared Chiswick, sleep came to her help and ours.

THE VOICE OF THE SIREN

After that, the night seemed to me like a dream. The serving man lay snoring in the prow, and only we three sat up to feast on the beauty of the night. The moon rode high above our heads, changing the river into a silver band, and deepening the mysterious shadows of the crowding woods on either bank. Not a sound was heard but the regular plash of our blades; naught moved but our gliding boat, and the silent water which bore us. Ludar, lugging steadily at his oar, spoke not a word. Yet I knew, though I was at his back, where his eyes rested, and what was the big content in his heart. As for me, lulled by music of our oars, and entranced by the balmy brightness of the night, I forgot my great sorrow, and with my eyes on naught but one fair face, felt a strange peace. Nor I think was she, as she sat there, erect, in the stern, her form clear cut against the silver water behind, indifferent to the restfulness of the scene. Her eyes, gazing far away, seemed to gather in them the wandering rays of the moon; and when presently, scarce heeding, perhaps, what she did, she broke into a soft murmuring chant, which rose and fell with the cadence of our oars, I, at least, felt the bewitchment complete.

Little dreamed any of us how soon the peace of that brief voyage was to be broken.

When the midsummer dawn chased the moonbeams from off the water, we had reached Battersea, on a fast failing tide. Before we reached Lambeth, the stream was turning against us; and it needed all the strength of our arms after that to make headway. Yet how could we tire? She never drooped the livelong night, nor, when she perceived what vigour her music lent to our rowing, did she weary of chanting to us. Keeping close under the marshy southern bank to escape the current, we slowly made our way, till we came at length within sight of the Bridge.

Then ensued a toil beside which the labours of the night were as nothing; for the angry tide swirled fiercely through the narrow way, threatening, when we approached it, to drive us back up stream. Yet, by dint of much effort and clinging to the piles, and, more than all, Ludar's notable exploits with the oars, we won through at last.

The first sound that met our ears was a cheery " Yeo-ho ! " somewhere near, and looking up, I saw the Frenchman, with

SIR LUDAR

the Queen's flag at his masthead, making ready, so soon as the tide turned, to weigh anchor and drop seaward.

He looked over at us doubtfully, as we hailed him and came alongside; but when he saw me and heard what was in the wind, he lowered his ladder and had us up into the ship.

He was a poor man, he said, and his ship ill-fitted for so brave a company; yet if we misliked not his price, and the ladies would put up with the rest, why, then, he would take us.

Then the maiden told him to make himself easy about the price. She had wherewithal to satisfy him on that score. Whereupon the Frenchman grew monstrous civil and bade her consider the ship as her own; while as for Ludar and the serving man and me, what we lacked in money, said he, he would take out of us in work. This suited us well, and the business was settled.

As it wanted two hours yet to the turn of the tide, I begged my new captain's leave, while we waited, to take the boat in which we had come to where it would be restored to its rightful owner. The Frenchman agreed, not without difficulty; "For," said he, "so soon as the tide gives, I must weigh anchor, with you, or without you. Nevertheless, if you must go, go."

Ludar, too, dissuaded me from venturing. But the maiden said: "Why hinder him, Sir Knight? Humphrey is no child that he cannot be trusted; and to prove it, my friend," said she, drawing forth her purse, "as you return, pray buy me a large warm cloak for my good old nurse, who is ill used to the sea and is shivering already. Spend what you need, and bring me back the rest."

The purse was a heavy one, and I wondered at her freak in trusting it all to me, when one piece from it would have sufficed. However, it was not for me to question her; so, promising to be back in good time, I let myself down to the boat, and rowed lustily to the steps below the Bridge. I durst not venture further citywards where I was known; but I remembered my old enemy, Will Peake on the Bridge, and resolved to commit the boat to his care, knowing him for an honest 'prentice who would see it duly returned to its owner. Besides, where better, thought I, could I find a shawl for old Judy than among the Mercers on the Bridge?

So up to the Bridge I clambered, merry to think how

I AM SENT A-SHOPPING

soon I, and all I loved best, would be far away on the free sea, with our enemies all behind, and our hopes all before.

Will Peake hailed me civilly, and hearing of my plight, readily charged himself with the business of the boat. Then it seemed to me I could not do better than consult him about the cloak, and I did so; whereat he puffed himself very big, and said, if I meant to make the garment myself, he could sell me the stuff, if not, I must go into Cheap, and buy one ready made at the shops. So I thanked him, and hastened with quick strides citywards.

I had hoped to get my merchandise over on the Bridge. Yet there was ample time to spare even without haste. For all that, I ran, longing to be safe back on the *Miséricorde*.

Now, just as I came near the Steel yard (where you turn by Dowgate towards Wallbrook) I met a party of soldiers loitering in the road, as it seemed in quest of somebody. Seeing me running their way, they closed upon me as I came up, and bade me halt. I bade them, angrily enough, unhand me and let me go by, as I was an honest citizen, and pressed on an errand to Cheapside. At this they laughed, and said that was what every man they caught vowed, and since they did not like the looks of me, I must away with them to see what their captain would think of me.

I protested in vain that I was in urgent haste; they laughed over again, and had me away to a tavern hard by, where, said they, their captain lodged and would see me anon.

All this time the minutes were flying, and I was at my wits' end what to do. It seemed to me wisest, if I could, to humour them, if perchance they might be cajoled to let me go. But when, after waiting half-an-hour, the captain did not appear, I felt I must do something, or give up hope of reaching the ship in time. So I beckoned the leader of the band to me."

"Friend," said I, as civilly as I could, "indeed I am not the man you take me for; I am a sailor, bound to a merchant vessel, which in half-an-hour is to sail on the tide for sea——"

"A sailor!" quoth he, "nay, by my body, thou'rt a soldier now, my lad, and a brave one to boot. We want lads of thy build for the wars; so rest thee content to travel by

SIR LUDAR

land instead of by sea. Here's money on it," thrusting silver into my hand, " let's see how neatly thou can'st turn up a tankard to the Queen's health ! "

" No," cried I, letting the money drop, " I am no soldier. And as for money," said I, pulling out my lady's purse, " here is an angel for you, good man, if you but let me go."

" Oh, ho," cried he, " 'tis a lad with a purse, is it ? So much the better for us. Here, comrades," cried he.

But I waited for no more. The bells of Cheap were already chiming the hour. With a blow of my fist I felled him, and breaking through the rest of them before they comprehended what I was about, I took to my heels.

Then ensued a hue and cry the like of which Thames Street had not often witnessed. The soldiers, encumbered as they were with their harness, could only shout and raise the town. Others, more fleet, pressed me hard ; others, coming to meet the uproar, hustled me, and struck me at, and tripped me as I went by. But I had not wrestled and played football in Finsbury Fields for naught. At length the crowd became so great, all running one way, that not a man knew why he ran, or what it was all about. As for me, when I saw that, I mingled with the crowd, and shouted, " Stop thief ! " with the loudest of them. Then, when no one thought of me, I slipped quickly down to the water's edge, and flung myself into the first wherry I found.

But by this time the hour was long gone by. For we had been chasing half-an-hour up and down ; up Watling Street, across Cheap, behind the New Exchange, up Cornhill, down Gracious Street, and along the new Fish Street towards the Bridge ; so that when, more dead than alive, I struck out into the stream and shot the Bridge, not a sign was there of the *Miséricorde*.

I was tempted to give it up then, and let who would take me. And, indeed, there seemed a good chance of that. For the owner of my wherry, supposing me to be the thief I seemed, was already out after me, and in another few minutes the hue and cry by water would be as loud as that by land. So on I went on the rapid ebb for dear life. And casting my eyes upward, I noticed that the air was still and windless ; so that wherever she was, the *Miséricorde* could be getting little help from her canvas. And if she were only drifting on the

TOO LATE

tide, why should not I with my oars make as good or better pace than she?

Yet I confess I was sorely vexed to think that they had gone without me; and when I remembered further that I had the lady's purse with me, I could have thrown myself, in despair, over my boat's side. What would they think and say of me!

I could see the waterman's boat behind me come through the Bridge, and guessed well enough that some other craft near it were joining in the pursuit. So I pulled desperately, and made my boat fly down the stream. Yet ever as I turned and looked ahead there was no sign of the *Miséricorde*. Worse still, a flutter of breeze on my brow showed that the wind was already coming, and then, I knew I might row my arms off, and never catch her. The dogged waterman behind me still held on and seemed to be gaining. Little wonder if he did, for I had been rowing all night, and now my arms began to flag. Yet what was his stake on this race compared with mine? So away down the stream I pulled past Deptford, and the Queen's Palace at Greenwich (Heaven save her!), turning my looks now forward, now backward, and praying each minute for a sight of the *Miséricorde*. A little past Greenwich I was near meeting my end; for, looking eagerly for a sight of my pursuers behind, I failed to perceive a boat crossing the river ahead of me; nor was it till my boat's nose struck her full in the side that I was aware of the obstacle. The man and woman in the boat (which seemed to be a floating pedlar's shop plying among the ships) swore at me roundly, and I had much ado to persuade them that no harm was done, and that if any one had a right to complain, I had. I was rowing on, to put an end to the parley, when my eye caught sight of a bundle of garments on the boat's poop.

"Stay," cried I, "to show I bear you no malice, I will even make a purchase of you, if you have what I require."

"Name it," said they, doubtfully.

"Have you a cloak, warm enough and smart enough, to wrap my poor old mother in, when I take her on the water?" said I.

"That have we," cried the woman, fumbling in the heap, "but 'tis more than you will pay."

SIR LUDAR

"How much?" I remanded.

She said a half-angel; but when I too eagerly pulled out my mistress's purse to pay her, her eyes gleamed and she said she was mistaken, she had no cloak there for less than a gold angel.

"Show it me," said I, coming alongside.

It was what I wanted, yet I durst not say so. So I snatched it by force, and tossing the woman an angel, made off with my prize, leaving them amazed and swearing by all the heathen gods they had been robbed and left beggars.

While I delayed thus my pursuers had gained rapidly upon me, and I saw I must pull away in earnest if I was to avoid them. So, comforted to have the cloak, and resolved, if I rowed all the way from here to the sea, I would overtake the *Miséricorde*, I cast aside all languor and made my craft once more leap through the water. The wind was freshening fast and helped me on. Alas! I well knew it would soon do the same both for the Frenchman's sails ahead, and for my pursuers behind. I own these latter were stronger rowers than I, for still they seemed to be creeping up upon me at every stroke, and by nothing I could do was I able to put more distance between us. Should they overtake me, there would be more delay, and that, whatever came of it, meant that the ship would be gone beyond all reach. However, when at length I swung round the point and looked up the broad reach that leads to Woolwich, there to my joy, half a mile ahead was the *Miséricorde*, setting her sails and waiting on the coming breeze.

I paused not to shout, but gathered together all my powers, and let out with my oars until I thought they would crack. For half-an-hour I could not say whether I was gaining on her, or my waterman on me. At length I resolved to risk the short delay of a signal. So I stood in my boat waving the cloak over my head and shouting "Halloo!" with all the breath in my body. I durst not wait more than a moment to watch for a reply. None came, but instead, the yards bellied with the wind. I flung myself with a groan on my seat, and took back my oars. Already the waterman was within shouting distance, and his comrades not far behind. But I heeded not their cries, and plunged my oars once again in bitter chase. It was long before I durst look round. Then,

A STERN CHASE

to my surprise, I saw her standing away in to the Essex shore with all her sails full of wind.

Then all seemed lost, till I reflected that she must come back for another tack before she could clear the bend. If so, I was safe. So I kept steadily on, scarcely holding my own with my pursuers, until at length, to my joy, I saw her put about and bear down full upon me. It was an anxious time as she came up. No one on board, it was clear, guessed who I might be ; nor, I think, did any one perceive me as I lay there, except the man at the prow, who, seeing me resolved to be run down, left me to take my will. By this time my pursuer was a hundred yards away, thinking himself sure of me at last, and saving his breath. It was a race whether he or the *Miséricorde* would be upon me the sooner, but I settled that. For, as the ship came up, slowing towards the end of her tack, I took a few strokes out to meet her, and then turning my boats' head quickly slipped close under. I had already marked a rope that hung from the poop within reach, and on this, when the moment came, I ventured my all. Taking the cloak over my shoulder, and casting away my oars, I sprang to my feet, and gave one leap which sent my empty boat staggering back into her owner's hands, while it left me hanging 'twixt heaven and earth.

To haul myself aboard was the work of a minute ; even as I did so, I could see out of the corner of my eye my pursuer staring round at me, amazed, while he reached out to secure his truant craft. But that was all I saw of him, for next moment I stood on deck half fainting, face to face with Ludar and the maiden and a stranger.

CHAPTER X

How we sailed with a Poet of the First Water

LUDAR told me, when presently I had revived enough to hear his story, that when the tide turned and I did not appear, the Frenchman laughed and bade them haul the anchor and thank Heaven they were rid of a thief. " Whereat," said Ludar, " we came to words, and the maiden took your part and besought the fellow to wait a half-hour. But he would hear none of it. He said he was master here, and, if we liked not the ship, we might go out of it. Indeed," added he, " he had a mind, he said, to put us all out and be rid of so ill a company. Then there was nothing left but to let him have his will, and we sailed. Yet I was not surprised to see you back."

" And she—she did not deem me a traitor ? " I asked.

" That maiden," said Ludar, gravely, " knows not what traitor means."

Whereat I felt partly humbled, partly comforted.

" Yes," said Ludar, " I am glad to have you back, Humphrey, for this voyage bodes uneasily."

" How do you mean ? " I asked.

" Our messmates," said he (and then I noticed that he wore a sailor's jacket), " are a scurvy crew, as you will presently discover. The captain already repents that he has taken us. The old nurse is hard to please." Here he sighed. " The serving man is a fool. And the stranger—— "

" Aye, what of him ? Who is he ? "

" He is a half-witted spark, a fugitive from justice, and, to boot, an impudent coxcomb whom I have had ten minds already to pitch over the ship's side. He was hidden here on board before we came, having killed a man at Court, he brags, and seeking shelter in Scotland till the storm be past. But here he is."

The stranger was a slim, well-shaped youth, with a simpering

A STRANGER ON BOARD

lip, and dainty ringlets descending to his shoulders. He was dressed extravagantly even for the land, and for the sea ridiculously. His doublet was of satin, bravely slashed and laced, and puffed to the size of a globe on either thigh. His hose were of crimson silk, gaily tied with points and knots. His shirt was of the same hue, with a short taffeta cloak over, bound at the neck by a monstrous ruff, out of which his face looked like a calf's head from a dish of trimmings. To crown all, a white plume waved in his hat, while the rapier at his waist was caught up jauntily behind him, so that the point and the hilt lay on a level at either hip. His face was both cheerful and weak; and, as he strutted up to where Ludar and I stood, his gait reminded me much of a chanticleer amidst his spouses.

He was delivering himself of some poetic rapture, addressed, as it seemed, to the mud banks of the Essex shore, and feigned to perceive neither Ludar nor me till he came upon us.

"So," said he then, eyeing me, "here is our Flying Dutchman, our bolt out of the blue, our dragon's tooth turned to man. And, by my sword, a pretty fellow too. Count me as thy patron, my Hollander, and if, as I judge by thy face, thou hast a tooth for the honey of Parnassus his garden, and the dainty apples of the Muses' orchard, thou shalt not starve verily. To be brief, I favour thee therefore, thy fortune is made."

I was bewildered enough by this speech, not a tithe of which could I understand. I took it ill to be called Dutchman, and dragon's tooth; nor, albeit I was a printer's 'prentice, did I know what he meant by Parnassus. Still, as he seemed friendly disposed, I answered:

"I thank you."

"Thank not me," said he, raising his hand. "Let not the groping man thank the lamp, nor the briar the brook. Thank the sun whence the lamp hath his light, and the ocean to whom the brook oweth his waters. Thank that incomparable paragon, that consummate swan, that pearl of all perfection, my mistress, of whose brightness I am but the mirror and medium."

"Pardon me, sir," said I, feeling very foolish to comprehend not a word of his fine talk, "if you have anything to tell me, pray, say so; but, for the life of me, I cannot discover what you mean by all this."

SIR LUDAR

"I mean," said he, "that she, my lady, the Aphrodite who rules these waves, the star who guides our course, the nymph who suns her locks on this poor ship, the same condescends to call you her servant; wherefore, owe it to her, that thou mayest also call me thy master."

I began to weary of this jargon. Moreover, the fellow now seemed to be talking about matters which he had better leave to Ludar and me. So I said:

"You are none of my master. I have a better."

He looked a little hurt at this, I thought, and said:

"Can an ass call the horse its master when a man claimeth both? Who is this mortal, sirrah, that I may scorn him?"

"This gentleman is my master," said I, growing very hot, and laying my hand on Ludar's arm.

The gallant laughed.

"Pretty, on my life! The dog hath its parasites, the scullion his menial, the earthen pot his mug, and each puffeth himself into a gentleman thereby. And who may you be, forsooth?"

"Ludar McSomhairle Buidhe McDonnell of the Glyns," said Ludar, solemnly.

The fellow laughed outright.

"I do remember," said he, "a pretty jest of Dan Æsopus about a jackdaw who thought himself a peacock because he had a monstrous long feather to his tail. Prithee, thou silly son of Neptune, knowest thou not that if I did bid thee carry me my box from the fore-deck there to the poop, thou must crawl with it like my jack-porter? And, by my soul, I have named the very service that brought me hither. Therefore, my lord Sir Ludar McSurley Boy McNeptune McMalapert McDonnell of the Glyns, fetch my box below. And should the burden be too heavy for thy dainty fingers, pray thy serving gentleman here to lend thee a hand."

Ludar, who was leaning against the mast, yawned; whereat, the gallant dropping his fine speeches, turned as red as a lobster, and with a loud French oath, drew out his rapier and flourished it.

Ludar watched him contemptuously for a while, until the blade, getting courage at every pass, ventured a modest prick. Then he leapt out like a cat on a mouse, and caught the silly fellow such a grip of the wrist as sent his sword spinning on

A SCURVY CREW

the deck. Picking it up, he quietly broke it over his knee into three pieces, which he pitched one after the other overboard.

"Now, master jackanapes," said he, returning to his adversary, and catching him by his starched ruff. "You shall follow your sword."

Then the poor fellow, scared out of his wits, let go a string of oaths, and vowed to heaven he did but jest, and loved us both like his own brothers, and, would Ludar but unhand him, he might count on him as a friend for life, and so forth. Even Ludar could not help laughing at the figure he made; and having lifted him a little on to the gunwale, let him down again with a "get you gone then."

'Twas wonderful how the gallant's courage came back as soon as he stood free.

"By my soul," said he, with a gay laugh, "thou'rt a brave lad, and I like thee for 't. A jest is like marrow in a dog's bone, and life without sport is a camel's track. Come, thou and I shall be friends, I see; and crack more jokes than one ere this voyage be over. And, in sooth, Achilles doth well to make proof now and again of the strength of Hercules. Why, my Hercules, I warrant thou couldest lift that box of mine with thy finger and thumb. I pray thee, for my admiration, see if thou couldest so carry it from where it now lies to my cabin in the poop; and our flying Dutchman here shall be judge that the feat be fairly done."

Ludar, with a grim smile, owned that he had the worst of this encounter, and made the fellow happy by carrying his box in one hand; although he alarmed him not a little by offering to carry him in the other.

When this little jest was over, the captain came to us with orders to join the crew in making all things ready for presently meeting the sea breezes at the river's mouth; so we had no more time just then to think of Master Coxcomb.

It moved my admiration to see with what a will Ludar worked at his task. He made no question of the Frenchman's right to order his services; and methought, as he hauled away cheerily among his ill-favoured messmates, he looked as noble as had he been marching at the head of an army. The ship's crew was, to tell the truth, a scurvy company. Not counting us, there were but eleven of them, mostly French, who talked and cursed while they worked

SIR LUDAR

and three English, who sulked and grumbled. They stared in no friendly way at Ludar and me when we joined them; nor did they like us the better that, without much knowledge or seamanship, we yet put our backs into what we did, and bade them do the same. Ludar, indeed, born to command, was not sparing in his abuse of their laziness; and it vexed me a little to see how he thereby made himself an enemy of every man among them.

Towards nightfall we were all ship-shape, and the watch being set—of which Ludar was one—I had leisure to go below to seek the sleep I sorely needed. I would fain, before doing so, have visited the maiden to satisfy myself that all went well with her. But I durst hardly venture so far without her bidding. I sought my berth below, therefore—and a vile, foul corner of the hold it was—and laid myself down, wondering what would be the end of all this journeying.

There was a sailor—one of the Frenchmen—down beside me, who, when he saw who I was, sat up and began to talk. In a foolish moment I betrayed that I understood some of his French lingo, whereat he—being more than half drunken—waxed civil, and his tongue loosed itself still more.

"Who is *she*?" he whispered presently, in his foreign tongue.

"A lady," said I, shortly.

"So! and monstrous rich, by our lady! Comrade," said he, "I helped carry her box on board. Do you take me for a fool? There is something weighs more in that than a maiden's frocks—eh, my friend?"

"You are a fool," said I.

"A fool? Ha! ha! 'Tis well. And I am fool enough to——you be her man, they say? and an honest fellow? Ha! ha!"

"Aye, aye," said I, drowsily enough, "let me go to sleep."

"Aye, aye," said he, "even if it be silver pieces and not gold, 'twill be enough to make men of thee and me. Dost hear, sluggard? Thee and me, and no more planks and ropes, and——"

I had ceased to hear his maunderings, and was sound asleep.

When I awoke, it was to hear the thundering crash of a wave on the deck overhead, and I knew we were at last on the open sea. Alas! when I turned over to recover my

SEA IS NO RESPECTER OF PERSONS

sleep, I fell into so horrible a fit of shuddering and sickness that I believed the hour of my departure was come. The ship rolled heavily through the uneasy water, and at every lurch my heart sunk—I know not whither. I could hear the shuffling of steps overhead, and the dash of the waves against the ship's side, and the voice of the sailors at their posts. Little recked they of the comrade who was dying below !

Presently a call came for the new watch to turn up on deck. I was helpless to obey, and lay groaning there, not caring if the next lurch took us down to the bottom. At last, after much shouting, the captain himself came down and shook me roughly.

" Leave me," said I, " to die in peace."

" Die ! " cried he, " thou sickly lubber. If you rise not in a minute's time, we will see what a rope's end can do to 'liven thee. Come, get up."

I struggled to my feet, but in that posture my sickness came back with double violence, so that I tumbled again to the floor, and vowed he might use every rope in the ship to me, but up I could not get.

I do not well recall what happened those next few days. I believe I staggered upon deck and went miserably through the form of work, jeered at by my fellow sailors, despised by my captain, and wondered at by Ludar. But when, after the sickness gave way, I one day found myself in a fever, with my strength all gone, I was let go below and lie there without more to do. I know not how it came to pass, but ill I was for a day or two ; perhaps it was the vexations of the last few weeks, or the weakness left by the sickness, or a visitation of the colic from heaven ; however it was, I lay there, humbled and ashamed of my weakness, and wishing myself safe back outside Temple Bar.

At these times, Ludar was a brother to me. He came often to see me, and talked so cheerily, that I almost forgot how solemn his looks used to be. More than that, he fetched me dainties to eat, without which I might have starved; for, while the fever lasted, I could not stomach the strong ship's fare. And I suspected more than once that he had secured my peace from the captain by offering himself to do a good piece of my work as well as his own.

He spoke little enough about the maiden, though I longed to hear of her. Once, when I asked him, his face grew overcast.

SIR LUDAR

"That maiden," said he, "is never so merry as when the waves are breaking over the deck. Yet I see her little, for, in sooth, the old nurse has been nearer death than you, and will allow no one to go near her but her young mistress. Nor dare I offer myself where I am not bidden. Humphrey," added he, "I prefer to talk of something else."

Now, I must tell you that, to my surprise, I found I had another friend in these dark days; I mean the poet. Contemptible as was my plight, and mean as was the cabin I hid in, when he heard I was ill, he came more than once to see me. It suited him to make a mighty to do about it, as if his condescension must heal me on the spot. Yet the kindness that was in him, and the wonder he afforded me, made up for all these airs and graces.

"Alack and well a day!" exclaimed he, when he first came. "Vulcan hath fallen from the clouds and lieth halting below. The apple which was rosy is become green, and the Dutchman who of late flew is now become ship's ballast. Nay, my poor ruin, thank me not for coming; 'tis the common debt the high oweth to the low, the sound to the broken, the poem to the prose; nay, 'tis the duty a knight oweth to his lady's humblest menial."

"And how is the lady?" said I; for I wearied to hear of her, even from any lips.

"Hast thou seen the swan with wings new dressed float on the summer tide? Hast thou heard the thrush, full-throated, call his mate across the lea? Hast thou watched the moon soar up the heavens, sweeping aside the clouds, and defying the mists of earth? Hast thou marked, my Dutchman, the summer laughter on a field of golden corn? Hast thou tracked the merry breeze along the ripples of a dazzled ocean?——"

"Yes, yes," said I, "but what has that to do with the maiden we speak of?"

He smiled on me pityingly.

"Such, poor youth, is she; and such, methinks, am I become, who sit at her feet and sun myself in her light——"

"'Tis dark down here," I said, "but you seem to me neither swan, nor thrush, nor moon, nor a corn field, nor an ocean. But I thank you, even as you are, for coming."

"'Tis a sign of a sound mind," said he, "when gratitude

POETIC CONSOLATIONS

answereth to graciousness. And now, prithee, how do you do?"

I told him I was better, and that I might not have mended so far, but for my dear master, Sir Ludar.

Then he bridled up and his cheeks coloured.

"Ah, Hercules is a good sailor, and a strong animal. 'Tis fit he should wait upon you, since you be in my present favour. Moreover, like cureth like, as it is said; therefore he is better here tending you, than casting sheep's eyes on one who is as the sun above his head. I have had a mind to admonish him to remove the offence of his visage from her purview, for I perceived, by my own mislike of it, that it was a weariness to her. The pure glass is dimmed by the breath of the beholder, and a face at the window darkeneth a chamber."

"Sir Ludar will be here soon," said I; "I pray you stay and tell him this."

"No," said he, looking, I thought, a little alarmed. "If the cloud withdraw not from the sun's path of his own motion, neither will he scatter for our bidding. Therefore, let him be. And, indeed, I stay here too long, my Dutchman. Who shall say but the dove sigheth already for her truant mate? So farewell; and count me thy patron."

He came often after this, always with the same brave talk.

One day, however, he seemed more like a plain man and said: "'Tis time thou wert up, my Hollander. There is thunder in the air, the horizon is big with clouds, the dull sea rustleth with the coming storm, and I smell the wind afar off."

"Why," said I, starting up, "Ludar told me but just now the weather was fair and settled, and that the breeze was shifting to the south."

"I spoke not of the weather," said he. "Let it be. The thunder may hide beneath a brow, the lightning may flash from out two eyelids, and the storm may break in a man's breast."

"For Heaven's sake, speak plain," said I. "What do you mean?"

"Wait and see," said he, "I like not these French dogs. Only let thy eye be keen, thy ear quick, and thy hand ready, my Hollander, and stand by me when I call on thee."

SIR LUDAR

More I could not get out of him. When I spoke of it to Ludar afterwards, he said:

"Maybe the little antic is right. Yet they are too sorry a crew, and too small to do mischief. They suspect us of carrying treasure aboard, and your friend the captain, I take it, is the roundest villain of them all."

I vowed the captain was no friend of mine; yet I believed him honest. But as for the crew, it came to my mind then what the drunken fellow had blabbed out the first night; and I said it was like enough to be true.

That afternoon I rose from my sick-bed and came on deck. I remember to this hour the joy of that afternoon.

The day was bright and fair; land was nowhere to be seen; only a stretch of blue-green water through which the *Miséricorde* spanked with a light breeze at her stern. The white sails shone out in the sunlight, and the happy gulls called to one another above our heads. As I faced round and drank in mouthful after mouthful of the fresh salt air, my life seemed to revive within me, and I felt the strength rush back into my thews. But the greatest joy of all was that the maiden, seeing me stand there, came up and bade me a joyous welcome to the upper air once more.

"Alas," said she, laughing, "it has been dull times while you have been below, Humphrey. My good old nurse has not ceased to cry out that she was dying since we took our first lurch into the free sea. Your Knight of the Rueful Countenance flies from me whenever he sees me afar; your French captain might be an Englishman, he is so sulky; and as for your English paragon there,"—and she pointed to the gallant who was strutting on the forward deck—"he frightens me with his frenzies and raptures. Do you all make love that way in England?"

"No," said I, "I think not."

"Why, Humphrey, you talk as if you knew not; I would have vowed you had a sweetheart of your own, with the rest of them."

"Maybe I have," said I.

Just then to my relief, Ludar came up.

"Sir Ludar," I said, "this lady complains that you, who are so brave, run away whenever she looks your way."

Neither the maiden nor Ludar liked my clumsy speech.

HOW THEY MAKE LOVE IN ENGLAND

"Nay, Sir Malapert," said she, "I complain not of what contents me. Besides, Sir Ludar has been better employed in nursing you."

"If I be a coward," said Ludar, "it's because I dread a frown more than a battleaxe."

The maiden looked up at him, with the gentle light in her eyes which I had marked before now.

"If you dread frowns," said she, laughing, "never look in your mirror, Sir Ludar; for, by my faith, you glare at me now as if I were an English poet, such as now approacheth."

We looked up and there was our gallant at our elbows.

"As the loadstone to his star, as the compass to the pole, as the river to the sea, so come I, fair tyrant of my heart. For thy sake, I even salute these thy satellites, O moon of my vision! who derive from thee their lustre."

"Witness Sir Ludar's countenance," said the maiden. "But now that the sun has come on the horizon, Sir Poet, shall not we lesser lights all pale? Pray, did you catch any fish to-day?"

"Nay, mistress mine, how should the silly fish, dazzled by thy heavenly brightness, see the humble bait of a mortal?"

"I know not," said the maiden, "but I saw one sailor, an hour ago, catch three."

"Is it a wonder, since you watched the quivering line? Mark you, my humble friends," said he, turning to Ludar and me. "I relieve you of your further attendance on me and this lady. I thank you, and so farewell, till we summon you further."

"Nay, Sir Poet," said the maiden, "if you must be gone, adieu. As for me, Sir Ludar is about to teach me the mystery of the angle, and Humphrey waits on Sir Ludar. Therefore, concern yourself not for me; I am well attended."

"Oh," said he, rather chapfallen, "your condescension is a lesson for angels. When the planet deigns to shine into the humble pool, shall the star not do the same? I will even abide at your side, and be gracious too."

But his brave intention was thwarted. For a call came just then from the old nurse, which carried the maiden off to her side; while Ludar and I, receiving a summons from the captain, went forward, and so left the poet to his own devices.

A sterner summons was not far off, as you shall hear.

CHAPTER XI

How the *Miséricorde* changed her Crew

WE were, I reckon, somewhere off the Yorkshire coast; for we had been sailing a week, for the most part against foul winds. To-night, as I said, the light breeze had backed to the south and was sending us forward quietly at some six or seven knots an hour. All seemed to promise a speedy end to our voyage; and yet, as I stood there, drinking in the beauty of the evening, and rejoicing in my recovered strength, I would as soon we had been bound on a voyage ten times as long.

I was standing idly near the foremast. On the high poop behind sat the maiden, singing beside her old nurse, who, like me, was enjoying the air for the first time to-night. Ludar lolled near me, on a coil of rope, watching the sun dip as he listened to the singing, and betwixt whiles unravelling the tangles of a fishing line. On the forecastle, the French seamen sat and whispered, scowling sometimes our way, and sometimes laughing at the poet who strutted near them, intent on the sunset and big with some notable verses thereupon, which were hatching in his brain. An English fellow was at the helm, half asleep; while the captain, grumbling at the slackness of the breeze, paced to and fro, with an oath betwixt his lips and an ugly frown on his brow.

Suddenly I seemed to detect among the Frenchmen a stir, as if something had just been said or resolved upon in their whisperings. The captain at that instant was near them, turning in his walk; when, without warning, two of their number sprang out upon him. There was a shout, a struggle, the gleam of a knife, and then a dead man lay on the deck. All was so quick and sudden that the murder was done under my very eyes before I knew what was happening.

THE STORM BREAKS

Then, in a twinkling, the whole ship became the scene of a deadly fight. Three of the traitors threw themselves on Ludar; the poet reeled in the grip of another; two others made for me.

"Back, back!" shouted Ludar, in a voice of thunder, as he began his struggle.

'Twas well I obeyed him; for the two who had made an end of the captain were already rushing in the direction of the women, and had I reached the ladder a moment later, all might have been lost.

The men, I think, in laying their wicked plan, had scarcely taken me (who late was so weak) into account as a fighting man. They had reckoned to carry the poop, where lay the supposed treasure and the arms, without a blow; and once there, the ship would be theirs. It staggered them, therefore, to find me standing in the way and laying about me. The two women, as I said, were on the upper deck which formed the roof of the poop house. To that there was no access save by the small ladder, which I accordingly wrenched from its place and swung round with all my might at my assailants. The blow knocked over two of them; and before they could regain their feet, I had struck another a blow with my fist, which needed no second. The fourth varlet did not wait for me, but closed on me with his knife. Luckily the blade missed its mark, grazing only my ribs, and before he could strike again I had him by the wrist, and the blow he meant for me went home in his own neck. After that, 'twas easy work to hold off the other two, one of whom was the drunken fool who had blabbed his secret days ago, had I only heeded it, in my sick cabin. Finding me stubborn, and further passage barred, they sheered off with a curse and hastened forward. I durst not follow them; for it might be a feint to decoy me from my post. So, with all the haste I could, I threw up an out-work of lumber, sails, spars, and boxes across the deck some distance in front of the poop, and, relieving my two fallen assailants of their knives, I stood ready for whatever next might betide.

"Humphrey," called the maiden from above, "put up the ladder quickly and let me down."

"Nay," said I, "'tis no place for you, maiden. You are safe there. Stay."

SIR LUDAR

"Obey me, Humphrey," said she in so commanding a voice that I fetched the ladder at once.

She looked pale and stern; but otherwise was cool and collected as she descended.

"Now," said she, as she stood beside me, "go and bring down my nurse. Give me that knife; I will mount guard here till you are done."

I durst not waste time by arguing; she took the knife from me and motioned me to my task. The poor old lady, more dead than alive, was hard to move; nor was it till I wickedly threatened to cast her overboard, that she consented to come at all. As I was catching her in my arms, the man at the helm, whom I had all this time clean forgotten, sprang suddenly on me from behind with a pole which, had it been better aimed, would have ended my troubles then and there. As it was, the timber fell on my shoulder, almost cracking the blade. But I was in with him in a twinkling, and had him by the throat before he could strike again. Next moment, the wretch (woe to us that he was an Englishman!) was over the board, and the Lord have mercy on his soul!

The delay was pitiable for the old woman, whom, when I came to her again, I found to have swooned away. It was all I could do with my bruised arm to lift her and bring her to the ladder. How I got her down and into her cabin I know not; but when I came out again to my lady's side, the ship seemed to swim before my eyes. I remember a vision of Ludar, bloody and gasping, reeling across the deck towards us, fighting his way, foot by foot, with four or five savage devils who followed yelling at his back.

Then for a time all seemed dim and horrible. I knew that we were fighting desperately for our lives; that men fell heavily and with a groan on to the deck; that the maiden stood by us, undaunted; that presently there was a report of a pistol, followed by a hideous shouting and shrieking. After that, all seemed to grow still of a sudden, and Ludar shouted, "Look to Humphrey."

When I came to, we were still on the deck. The maiden was bathing my brow with water. Ludar, pale and blood-stained, stood gloomily by. Of the enemy not a man stirred. My swoon could not have lasted long, for the hues of the sunset lingered yet in the sky. I tried to gather myself

THE BATTLE IS SHORT BUT SORE

together, but the maiden gently restrained me. "No, Humphrey," said she, "lie still. There is no more work to be done. Thank God you are safe, as we are."

'Twas sorely tempting to lie thus, so sweetly tended; but the sight of Ludar shamed me into energy. I struggled to my feet. My arm hung limp at my side and my head throbbed; but for that, I was sound and able to stand upright.

Ludar, when I came to look at him, was in a worse plight than I. He was bleeding from a gash on his face, and another on his leg; while the jacket he wore was torn in shreds on his back. He came and took my arm, and then motioned with his head to the ghastly heap of dead men on the deck.

"Take her within," said he, "and then come and help me."

"Maiden," said I, "thank Heaven you are safe, and that we are alive to guard you. Your old nurse I fear is more in need of help than we. I left her senseless. Will you not go to her?"

I think she guessed what we meant; for she said nothing, but went quickly within.

Then Ludar and I went out to our task. Of the seven Frenchmen who had set on us, not one lived. Beside these lay the captain, the maiden's waiting man (who, Ludar said, had taken side with the traitors), and one other of the English sailors who had fought for us.

"What of the poet?" said I, when after much labour the ship had been lightened of all that was not living.

"He is safe at the mast-head," said Ludar.

There, sure enough, when I looked up, clung the poor gallant; peering down at us with pasty face, and hugging the mast with arms and legs.

"Let him bide there a while," said Ludar. "He is safe and out of the way. He skipped up at the first assault, and wisely cut the rope ladder behind him, so that no man could pursue him. But tell me, how do you fare?"

"I am less hurt than you," said I. "Only my arm is numbed by the whack the English knave gave me; while you, Ludar, are bleeding, head and foot."

"I was scratched," said he. "The villains who set on me were too quick, as you saw, and had me down before I could shut my fist. Why they did not despatch me then and there I know not; but in seizing me they carried their

SIR LUDAR

blades in their teeth, the better to use their hands, so that I was able to snatch one for my own use as I fell. It served only to rid me of one of the company. Yet I got my feet again under me, when the other two made at me, as well as the two who had fled from you. Among them all I got these scratches. When the fifth came, who had seen the poet aloft, I knew I could hold ground no longer; so I gave way, as you saw, and made for your barrier. After that you know, and how the maiden stood by us all through, and in the end fetched the pistol which finished the business. Had these villains but been armed, it is they who would have buried us. But come in now, Humphrey, and take counsel."

'Twas a strange ship's company that met that evening in the dead captain's cabin. The maiden, Ludar, I, and one of the English fellows, who had been sleeping below and knew naught of the fight till all was over. As for the poet, Ludar still refused to have him down till our conference was over.

Of all our party the maiden was, I think, the most hopeful. "God and His saints," said she, "have ordered this to try us, and see of what mettle we be. Shall we despair, Sir Ludar, when He has proved His goodness to us? The past is done, the future is all before us. You are our captain now, and Humphrey and I and this brave sailor here, aye and our poor poet aloft there, are your crew to follow where you lead. I can man a gun and haul a rope, as you shall see. Come, Humphrey, what say you?"

"I have vowed," said I, "to follow my master to the death. Nor can I think heaven will desert us while you who belong there, are aboard."

She blushed at this and turned it off.

"Nay, my friend, it depends on how we do the duty that lies to our hand whether we belong there or not."

Here Ludar broke in abruptly.

"Seaman, where be we now?"

The sailor got up and went out to ascertain our bearings.

"Maiden," said Ludar, then, more grave than I had ever seen him, "I can make no fine speeches, such as Humphrey here or yonder monkey at the mast-head; but I accept you as one of this crew with a prouder heart than if I were offered my father's castle."

Then he held out his great hand, and she lay her little

THE NEW CREW

hand in it, and her true eyes flashed up to meet his And I who stood by knew that the compact I witnessed then was for a longer voyage than from here to Leith.

I was glad when presently the man came in and reported.

"By your leave, captain, we be eight leagues east of Flamboro' with a southerly breeze falling fast. The ship lies in the wind and the tiller is swinging."

"Take the helm, master, and keep her head straight. Humphrey, fetch down the poet. He and I will mount the first watch to-night. Maiden, do you get what rest you may, ere your turn comes in the morning."

"Aye, aye, my captain," said she cheerily, and went.

"Humphrey," said Ludar, calling me back, when she had gone, "do you wonder that I love that maiden?"

"I do not," said I.

"Is she you love as fair, as brave, as noble?"

"She is," I answered, "every whit as fair, every whit as brave, every whit as noble."

"Then why," he asked, looking hard at me, "are you sad when you speak of her?"

"Alas," said I, "she loves me not. Ludar, talk not to me of her; I will go fetch the poet."

The poor fellow was by this time well-nigh at the end of his patience. For, though he had fixed himself cunningly in the rigging of the foremast, seating himself on the royal yard, and hugging the mast lovingly with his arms and legs, he found himself unable to budge, or even see what was going on below, by reason of the dizziness which afflicted him. How he had got up so far, and managed to cut the ropes behind him, he never could explain. But a man will do desperate feats for his life's sake.

It was no light task to dislodge him. With my maimed arm I could not haul myself up the rigging even to the lower topyard, much less carry up to him his dangling ladder. All I could do was to hail him and bid him be of good cheer till we had him down.

"Cheer," he cried, "cometh not in a voice from the void, neither is there help in empty breath. Come up, for I am weary of my perch; and verily, if the mountain come not to Mahomet, the prophet must abase himself to the mountain. In short, my man, I am near tumbling."

SIR LUDAR

"Hold on," cried I. "I shall fetch help and all will be safe."

"Oh, that the giants would pile Pelion on Ossa and get me out of this heaven!" I heard him say. Methought, however, the fellow could not yet be in desperate straits to talk thus.

At last the seaman scrambled up and fetched him down, not without many protestations and caveats by the way. Once down, however, he shook his fluttered plumes, and crowed like any chanticleer.

"*Facilis descensus Averni*, as our Maro hath it. As the muse droppeth from the heights, and the golden shower descendeth, so visit I once more the Arcadian plains. Which remindeth me, where is my Danaë, and how fareth she? Apprise her, I pray you, of my return. And, by the way," added he, puffing himself valiantly, "where is the varlet that late sought my life. He and I must settle scores before this night be an hour older. Fetch him hither and by my——"

"See here, Sir Popinjay," said Ludar, coming forward impatiently, and cutting the speech in twain, "the time is gone past for this fooling. If you be a man, you may prove it now. If not, on my soul, you shall go aloft again. Come, you share this watch with me. Put some food into your body, and then keep sharp look-out ahead. You see the entire crew of this vessel, save the two women; therefore, cease to be half a man and make yourself two."

The fellow turned pale at this news, and cast a glance up and down the empty ship. Then, without a word, he took up half a loaf and a mug of beer from the cabin table and walked forward.

"Humphrey," said Ludar, "get to bed, your turn will come."

But to bed I could not go; and Ludar for once, I found, was not hard to persuade.

There was in truth much to be done before we could think of rest. Together we overhauled the ship's rations, and found what would last us for long enough yet. We examined, too, our ordnance, which was but meagre and ill-fashioned; we had three pieces on either side, besides a small swivel gun on poop and forecastle. The ammunition was sufficient for these and for the few pistols and muskets which

AFTER STORM, PEACE

we found in the Frenchman's cabin. Further, we looked long and hard at our charts, which seemed well marked for the passage we were bound on. The English fellow, we discovered, had been several times that way; and, though he was no pilot, he said he yet knew the Bass Rock from a mud bank, and, provided we fell in with neither pirates, tempest, nor the Spaniard, could put us into Leith Roads right side uppermost as well as any man. Whereat we felt easier in our minds than we had been.

By the time all these consultations were ended, the watch was half spent. Ludar therefore ordered me below, whether I would or no, to rest. In truth I was ready for it, and fell asleep almost before my head touched my pillow.

When I awoke, Ludar stood beside me.

"Up!" said he, "all goes well, and your watch-partner awaits you."

"Ludar," said I, springing up. "Why do you give me the partner who belongs of right to you?"

"'Tis a time for work," said he, with a smile, "not for play. Am I not captain here? To your watch, Humphrey."

I went on board. There stood she on the forecastle, looking ahead and singing softly to herself.

I left her and went aft. The sailor was still at the helm, having volunteered a double watch to see us through the night. All behind was shipshape and trim. Ludar had been busy, clearing the decks and bringing back to order the confusion left by the late battle. There was nothing for me to do. Therefore, with beating heart I walked forward once more.

She turned at my coming and greeted me frankly.

"Welcome, messmate," said she. "Is all well?"

"All is well," said I. "The Captain has done the work of ten men, and nought is left for me and you but to look ahead."

"And he is resting?" asked she. "Think you his wounds were dressed?"

"I helped him tend them before I went below," said I. "They were but scratches."

"And your arm," said she; "it still hangs heavy. May I not bind it for you, Humphrey?"

I wished I was the heathen Briareus then, with an hundred

arms. There was magic in her touch; and no charm of witch or fairy could have mended my bruised limb as did she.

After that, we sat silent awhile, looking out to sea. The soft light was spreading on the east, heralding the coming day. The slack breeze flapped lazily in the sails overhead and scarce ruffled the drowsy ocean. The stars one by one put out their little lights and vanished into the blue. There was no sound but the creaking of the yards and the gentle plash of the water on the hull; only these and the music of a maiden's song. It went hard with me, that night. For a while, as I sat there, gazing into her face and listening to her music and feeling the touch of her hand on my arm, I was fool enough to think all this—all this peace, all this beauty of the ocean dawn, all this lulling of the breeze, all this music, this gentle smile, this tender touch, spelt love; and there came a voice from the tempter that I should tell her as much then and there. What hindered me, I know not. 'Twas not alone the thought of Ludar, or the remembrance of my own honour, or the fear of her contempt. Be it what it may, I was helped by Heaven that night to be a man, and with a mighty effort to shake off the spell that was on me. So I rose to my feet and walked abaft. Many a time I paced to and fro cooling my fevered brow ere I ventured to return. But when at last I did, I was safe. She stood there motionless, radiant with the first beams of the royal sun as he leapt up from the sea.

"Look, Humphrey," she cried. "Is not that worth keeping watch for?" Then she broke again into song.

"Is that an Irish song you sing?" I asked.

"It is. How knew you that?"

"I guessed it. What does it mean?"

She blushed.

"'Tis a song the maidens sing at home—an old, old song," said she, "that I learned from my nurse."

"I pray you, sing it again," said I.

She turned her face to the rising sun, and sang, in English words, as follows:

> Who cometh from the mountain like the sun for brightness?
> Whose voice ringeth like the wave on the shingle?
> Who runneth from the east like the roe?
> Who cometh?

THE MAIDEN'S HOME

Is it the wind that kisses my tresses?
Or is it the harp of Innis thrilling my ear?
Or is it the dawn on Ramore that dims my eyes?
Who cometh?

Is he far? Is he near? Whence comes he riding?
Dazzling in armour and white of brow?
Is it for me that he filleth the mountains with music?
Who waiteth?
Who cometh?

" 'Tis a wild song, full of riddles," said I. " Maybe there is a song somewhere which has the answers."

" I know it not," said she.

" Not yet," said I.

She looked up at me quickly as if she doubted my meaning. But I looked out seaward and asked:

" Where in Ireland is your home, maiden? Is it near Ludar's castle on the sea? "

" Hard by," said she. " The M'Donnells and O'Neills are neighbours and foes." And her brow clouded. " My father, Humphrey, is the bravest of the O'Neills as Ludar's father is the bravest of the M'Donnells."

" And does your father hold Dunluce? " asked I.

" I know not," said she. " I have never seen my father, Turlogh Luinech O'Neill, though I love him as my life. At two years I was sent away to England with my English mother, who was but a handfast bride to the O'Neill."

" And what may that be? " I asked.

" 'Tis a custom with us," said she, " for the chiefs to take wives who are theirs only so long as a better does not present herself. My mother, Alice Syngleton, the daughter of my father's English ally and preserver, Captain Syngleton, was thus wedded, and when I was two years old—so my old nurse tells me—he married the great Lady Cantire of the Isles. Wherefore my mother was sent home to England with me, and there we lived till she died three years ago; since when I have pined in a convent, and am now, in obedience to my father's summons, on my way to my unknown home. My father, being, as I understand, allied to the English, who have dispossessed the M'Donnells, I was to come over under the escort of an English officer of Sir William Carleton's choosing, who was my mother's kinsman. You know what peril that brought me to, and how, thanks to you, I am now making a safer journey, and a happier. Humphrey," said she, " till I met you and Sir Ludar, I had thought all men base; 'twas the one lesson they taught us at the convent. I have unlearned the lesson since."

"Pray Heaven you never have to relearn it," said I, groaning inwardly to think how near I had been to giving her cause.

Thus we talked that morning. At every word, what little hope I had once had of her love faded like the stars above our heads. Yet, instead of it came the promise of an almost sisterly friendship, which at the time seemed poor enough exchange, but which was yet a prize worth any man's having. She bade me tell her about myself, and heard me so gently, and concerned herself so honestly in all that touched me, and praised and chid me so prettily for what I had done well and ill, that I would my story had been twice as long and twice as pitiful. The only secret I did not tell her, you may guess. She did not. But she heard me greedily when I came to tell of my meeting with Ludar and of our adventures near Oxford; and for his sake, as much as for my own, she thought kindly of me and promised me her friendship.

Our watch was ended, and we were in the act of quitting our post, when the maiden, taking one last look seaward, cried: " Is not that a sail away there ? "

Sure enough it was, sparkling on the westward horizon, some two leagues to the larboard.

" Who cometh ? " said I to myself, echoing the maiden's song.

CHAPTER XII

How we sailed into Leith

A STRANGE joy seized me as I sighted the unknown ship. For my heart told me she was no friend, and I was just in the humour for a fight. I was one too many on board the *Miséricorde ;* and a brush with the Queen's foes just now would comfort me amazingly. And yet, when I came to think of it, she lay in nearer the English coast than we, and was like enough to be no Queen's enemy after all, but a Queen's cruiser on the look-out for suspicious craft like ours. For we floated no colours aloft. After the late fight Ludar had hauled down the Frenchman's flag ; but it was in vain I begged him to hoist that of her royal Majesty in its place. He would not hear of it.

"No," said he, "I sail under no false colours. This is a voyage for safety, not for glory, else I know the flag would fly there. As it is, Humphrey, 'tis best for us all to fly nothing. The masts shall go bare. The blue of a maiden's eyes is colour enough for you and me to fight under."

I could not gainsay him. We were in no trim for receiving broadsides, or grappling with sea-dogs, however merry the ports might be for a man in my plight. Our business was to bring the *Miséricorde* safe into Leith Roads, and to that venture we stood pledged.

Ludar ordered the maiden to her quarters and me to my cabin.

"In this calm," said he, " 'twill be hours before we foregather if foregather we may. So below, while the poet and I whistle for a breeze."

Towards afternoon we lay much as we were, drifting a little westward. But then came some clouds up from the south-east and with them a puff into our canvas.

SIR LUDAR

"We may be glad to take in a reef on her before daybreak, Captain," said the seaman.

"Time, enough till then," said Ludar. "Take all you can now."

We had not long to wait before the *Miséricorde* had way on once more. Then Ludar called his crew to him and said:

"To-night, be yonder stranger who she may, we run a race. Maiden, you have the keenest eyes; keep the watch forward. Humphrey, do you and the poet see to the guns and have all ready in case we need to show our teeth. Pilot, budge not one point out of the wind; but let her run. We may slip past in the dark, and then we are light-heeled enough to keep ahead. Old nurse, I warrant you have loaded a piece before now—we may need you to do it again. Meanwhile, to bed with you."

Then the race began. The wind behind us freshened fast, so that in an hour's time our timbers were creaking under stress of canvas. Before that, the stranger ship, though still a league and a half to larboard, had caught the breeze and was going too, canvas crowded, with her nose a point out of the wind into our course. For a long while it seemed as if we were never to come nearer, so anxious was she to give us no more advantage than she could help. But towards sundown we may have been a league asunder running neck and neck.

"She's an English cruiser, Captain," cried the helmsman, "and takes us for a Spaniard—that's flat."

"Then run as if we were so," said Ludar. "Budge not an inch from your course even if we scrape her bows as we pass."

So we held on straight down the wind, while the Englishman, closing in at every mile, held on too; and no one was to say which of us gained an inch on the other.

The sun tumbled into the sea and the brief twilight grew deeper, while behind us the wind gathered itself into a squall. Just before daylight failed, we could perceive the cruiser, not two miles away, leaning forward on her course, with the Queen's flag on her poop, and a row of portholes gaping our way. Then we lost her in the dusk.

The poet, who stood near me at the gun, said:

"Night is as a cave of which none seeth the end from the

A RACE

beginning; and a man hooded feeleth what he before saw. My Hollander, I bargained not for this when I took passage here. I wish it were to-morrow. Why do we not, under cover of night, change our course?"

"Because, since that is what our pursuers will expect of us, it will delude them the more if we keep straight on."

"O truth, many are thy arts!" said he. "But if, my Soothsayer, the wolf's cunning be a match for that of the lamb? What then?"

"Then you may want your match, and your knife too," said I.

He shivered a little.

"My Hollander," said he, "if I fall, say to my lady 'twas for her; and I pray you give her the gem in my bonnet. Say to her its brightness was dimmer than the remembrance of her eyes; and its price meaner than the dewdrop on her lip. Bring her to see me where I lie; and compose my face to greet her. Tell me, my Dutchman, doth a cannon ball give short shrift, or were it easier to die by the steel?"

"A peace to your nonsense," said I. "You have more sonnets to write before we need think of laying you out."

He was comforted at this, and we resumed our watch in silence.

The night grew very dark, and at every gust our masts stooped further before the wind. The *Miséricorde* hissed her way through the water, and still our pilot turned not his helm an inch right or left.

Presently, Ludar came up to where we stood. I could see his eyes flash even in the dark.

"Go forward now," said he to me. "Should we both be running as we were, and as I think we are our courses ought to meet not far hence. Send the maiden to me—I need her to take the helm while we three stand to the guns. Pray Heaven we win clear; if not, it will go hard with you, friend, in the prow. Let go your pistol at first sight of them, and, if you can, come abaft to join us before we strike."

I could tell by the tone in which he spoke that he took in every inch of our peril, and trembled, not for himself, but for some one else.

The maiden was loth to quit her post; for she, too, knew the risk of it and claimed it as her right. But when I told her

SIR LUDAR

the Captain had so ordered, and required her at the helm, she obeyed without another word.

Then followed a quarter of an hour that seemed like a lifetime. As I stood craning my neck forward, gazing under my hands seaward, there crowded into my memory visions of all my past life. I seemed to see the home of my boyhood, and looked again into my mother's face. And I stood once more before my case in the shop outside Temple Bar, and listened to Peter Stoupe humming his psalm tune, and heard my types click into the stick. I marched once more at the head of my clubs to Finsbury Fields, and there I saw Captain Merriman—drat him!—with his vile lips at a maiden's ear. And I passed, too, along the village street at Kingston where met me my mistress and her sweet daughter; and as I looked back, Jeannette turned too and——

What was that? Surely in the darkness I saw something! No. All was pitch black. The wind roared through the rigging, and the water seethed up at the plunging prow. But though I saw nothing, I felt the pursuer near; so near, I wondered not to hear the swish of her keel through the waves. On we went and nearer and nearer we seemed together. Oh for one sign of them, were it even a gun across our path! But sign there came none. The darkness seemed blacker than ever and——

All of a sudden I seemed to detect something—a spark, or a glow, or the luminous break of a wave. So swiftly it came and went, that it was gone before I could look. A trick of my vision, thought I. No! there it was again, this time nothing but a spark, close by, on a level, perhaps, with our mizzen. So near was it, I wondered whether it might not be the lighting of a match at our own guns. It went again: and as it did so, my finger, almost without my knowing it, tightened on the trigger of my pistol and it went off.

At the same moment, there was a blaze, a roar, a crash, and a shout. For an instant the *Miséricorde* reeled in her course and quivered from stern to stern. Then, another shout and a wild irregular roar astern. Then our good ship gathered herself together and leapt forward once more into the darkness, and the peril was passed.

All was over so suddenly that the pistol was still smoking in my hand as I leapt from the forecastle and rushed aft.

A SHOT INTO THE DARK

"Is all well?" I shouted.

"All well," said Ludar, quietly. "She grazed our poop and no more."

"And the maiden?" said I.

"All well," cried she, cheerily from the helm, "and fair in the wind."

"Stand at your posts still," cried Ludar.

So for another half-hour yet we stood at our posts, just as we had stood before the crisis came; and not a word said any one.

Then in the stormy east came a faint flush of dawn, and we knew that this perilous night was over.

"Seaman," said Ludar, "relieve the maiden at the helm, and bid her come hither."

She came, radiant and triumphant.

"Sir Ludar," she said, "I thank you for letting me hold the helm this night. You gave it me as the place of safety; but I had my revenge, since it proved the post of honour."

"It was indeed the post of danger," said Ludar. "Had you swerved and not held straight on, we might not have been here to honour you for it. But say, did none of the Englishman's shot reach the poop?"

"Some of it. Witness the sail there and the rail and the stern windows; but it spared me."

"I think," said Ludar, "we maimed them in one of their masts in passing, and their bowsprit broke short when it touched our stern. I doubt if we shall find them following us."

"As for our Hollander," said the poet, who had been wondrous silent thus far, "he hath this night proved himself twice a prophet. He said we should win this race; he said, moreover, I should live to write another ode. And lo! he spoke true. By your leave, Captain, I will go celebrate this notable occasion in a strain worthy of it and to the glory of my fair Amazon who——"

"Go below and cook this company some pottage," said Ludar, "and see you be not long over it."

Whereat the poet, with the muse taken out of him, departed. We stood watching the dawn till there was light enough to look back on our night's work. There was the Englishman with her mainmast gone, and draggled about

SIR LUDAR

the bows, beating up under reefed sails for the coast. It was plain to see, although we were two long leagues away, that she had had enough for one night and was going to leave us in peace. For myself, as I looked, I could not wholly glory in having thus flouted her Majesty's flag; but I considered that we had run that night for our lives, so I hoped the sin would be forgiven me.

And now, when we come to look round us, we found the wind still running high, and shifting a point or so to the eastward, promising a stormy day. So Ludar bade us shorten our canvas and put out our ship's head a bit, so as to give the coast a wide berth.

And, in truth, as the day wore on, the wind freshened into a gale, and the gale into a tempest, so that if we had promised ourselves relief after the perils of last night, our hopes were dashed. The sea, which so far had been easy, ran now high, and washed over our prow as we stood across the wind, and it was plain we were going to find out before long of what mettle our brave timbers were.

'Twas no light thing to face a night like this, even with a good crew—how much less with but four men and a maid? Yet I never saw Ludar more at his ease. In the danger of last night his face had been troubled and his manner excited. Now he gave his orders as if this were a pleasure trip on a quiet lake.

"What is there to mind," said he, "in a capful of wind? 'Tis sent to help us on our way; whereas, had we been taken last night where should we be now? Come, my men, help me shorten sail, for a little will go a long way a night like this. Maiden, to you I trust the helm with a light heart. 'Twill tax your strength more to keep her head thus than to run, as you did last night, clean before the wind; but you are strong and brave, and teach us to be the same."

The subtlest courtier's speech could not have won her as did these blunt words. She said no more than "I go, my Captain." But the look of her eyes as they met his spoke volumes of joy and gratitude, a tithe of which would have gladdened me for a lifetime.

Then we fell to shortening our canvas—a perilous task. When that was done, leaving only the topsails spread, Ludar bade us make good the hatches, and fall to and eat. Which we did, all but the poet, who, being either big with his ode, or misliking the wildness of the night, sat idle.

"Come, Sir Popinjay," said Ludar. "Eat, for no man can work on an empty stomach, and even poetry will not help haul a rope."

"We avoid Scylla, my Captain, only to fall into Charybdis. Methinks Scylla were the better fate. At least I might have passed this night recumbent. The eagle, at the day's end, flieth to his nest, and the lion hath his den; to all toil cometh an evensong, save to the shuttlecocks of Æolus."

"Nay, Sir Poet, you did bravely last night. Fall to and eat now, and we shall see you do more bravely to-night."

"Orpheus, his weapon, is a harp, not a gun. Nevertheless, I am one of five, and shall yield me to a man's bidding for the sake of her, my mistress, to whose glory I have this day indited my ode, and into whose sweet ear I will even now go recite it."

"No, no," said Ludar, "stay here and eat, and then go make a better one on the starboard bow, with your hand on the forestays, and your eye seaward."

He obeyed at length and swallowed his supper. Then, lamenting the maiden's fate at being deprived of his ode, he went gallantly forward.

"There goes a brave man in the garb of a fool," said Ludar. "Humphrey, in this wind, the maiden will be hard put to it to keep her post on the poop. 'Twould help her to lash her to her helm. Will you go and do it?"

"That task belongs to the Captain," said I. "She will suffer it from you." He smiled at me grimly and went astern. And, as I said, the maiden let him have his way; and there she stood, as night closed, erect and steadfast, with her hands on the tiller and her brave face set seaward.

'Twas a fearful night of shrieking wind and thundering wave. Often and often as the brave *Miséricorde* reared and hung suspended on a wave's crest, we knew none of us if she would ever reach the next. Lucky for us we were a flush-decked ship and our hatches sound, for the seas that poured over us would have filled us to the brim in an hour. Lucky, too, the Frenchman's cargo had been snugly stowed, or we should have been on our beam-ends before midnight. Half way through the night, there was a loud crack and over went our main topmast with her sails in ribbons. We had scarce time, at great peril, to cut her away, when another burst snapped our mizzen almost at the deck.

"That lightens us still more," said Ludar. "Let go all the forward canvas, and cut away. We must put her into the wind and let her drive under bare poles."

With that he went to the helm, where indeed the maiden must have needed succour. And there he stayed beside her till the night passed.

Afterwards he told me that he found her there, half stunned by the wind, but never flinching, or yielding a point out of the course. "I know not if she was pleased to see me there," said he. "She said little enough, and hardly surrendered me the tiller. But when we put the ship into the wind, there was little to do, save to stand and watch the sea, and shield ourselves as best we might from the force of the waves that leapt over the poop."

And fierce enough they were, in truth. But what was worse was that our course now lay due west, bringing us every league nearer the coast. Should the tempest last much longer we might have a sterner peril to face on the iron Northumbrian shore than ever we had escaped in the open sea.

The night passed and morning saw us driving headlong, with but one mast standing and not a sail to bless it. The maiden who had stood at her post since sundown yielded at last and came down, pale and drenched, to her quarters. The poet too, who had clung all night to the halyards, looking faithfully ahead and polishing his ode inwardly at the same time, also crawled abaft, half frozen and stupid with drowsiness. Indeed, there was little any of us could do, and one by one Ludar ordered us to rest, while he, whom no labour seemed to daunt, clung doggedly to the helm.

Thus half that day the wind flung us forward, till presently, far on the horizon, we could discern the sullen outline of a cliff.

"We are lost!" said I.

"Humphrey, you are a fool," said Ludar. "See you not the wind is backing fast?"

So it was, and as we drove on, ever nearer the fatal coast, it swung round again to the southerly, and the

THE POET'S LAMENT

sun above us blazed out fitfully from among the breaking coluds.

"Heaven fights for us," said Ludar. "Quick, rig up a sail forward and fly a yard; and do you, seaman, look to your charts and say where we are."

"That I have done long since," said the sailor. "We are scarce a league from the Holy Island, and 'tis full time we put her head out, sir."

"Come and take the helm then."

For a while it seemed as if we were to expect as wild a tempest from the south as ever we had met from the east. But towards evening, the wind slackened a bit, and, veering south-east, enabled us to stand clear of the coast, and make, battered and ill canvassed as we were, straight for the Scotch Forth.

The maiden slept all through that night, and when at dawn she came on deck, fresh and singing, we were tumbling merrily through a slackening sea, with the Bass Rock looming on the horizon.

"Methinks the jaded Greek felt not otherwise when, leaving behind him the blood-stained plains of Troy, he espied the cloud-topped mountains of Hellas," said the poet, who joined us as we stood.

"Which means," said the maiden, "you are glad?"

"Shall Pyramus rejoice to see the wall that hides him from his Thisbe? or Hector leap at the trumpet which parts him from his Andromache? Mistress mine, in yonder rock shall I read my doom?"

"Rather read us your ode, Sir Poet," said she. "It has had a stormy hatching, and should be a tempestuous outburst."

"As indeed you shall find it, if I have your leave to rehearse it," said he.

"I beg no greater favour," said she.

Then the poet poured out this brave sonnet:—

> "Go, grievous gales, your heads that heave,
> Ye foam-flaked furies of the wasty deep,
> Ye loud-tongued Tritons, wind and wave,
> Go fan my love where she doth sleep,
> And tell her, tell her in her ear
> Her Corydon sits sighing here.

SIR LUDAR

The tempest stalks the stormy sea,
  The lightning leaps with lurid light,
The glad gull calls from lea to lea,
  The whistling whirlwind fills the night;
Bears each a message to my love,
Whose stony heart I faint to move."

" 'Tis too short," said the maiden, " we shall be friends, I hope, long enough to hear more of it."

"Meanwhile, Sir Poet," said Ludar, who chafed at these civilities, "go forward again, and keep the watch. Call if you spy aught, and keep your eyes well open."

Fortune favoured us that day, as she had handled us roughly in the days before. The wind held good, and filled our slender canvas. The pilot's charts deceived not; nor did friend or enemy stand across our path. Before night we had swept round the rock and found the channel of the Forth, up which, on a favouring tide, we dropped quietly that evening; and at nightfall let go our anchor with grateful hearts, albeit weary bodies, in Leith Roads, where for a season the *Miséricorde* and we had rest from our labours

CHAPTER XIII

How we brought the Maiden to her Father's House

A MONTH later, Ludar and the maiden and I stood on a cliff in Cantire which overlooks the Irish coast. The September sun was dipping wrathfully on the distant Donegal heights, kindling, as he did so, the headlands of Antrim with a crimson glow. Below us, the Atlantic surged heavily and impatiently round the rugged Mull. Opposite—so near, it seemed we might almost shout across—loomed out, sheer from the sea, the huge cliff of Benmore, dwarfing the forelands on either hand, and looking, as we saw it then, anything but the Fair Head which people call it. Scarcely further, on our right, lapped in the lurid water, lay the sweet Isle of Raughlin, ablaze with heather, and resounding with its chorus of seabirds. A finer scene you could scarce desire. A scene which one day, when the sun is high and the calm water blue, may glisten before you like a vision of heaven; or, on a wild black day of storm, may frown over at you like a prison wall of lost souls; or (as it seemed to-night), like the strange battlements of a wizard's castle, which, while you dread, you yet long to enter.

We looked across the narrow channel in silence. I could mark Ludar's eyes flash and his great chest heave, and knew that he thought of his exiled father and his ravished castle. The maiden at his side, as she turned her fair face to the setting sun, half hopefully, half doubtfully, thought perhaps of her unknown home and her unremembered father. As for me, my mind was charged with wonder at a scene so strange and beautiful, and yet with loneliness as I recalled that for me, at least, there waited no home over there.

"The sun has gone," said the maiden presently, laying her hand on Ludar's arm.

SIR LUDAR

He said nothing; but took the little hand captive in his, and stood there, watching the fading glow.

Then she began to sing softly; and I, knowing they needed not my help, left them.

I remember, as I made my way, stumbling through the thick heather, towards the little village, feeling that this trouble of mine would be less could I tell it to some one; and then, I know not how, I fancied myself telling it to sweet Jeannette; and how prettily she heard me, with her bright eyes glistening for my sake, and her hand on my arm, just as a minute ago I had seen that maiden's hand on Ludar's. Heigho! I who called myself a man was becoming a girl! Happily the heather was thick and the path steep, so that I presently had some other care for my head to busy itself with.

So I came down to the little bay, and set the boat in readiness for to-morrow's voyage, and then, having nought else to do (for the old nurse was abed already), I curled myself up in my corner and fell asleep, dreaming of I know not what.

Now, you are not to suppose that from the time we dropped anchor in Leith Roads till now our travels had been easy. On the contrary, the perils we had met by sea had been nothing to those we encountered by land. Well for us, in parting company with the *Miséricorde* (which we left in the hands of the honest pilot to render up to the Frenchman's agents in Scotland), we had taken each our pistol and sword. For scarce had we set foot in Edinburgh, but we were called to use them. Sometimes it was to protect the maiden from the gallants of the Court, who deemed each pretty face their private game, and were amazed to find Ludar and me dispute their title. Sometimes it was to defend ourselves from the hungry redshanks who itched to dig their daggers into some body, little matter whose. Sometimes it was from rogues and vagabonds whose mouths watered at the sight of the box. Sometimes it was from the officers, who took us one day for English spies, and the next for lords in disguise. As for the poet, the day of our landing he had fled for his life from the terrors of the place, and so we lost him.

I cannot tell what battles we fought, what knocks we got, or what we gave in return; how night by night we slept, sword in hand, at the maiden's door; how day by day we sought to escape from the city and could not; how at

RECEIVED BY THE M'DONNELLS

length, under cover of a notable fray in the streets, we fled back to Leith, where we found a boat and so reached Falkirk. From there, how like so many gipsies we wandered over the hills and among the deep valleys till we came to Lennox, and so once more met the sea on the other side. Then, by what perils of storm and current, in a small row-boat, we crossed to the wild Isle of Arran, on which we were well-nigh starved with hunger and drowned with the rains. And at last, how, using a fine day, we made across to Cantire, where, so soon as Ludar declared his name, we were hospitably received by the M'Donnells there, and promised a safe conduct over to Ireland.

From the wild men here—half soldiers, half mariners—we heard—not that I could understand a word of their tongue, but Ludar and the old nurse could—that Sorley Boy, Ludar's father, was already across, hiding in the Antrim Glynns, where, joined by many a friendly clan, he was waiting his chance to swoop down on the English and recapture his ancient fortress. Turlogh Luinech O'Neill, the maiden's father, we heard, was still lending himself to the invaders, and in return for the Queen's favour, holding aloof, if not getting ready to fall upon the M'Donnells when the time came. Of these last, Alexander, Ludar's brother, first and favourite son of the great Sorley Boy (for Donnell, the eldest of all, had been slain in battle), was reputed, next to his father, the bravest; he was also in the Glynns; but James and Randal, his other brothers, were in the Isles, raising the Scots there, and waiting the signal to descend with their gallowglasses on the coveted coast.

Ludar, had he been alone, would have stayed, I think, to join them. But, with the maiden there, he could think of naught until he had rendered her up safely to her father, foeman though he might be. So to-morrow we were to sail for Castleroe, Turlogh's fort on the western bank of the River Bann, whence, having left our charge, we would repair, Ludar said, sword in hand to his father's camp.

At daybreak we quitted the M'Donnells' hut in which we had sheltered and went down to the little harbour in the bay. The long Atlantic waves thundered in from the west as if they would bar our passage, and I wondered much at the peril of crossing that angry channel in so frail a craft.

SIR LUDAR

But Ludar laughed when I questioned him.

"These galleys," said he, "have carried my fathers on stormier seas than this—aye, and the maiden's fathers too; therefore they may be trusted to carry you now, Humphrey."

"I care naught for myself," said I, "and you know it. Nay, Ludar, if it comes to that, I had as soon be under those waves as upon them."

He looked at me in his strange solemn way.

"Friend," he said, "you are unhappy. Was it always so, or is it because I, with a great happiness in me, see more than I once did? Humphrey," added he, "that maiden has said to me that she loves me. Can you credit it?"

I locked his hand in mine. Would that I could show him to you as he stood there; his face ablaze with triumph, yet almost humbled with his good fortune. Then, as he looked on me, the blaze softened into a look of pity.

"I am selfish," said he, "while you are far away from her you love. Yet I could not help telling it, Humphrey. Heaven give you the same secret one day to tell me! But here she comes. Take her beside you at the helm. As for me, the light is too strong in my eyes for me to steer. I must be alone here in the prow, till the world take shape again."

The galley was a long open boat with a single square sail, and thwarts for twelve rowers. To-day six sturdy Scots took the oars, all M'Donnells, who wondered much that Ludar should lie forward, leaving the fair maid and me at the helm. As for the old nurse, whose courage revived as the opposite headlands rose up to view, she ensconced herself amidships, and croned in her native tongue with the rowers. We needed to row many a mile, round the island, before we could hope to hoist our sail. Yet, I could not help marvelling at the vigour of the oarsmen, and at the speed and steadiness of our boat over the billows.

The maiden, who by her blushes when we first met that morning had confirmed Ludar's story, was content enough to sit in the stern with me, while he courted solitude in the prow. She sat a long while silent, looking seaward, and, I think, with the self-same light in her eyes which dimmed those of Ludar. Presently, however, she turned her face to me and said, almost suddenly:

HUMPHREY AND THE MAIDEN

" Humphrey, tell me more of that maiden you spoke about. Why does she not love you ? "

I knew not what to say, the question was so unlooked for. I tried to laugh it off.

" Ask her that," said I. " Why should she ? I am not Sir Ludar."

" No," said she gently, and then her face blushed once more, and she dropped silent, looking away seaward.

I was sorry for my churlish speech, and feared it had given her offence. But here I was wrong, for presently she said again :

" Is she the little maid who talks to you at home in French, and whom you carried in your arms. Tell me more of her, Humphrey."

To please her I obeyed. And somehow, as I recalled all the gentle ways of my sweet little mistress, and the quaint words she had spoken, and, in fancy, saw once again her bright face, and remembered how she had always taken my part and chased away the clouds from my brow—somehow I knew not how, the memory seemed very pleasant to me ; and I called to mind more yet, and wondered with myself how little I had had her in my thoughts since last we parted that cruel day in Kingston street.

As I talked, the maiden listened, her eyes stealing now and again to where Ludar lay wrestling with his mighty happiness in the prow, and then returning, half frightened, half pitying, to encourage me to tell her more. Which I did. And then, when all was said, she asked again :

" And why does she not love you ? "

" Indeed," replied I, " I never asked her. Nor do I know if I love her myself."

She smiled at that.

" May I answer for you ? No ? At least I love her, Humphrey, and for her sake and yours she shall be a sister to me and—— "

" And Ludar," said I, as she stopped short.

" Yes, to me and Ludar."

Then we fell to talk about Ludar, and so the day wore on, till, as the sun stood over our heads, we breasted the fair Island of Raughlin.

Here Ludar, with gloomy face, came astern to tell a story.

SIR LUDAR

'Twas neither brief nor merry; but, as he told it with flashing eyes and voice which rose and fell with the dashing waves, we listened with heaving bosoms. 'Twas of a boy, who once played with his comrades on that self-same Island of Raughlin. How in the pleasant summer time he had learned from his noble brothers to draw the bow, and, child as he was, to brandish the spear. How maidens were there, some of whom he called his sisters; and how they sang the wild legends of the coast and told him tales of lovers and fairies and heroes. And how, now and again a white boat came over from the mainland, and on it a noble warrior, gigantic in form, with his yellow locks streaming in the breeze, and the sun flashing on his gilded collar and naked sword. That noble man was the boy's father, and the scarcely less noble form at his side, less by a head than his sire, yet taller by a head than most of his clansmen, was the boy's elder brother. And how the boy followed these two wherever they went, and begged them to take him to the wars on the mainland; and they smiled and bade him wait ten years. So he was left with the women and children on the island, while the men went off in galleys to fight the invader. Then one fatal day, how they woke to see white-sailed ships in the offing and boats of armed men landing on the shore, and how in doubt and terror women and children and old men hastened to yonder castle on the hill, and begged the few armed men there stand to their guard.

"Then," said Ludar, with thunder in his face, "the strangers spread like flies over the fair island and surrounded the castle. To resist was useless. The armed men offered to yield if the women and children and old men were spared. 'Yield, then,' said the captain, and the gate was opened. Then the false villains shouted with laughter, and slew the armed men before the eyes of the helpless captives. 'Bring a torch!' shouted some. 'Drive them back into their kennel!' shouted others. Then a cry went up, so terrible that on the light summer breeze it floated to the mainland, to where on the headland the noble father of that boy stood, like a statue of horror, as the flames shot up. The wretched captives fought among themselves who should reach the door and die on the sword of the enemy rather than by the fire. That boy saw his playmates tossed in sport on the swords of

A GRUESOME STORY

their murderers, and heard his sisters shriek to him—boy as he was—to slay them before a worse death befel. Then he forgot all, except that when, days after, he awoke, he was in the heart of a deep cave into which the sea surged, carrying with it corpses. For a week he stayed there, tended by a rough shepherd, living on seaweed and fish, and well-nigh mad with thirst. At last came a boat ; and when that boy woke once more he was in the castle of his noble father, whose face was like the midnight, and whose once yellow hair was as white as the snow."

"That is the story," said Ludar. "I was that boy."

"And the murderers," said I, falteringly, for I guessed the answer.

"The murderers, Humphrey," said he, "were of the same race as your worst enemy and mine."

This gloomy story cast a cloud over our voyage ; until, after long silence, during which we sat and watched the rocky coast of the ill-omened Island, the maiden said :

"Sir Ludar, there are older stories of Raughlin than yours. Listen while I sing you of the wedding of Taise Taobhgheal, which befel there when yonder hill was crowned by a beautiful white city, with houses of glass, and when warriors shone in golden armour."

Then she sang a brave martial ballad of a famous battle, which was fought on those coasts for the hand of the beautiful Taise Taobhgheal. And the clear music of her voice, to which the rowers lent a chorus, helped charm away the sadness of Ludar's tale, and while away the time till, having rounded the island, we hoisted our brown sail and flew upon the waves past the great organ-shaped cliffs of the mainland.

The sun had long set behind the western foreland ere we caught ahead of us the roar of the surf on the bar which lay across the river's mouth. Our rowers had passed that way many a time before, and plunged us headlong into the mighty battle of the waters where river and sea met. For a short minute it seemed as if no boat could live in such a whirl ; but, before we well knew the danger, we were in calm water within the bar, sailing gaily down the broad, moonlit river.

Then Ludar and the maiden grew sad at the parting which

SIR LUDAR

was to come; and I, being weary of the helm, left them and went forward.

Beautiful the river was in the moonlight, with the woods crowding down to its margin, broken now and again by rugged knolls or smooth shining meadows. To me it was strange to be in Ireland and yet have all remind me of my own Thames, all except the wild chant of the foreign rowers.

Many a mile we rowed then, or rather glided. For Ludar bade the men slacken speed and let the night spend itself before we presented ourselves at Castleroe. Therefore we took in the oars after a while and floated idly on the tide.

The old nurse came forward to where I sat, very dismal and complaining.

"Ochone!" said she. "This has been a sore journey, Master Humphrey. My bones ache and my spirits are clean gone. Musha! it's myself would fain be back in London town after all. There'll be none to know Judy O'Cahan here; and I've nigh forgotten the speech and manners of the place mysel'. And my heart sinks for the sweet maiden."

"Why, what ails her?" I asked. "Has she not come to her father's house?"

"Aye, aye, so it's called, so it's called. 'Tis Turlogh owns Castleroe, but 'tis my Lady of Cantire owns Turlogh. He durst not bless himself if she forbid. She wants no English step-daughters, I warrant ye; or if she do, 'twill be to buy and sell with, and further her own greedy plans. I know my Lady; and I know how it will fare with my sweet maid. I tell thee, Master Humphrey, Turlogh, brave lad as he was, must now do as his grand Lady bids, and 'twere better far the maiden had stayed in her nunnery school."

"Why, Judy," said I, "you forget he sent to England for her; and that now, since this voyage began, she has found a protector who will ease both the lord and lady of Castleroe of her charge."

She laughed.

"Little you know, master 'prentice. But there comes the dawn."

Sure enough, in the east, the grey crept up the sky; and at the same time the banks on either side of us rose steeply, while the roar of a cataract ahead warned us that our journey's end was come.

OUR JOURNEY'S END

We waited yet another hour, moored under the bank till the sun lifted his forehead above the hill. Then the note of a bugle close at hand startled us, and Ludar bade us disembark.

Castleroe was a house perched strongly on the western bank of the river, with a moat round, and a drawbridge separating the outer courtyard from the house itself.

As we approached we were loudly challenged by a sentry who called to us in broad English.

"Who goes there ? Halt ! or by my life you shall have a taste of my musket if you advance further."

My heart leapt to my mouth. 'Twas not at hearing the English speech once more, but because the fellow's voice itself was familiar to me. And when a moment later its owner came in view, I saw the man I had met once on the road to Oxford, the same Tom Price who had gone near hanging me for a Jesuit, and afterwards had tempted me to take service in the troop of his master, Captain Merriman," for these Irish wars.

Was it much wonder I gasped aloud, as I saw him ?

"Tell Turlogh Luinech O'Neill," said Ludar, advancing, " that his daughter is come from England, with her ancient nurse. And take us to him, that we may deliver our charge safely into his hands."

"Ludar," cried I, taking him by the arm. "Halt, for Heaven's sake ! This is one of Captain Merriman's men ! "

The soldier looked round as I spoke, and recognised me in a trice.

"Hillo ! " cried he "what have we here ? My little Jesuit, Lord Mayor of London, as I'm a sinner ! And in what brave company ! Sure, they told me my lady expected visitors ; and here he is with his sweetheart, and old mother, and private chaplain. Woe's me, the flag is not aloft ! So, lad, thou'rt come to join our wars after all, and tell the captain about that duckweed ? And thou shalt, my little Humphrey —you see I even remember your name."

"One word, Tom Price," said I, breathlessly, "as you are an honest man. Is the captain here ? "

"Here ! He is my lady's honoured guest this three weeks, since he arrived here in a temper enough to sour the country-side. Why, hadst thou run away with his own sweetheart, thou couldst not—— "

SIR LUDAR

"Is my father, is Turlogh Luinech O'Neill here, then?" asked the maiden, coming up.

"Thy father!" said the soldier gasping. "Why I took thee for—— And art thou, then," said he, pulling off his cap, "art thou——"

"Yes, yes," said she, "I am Rose O'Neill. Pray say, is my father here?"

"Madam," said he, "he left us a week ago for his Castle at Toom. Howbeit my lady——"

"Ludar," said the maiden, "back to the boat, quick! I will not go in here."

"Nay, fair angel," said a voice at our side, "now we have found our truant bird, we must cage her."

It was Captain Merriman himself, smirking, hat in hand.

Before he could well speak the words, Ludar had sprung at his throat, and hurled him to the ground.

Then ensued a pitiful uproar. The guard, in a moment, turned out upon us. It was useless for two men to stand against twenty; our M'Donnells at the boat were beyond call. We fought as long as we could; nor was it till Ludar received a gun shot in his arm, and I a slash that laid bare my cheek bone, that we knew the game was up. The maiden had been carried off into the house; the old nurse lay in a swoon; three men, besides the captain, were disabled. As for us, we could but stagger to the gateway more dead than alive. Once outside, the gate was closed. The guard from within sent a few flying shots after us, one of which lightened me of my little finger, and another missed Ludar's knee. Then, seeing us gone and hearing the shouts of our M'Donnells, who, at the noise of the shots, had come up to help us, they forbore to follow further and let us get clear.

And it was in this manner we brought Rose O'Neill safely to her father's house at Castleroe.

CHAPTER XIV

How Ludar fired the Beacon on Knocklayd

I THINK, had it not been that Ludar immediately fell into a swoon with the wound in his arm, we should never have got him back to the boat. For such was his wrath and despair that he would have turned and invaded the castle single-handed, preferring to meet his death thus to leaving the maiden in so dire an extremity. As for me, 'twas well I had this new care thrust upon me, or I too might have fallen into a despair scarce less than his.

I guessed, so soon as the panic was over and Captain Merriman brought round, that order would be given to follow and capture us at all hazard. Therefore, so soon as our M'Donnells arrived, we bore Ludar among us to the boat, and cast loose without delay. In this we were none too soon, for we had not been long rowing ere a noise of bugles and shouting at the castle gave us to know that the pursuit was begun. Lucky for us, the woods on either bank were too dense to allow them to get within shot of us. Nor, after we had got safely past the town of Coleraine, was there much fear that they (being unprovided with boats) could get at close quarters with us.

Once clear, we looked to my comrade's wounds. The bullet which had gashed his arm had happily not lodged there ; but it had lost him so much blood that, although we bound it up and stanched the flow, it was yet a long while before he recovered life enough to open his eyes. Then he said :

" Whither are we going ? "

" Seaward," said I.

" Leaving her amid wolves," said he, bitterly.

" 'Twould do her no good if we returned," said I, " to be slain before her eyes. So long as she knows we are safe, there will be hope for her ; and she is brave enough to defend herself till we come again."

Ludar smiled bitterly. He knew, as I did, there was nothing in the words.

"My men," said he presently to the Scots, "wherever Sorley Boy, my father, is, take me."

"Sorley Boy is a fox that leaves no tracks," said one of the men, "but we last heard of him at Bonandonnye."

"Sail thither," said Ludar, and fell into silence.

'Twas a strange return voyage that, down that broad river, on the ebb of the self-same tide which had carried us up. Neither of us spoke a word, but as we watched the banks and one another, we wondered if this could be the same world and the same men as a few hours ago. It was a relief presently to meet the salt sea air on our faces, and to hear ahead once more the angry roar of the waves at the river's mouth.

Just as we reached the place where the channel, narrowing suddenly, tears its way through the sand into the ocean, a posse of horsemen dashed down on the western shore and shouted to us. So near were they, that I could see Tom Price among them, and beside him, that rascally Captain Laker, whom I had seen, or heard, last in Sir William Carleton's garden at Richmond.

One of the rowers pulled me down to the bottom of the boat just as a volley of shot whizzed over our heads.

"Up now, and row like fiends," cried our men when it had passed.

"Give me my pistol," said Ludar, "I have at least one arm."

So we tore through the water, letting fly at them as best we could while they stood reloading.

Ludar's aim missed, for he had only his left hand. Mine was more lucky, since it knocked over the villain Laker just as he raised his gun for a second shot.

This saved us ; for it gave us time to pull further beyond reach. So that when the next volley came, it pattered harmlessly in the waves around us.

This time we could not duck our heads, for our boat was already in the hurly-burly of the surf, and needed all our skill and all our strength to get her over that angry bar. More than once we were glad to fall back right side uppermost,

TO THE WARS

and more than once we looked to see every timber we had fly asunder. But at last, between two lesser waves, we slipped over, taking in half a boat of water as we did so, but winning clear of the peril; and leaving our pursuers, who had waited to see us perish, to turn back sullenly to report their ill success to their master.

'Twas a far cry to Bonandonnye, which lay behind the Eastern headlands, some four leagues beyond Benmore. Nor durst we approach it the shortest way, because our men had heard that the coast was closely guarded by the English, who made short work of all suspected craft. So we were fain to hoist our sail and stand out to sea, rounding Raughlin on the far side, and running back on Cantire.

There, for a week and more, Ludar lay in a fever, shouting to be taken to his father, yet too weak to turn in his bed. Tenderly his clansmen nursed him (and me, for the matter of that, for I had wounds too), until at least we were both in better trim.

Meanwhile, one of the men had rowed across to the mainland, and come back with the news that Sorley Boy was deep in the woods of Glenshesk, behind the great mountain of Knocklayd, where he was rapidly bringing his forces to a head for a swoop on Dunluce. This news decided Ludar to tarry not a day longer. That very night, as the sun set, we embarked on our boat. It was the time of the autumn gales, and hard enough were we put to it to get safely across. For that very reason, perhaps, we were able to land unobserved by the careless watchmen on the coast, who never dreamed to look for a boat on such a night. Whereas, had they known more of the M'Donnell oarsmen, they would have doubled their guard instead of going asleep.

I was glad to find that Ludar, having resolved on the journey, had strength enough to go through with it. Indeed, his step grew firmer every pace we took, and although his brow remained black, and he would, I think, have felled me to the ground had I mentioned the maiden's name in his ear, yet on other matters his spirits revived.

'Twas a difficult journey from the little bay where we landed to Glenshesk; nor dare we make it in broad daylight. We took care to clad ourselves like herdsmen; yet even so, it would have been a risk to accost a stranger or enter a hut for shelter. For the O'Neills and the English among them had overawed the peasants; and although it was commonly believed the Turlogh would hold aloof in this quarrel, yet he had his own grudge against the M'Donnells, and was not lightly to be run against. So we lay hid all day in the thick heather, and at night crossed rapidly at the back of Benmore, and plunged into the woods on the slopes of the dome-like Knocklayd. Ludar seemed to know his way by instinct. The M'Donnell had told us where we should meet with a friendly clansman, who would take us to the chief, and had warned us what paths specially to avoid in crossing the mountain. His instructions served us well; and at daybreak we came upon the friendly hut just where we had expected, a little below the summit on the seaward side of the hill.

The man would by no means let us lie in his hut for fear of being seen, but showed us a deep cave in the hill-side, where we (and a score of men beside, had it been needful) might hide.

As we lay there, waiting for night, Ludar, for the first time, referred to what had befallen at Castleroe.

"Humphrey," said he, "I am torn in two. How can I go out to take a castle, while she lies in the wolf's clutches yonder? Yet how may I, a loyal man, pursue my private quarrel while my brave father demands my service for the clan in this great enterprise?"

"Maybe," said I, "in doing the latter you will achieve both ends. For, assuredly, so soon as an alarm is raised for the safety of Dunluce, this Merriman and every trooper he has must come thither; so, the maiden will be left free of him. Besides," said I, "if what the old nurse says is true, my Lady Cantire is not the woman lightly to abandon her rights in the maiden. She is more likely to hold her as a bait to trap the Captain into some benefit to herself, and to that end she will at least keep her safe out of his clutches for a while."

Ludar groaned.

"Humphrey," said he, "you are a glib comforter. Tell me," he added, "from this height we should surely be able to see Castleroe."

THE SIGNAL BEACON

"Yes," said I, "I remember seeing this round hill, as we stood parleying with the sentinel."

Ludar said no more, but sat at the mouth of the cave, looking westward, till sunset.

Then a new resolve seemed to have taken hold of him. He led me to the cairn on the mountain top, where was piled a great heap of wood and briar ready for a beacon fire.

"When shall this be lit?" he asked our guide.

"When Sorley Boy is ready. 'Tis the last signal agreed upon. When Knocklayd is fired, friend and foe, the country round, will march."

"Then," said Ludar, "pile up more fuel, and fetch a torch."

The man and I stared at him in amazement.

"Do you hear?" he thundered. "Am I M'Donnell or are you?"

Then when the man, scared and terrified, went off to obey, Ludar said to me:

"I cannot help this, Humphrey. The signal must go out to-night, or all will be too late. Something tells me she is looking this way even now, praying for deliverance. Something tells me, too, that a day's more delay, and Dunluce is lost to us for ever. This shall bring all to a head, for better or worse."

"But your father," said I. "If he be not ready——"

"Sorley Boy M'Donnell is always ready," said Ludar, proudly.

So we stood silent and waited till the shepherd brought the torch.

"Can we see Dunluce from here?" I asked presently.

He took my arm and pointed to where, away in the west, a gleam of moonlight struck the sea.

"There," said he.

Then, as we both strained our eyes, there arose, as it seemed from that very spot, a strange wild sound, like the rise and fall of some wailing music, which moaned in the air and died away.

"What was that?" I asked.

"Hush!" said he. "Listen."

It came again, rising almost to a shriek, and sinking again into a sigh.

SIR LUDAR

Once more I looked at Ludar; and once more, with pale face, he motioned me to hold my peace and listen.

A third time the sound came, like a snatch of some mad song, ending in a sob. After it, you could almost feel the silence. We stood rooted to the spot, until presently the footsteps of the herdsman broke the spell. Then Ludar said:

"That is the Banshee. It means that in this business a M'Donnell of us will fall. Heaven help us!"

Then, scornfully throwing off the fear which for a moment had seemed to overtake him, he resolutely snatched the torch from the man's hand and plunged it into the pile.

We stood and watched the fire, as first it crackled amidst the underlayer of twigs and dry heather, then caught the branches above, and finally shot up in a grand tall column of flame skyward, showering high its sparks, and casting a fierce glow far and wide over land and sea.

'Twas a strange, a wondrous sight; yet, as I looked, the midnight fire itself was not so strange as the sight of Ludar standing there, noble, huge and motionless, illumined by the strong light, gazing out with shaded eyes into the far distance. To me it seemed like a scene in some weird play of which I forgot that I was myself an actor.

But as soon as the flame, bursting forth with a great roar, reddened the sky overhead, Ludar drew me to a little distance, and pointed seaward. Then I perceived, suddenly, on our right a twinkle of light which presently increased to a lurid flame. At the same instant on the left appeared a like fire, which in turn was taken up one by one from headland to headland, till the whole coast from Cushindun to Ramore was ablaze; even on the far distant Donegal headlands there glimmered a responsive signal. A wondrous sight indeed, with the Atlantic almost at our feet, reflecting angrily back the glare of the fire, and traversed by paths of light each seeming less fierce as the distance increased, until from the remotest there travelled but a tiny streak. Above, the sky still more fiercely carried the red signal; while from their rocks swooped up the great army of seabirds and flew crying out to sea.

Thither my two comrades still eagerly gazed. Though scarce five minutes had passed since the first flame shot aloft, the impatience of the herdsman became extreme, and he

THE ANSWER ACROSS THE SEA

muttered angrily through his clenched teeth as he strained his eyes into the irresponsive darkness.

"Altacarry!" exclaimed he at length, when presently, on the point of Raughlin, a light shot up.

"And Cantire!" he added, when, later, the eagerly looked for light on the Scottish mainland broke aloft and mingled its glare with that of the Antrim fires.

Then, at last, Ludar relaxed his motionless posture, and taking my arm, plunged hastily from the summit, with the herdsman before us for a guide.

Halfway down, the guide halted and pointed out two new signals inland. One to our right, the other straight before us.

"Yonder," said he, pointing to the right, "comes from the O'Cahan's country beyond the Bann, above Castleroe, where be English troops; that in front shows that Sorley Boy is afoot already. 'Tis a wily fox," added the man (talking as they all did in their Irish tongue), "among these score of lights, who shall say which is his, or whither he foregathers? But *we* know!"

Presently we dropped into the marshland at the base of the hill, and lost all save the red glare in the sky above us. By many a cunning path the man led us, between bogs, through woods, and over piled-up rocks, till we stood on a new hill side, and caught sight again of the distant beacons. That on Knocklayd, behind us, was already burning low; but it had done its work. For, as we mounted higher, a dozen new fires inland met our view; and, standing for a moment to look, our ears caught a distant sound of shouting, and the clattering of horses' feet.

We were now, our guide told us, looking down into the deep vale of Glenshesk, at the head of which the chieftain lay. A wild impassable valley it looked, crowded with forest, and flanked with rugged mountain. I could scarcely wonder, as I looked down, at the tales the man had told us, of how, in time of war, the country people would drive their cattle, together with the women and children, far into the depths of these glens for safety, while they went out to meet the enemy on the seaboard; or of how, tempting him to follow the booty up one of these, they had caught him many a time in a trap between two fires, and cut him to pieces.

The descent into the valley was perilous enough even

SIR LUDAR

for us. For the greater part of the way we had to swing ourselves down by the trees, many of which threatened to break under our weight and hurl us headlong to the bottom. But when, at last, we reached the stony land below, it was easier walking, and we reached the stream in safety.

Here we halted impatiently till morning.

"Humphrey," said Ludar, " by this time, unless we have ventured for naught, an alarm has gone out which will send Merriman out of Castleroe, and bring back Turlogh into it. So far, we have done well. But unless Sorley Boy reach Dunluce quickly, the enemy will be in the place before us, and we shall have done harm. Why do they not come ? If I had but fifty men like you, Humphrey, we need not be sitting thus."

But sit we did, till the sun looked at us over the hill. Then Ludar could wait no longer, but summoned me to my feet, and stalked up the valley. We had gone about an hour, when a loud tramp and shouting ahead, together with a vision of wild figures on the hills on either hand, told us that the long expected meeting had come at last. The next turn of the valley brought us full in view of the M'Donnell host. It stretched in a wild irregular line far up the glen, the men marching four or five abreast, armed, some with spears, some with swords and bucklers, others with bows, and a very few with firearms. They sang a loud wailing song as they marched, mingled with cries of defiance, and now and then of laughter. But what moved me most was the aspect of the two men who marched a dozen paces in the front of all.

The elder was a giant, huge of limb, towering above his clan like Saul, in the Bible, among his Israelites. His white hair hung wildly on his shoulders, and tossed defiantly with every step he took. He may have been seventy years of age, yet his face was knit as hard as a warrior's of thirty, and he stepped out as lissome and quick as his youngest gallowglass. Yet all this was as nothing to the noble sadness of his face and the blaze of his deep, blue eyes, which, had I not known it already, would have betrayed him to me anywhere as Ludar's father. The younger warrior at his side, a man of thirty-five, joyous of mien, his yellow hair glistening in the sunlight, and his massive form (only less massive than his father's) moving with a careless ease, it was not hard to guess

THREE MIGHTY MEN

was Alexander, the darling of the clan and the pride of his father's life.

Seeing us in the path, they suddenly halted, while the musketeers behind levelled their pieces.

But Ludar stepped solemnly forward.

"Father, I am Ludar," said he.

The old man uttered a quick exclamation and stepped back a pace to look at this stalwart man, whom he had seen last a young boy ten years ago. Then, with a face as solemn as that of his son's, he laid his great hand on the lad's shoulder and said:

"Thou art come in good time, Ludar, my son."

That was all the greeting that passed betwixt these two; for immediately the march began again, the old man stalking first alone, and the two brothers (who had kissed at meeting) following, arm in arm. 'Twas a noble sight those three great men—the old chief and his first and last born sons. But to my mind, much as I loved my master, Sorley Boy was the grandest of the three. While he was by, a man could look at no one else. Every gesture, every toss of the head, and swing of the arm had force in it; and to me it seemed a wonder that such a man should need an army at his back to carry him anywhere he willed.

He halted again presently, and wheeled round on his sons.

"Why did you fire the beacon?" he asked of Ludar.

"Because the time had come," said Ludar. "To-day Dunluce is slenderly guarded; to-morrow it will be full of the enemy."

Then he coloured up with a flush as he added:

"Father, I demand a favour—the first for ten years."

"It is granted, lad. I know what it is. You shall take the castle."

Then Ludar grew radiant, as he clutched his father's hand and thanked him for this mighty honour. And Alexander seemed scarcely less happy for his young brother's sake.

"We be a thousand armed man," said the old chief (he spoke in his own tongue, to which even I was growing somewhat familiar by now). "Take three hundred with you, Ludar, my son, and turn westward. Alexander, with three hundred more, shall march to the sea, northward, as we go now. I, with the rest, will strike eastward to Bonandonnye.

SIR LUDAR

To-morrow, boy, if Dunluce be not yours, Alexander shall come to take it for you. The day after, if you both fail, I shall be there myself with the clansmen from the Isles, who are already upon the sea. Here we part company, lads. When we meet again one of us shall not see the other two. Last night I heard the Banshee."

"And I," said Alexander.

"And I," said Ludar.

"Farewell, then," said Sorley Boy. "Do you, Ludar, choose your three hundred and begone. After you, Alexander do the same. I will take the rest. The pipers shall come with me to draw the enemy eastward."

The division was soon made. Ludar chose the clansmen who knew best the parts about Dunluce and the country we should have to cross to reach it. In an hour we were ready to start.

"Farewell," said the old chief. "We meet all at Dunluce two days hence."

"Dead or alive," said Alexander.

Then the order was given to march, and we turned suddenly up the westward slope of the glen, the men behind us shouting, "*Dunluce! Froach Eilan! Ludar!*" till our several parties lost sight of one another. Then Ludar ordered silence and speed; and so, all day long, we tramped over the rugged hills and across the deep valleys; till, near sundown, Ludar, having halted his men in a deep-wooded hollow, took me forward and brought me to the summit of a little green hill. Here he took my arm and pointed ahead.

"Dunluce!" said he.

CHAPTER XV

How Ludar took Dunluce

AT first I saw nothing but à jagged line of cliff-top, lower than where we stood, with the sea beyond. Then I perceived that where Ludar pointed the line broke suddenly, and disclosed a great naked rock standing alone, sheer out of the water which leapt wildly all round it and thundered into the cave at its base. I looked further. I saw a narrow bridge across the chasm, while what I had first thought to be rugged piles of rock took the form of grim battlements and towers, rising so straight from the edge of the rock that I had thought them a part of it. Across the bridge frowned an angry portcullis. As the place stood, it looked as if one man could hold it against a thousand, so unapproachable did it seem. On our side the bridge, on the mainland, was a large courtyard or barrack, with an outer wall and moat round it, of itself no easy place to carry; and when, beyond that, hung this angry castle, perched like an eagle over the sea, I marvelled not so much that the M'Donnells should hope to take it, as that they should ever have lost it.

I could understand Ludar's excitement as he stood there and gazed at this old fortress of his fathers, with the standard of the foreign invader floating above its topmast tower. He said nothing; yet, I could tell by the heaving of his chest, what thoughts were passing in his mind, what hatred of the usurper, what impatience to stand once more on those battlements and fling open the gate to his noble father.

The light faded from the sky as we stood there, until turrets and rock and flag melted away into a common blackness, and left us only the thunder of the waves in the hollows below, to tell us where Dunluce stood. Then Ludar led me quickly back to his men.

We found no little stir afoot. For the M'Donnells' scouts

had come in with a man of the English garrison whom they had found foraging for meat; while, almost at the same moment, a herdsman from Ramore (which was a district westward of us) had come to tell us news of the enemy.

Ludar heard the soldier first.

"We be but thirty men in yonder hold," said he. "For so soon as the alarm spread that Castleroe and the town of Coleraine were to be attacked, fifty of our guard and three cannon were drawn away thither this very morning. I know it, for I stood sentinel when Captain Merriman——"

"He! is he there?" demanded Ludar.

"No, in truth," said the soldier, "'twas he rode over from Castleroe and took away half our men, leaving us, in place, a parcel of puling women to mind, whom he might have kept with better grace at Castleroe."

"And who are these women?" asked Ludar with heightened colour.

"They say the fair one is a sweetheart of his own—a straight enough lass, but not of the sort I would willingly undertake myself. Some say she is kinswoman to the O'Neill or his lady, whom the captain was sent to guard hither; but, to my thinking, he was on his own business more than Turlogh's, and when this fighting be over we shall see him come back for his ladybird. I pray you, gentles," continued this man, who was of a careless sort, and distressed by no mischance, "permit me to return to the castle with this brace of birds. They are, in fact, for this same young lady, to whom our coarse fare hath little to recommend it, and who, being sickly, needs a dainty. I stand a fair chance to be shot for a truant when I get back; yet I may as well be that as hanged here by your worships. The only difference will be that the maiden will get her supper in one case, and miss it in the other."

"Go back," said Ludar. "If you be a liar, you are a rare one; if you be not, you are an honest fellow, and can be trusted to report nothing of what you have seen here."

"That will I not," said the man. "But when I see thee on the drawbridge, I shall let fly at thee, by your leave, as at an enemy of my Queen."

"You shall," said Ludar. "I would scorn you if you did not. But hearken, take the maiden this flower (and he

THE MOVEMENTS OF THE ENEMY

pulled a poppy flower from the grass) and tell her, before it droop he who sent it will be in Dunluce."

"Marry will I," said the soldier, laughing. "But thou wilt need to hasten, my master, for poppies fade fast. And if, as I expect, thou get no further than the bridge, or over the edge of it, you may trust me to look to the lady for your honour's sake."

So the man departed amidst not a few murmurings from our men, who understood not letting an enemy go scot free, unless it were to betray his party into their hands.

The other fellow, one of the men of the Route, who served which ever party he must, confirmed what the Englishman had said respecting the movements of the enemy. Sorley Boy had for weeks past let it be hinted, that when he came to strike, it would be at the Castle on the Bann on the one hand, and at Knockfergus, far to the south, on the other. Therefore, while Turlogh Luinech O'Neill tarried at Toome to watch what passed in the latter region, Captain Merriman strengthened Coleraine and the forts on the Bann in order to hold the former. Meanwhile, Sorley Boy, having thus made the enemy busy elsewhere, was coming down, as I have said, betwixt the two, at Dunluce. No doubt but the English suspected some scheme, for they withdrew only parts of their garrisons along the coast, depending on the natural strength of Dunluce and the other castles to hold off any attack till succour should arrive. But since the old fox never showed front till he was ready to spring, no one knew exactly where to expect Sorley Boy; whereby the enemy was forced to remain scattered, in little companies, all along the coast, from Larne to the Bann Mouth. At any rate, said the man, after the signals with Cantire last night, no one would expect the blow to fall till the Scottish clansmen were landed, which might be this time to-morrow.

Ludar bade the man remain in their company, and then called me and two others of his chief men aside.

"'Tis plain," said he, "our chance is now or never. Give the men time to sup, and then take forward your guns and have at them in front. You two," said he, addressing the two Scots, "with the main body are to carry the outworks, and pounding at the enemy's gate, keep him busy to landward. Humphrey, and I, and twenty more must try the sea front.

SIR LUDAR

As soon as you hear us shout from within, let drive every bolt you have, and the place is ours."

"But," said I, "you said that on the seaward side the place is unassailable."

"It is, except to M'Donnells. I did not play on these rocks for naught when a boy. Only pick me out twenty resolute men, and bring them round secretly to the first break in the cliffs eastward. I shall be there."

'Twas easy to find twenty men ready for the venture. Nay, the hard thing was to take no more than twenty, for a hundred were eager to come. No sooner were we started, than the main body, as agreed, leapt from their hiding-place, and marched rapidly on Dunluce.

Our guide took us a mile eastward of the castle, where at the head of the narrow gully that led from the cliff to the shore, stood Ludar, pistol in hand, waiting for us. He turned silently as we came up, and, motioning to us to follow, began at once the steep descent. The cleft was so narrow that one man could only lower himself at a time, and that swinging as often as not by his elbows and hands. For me it was harder work than for the active redshanks. As for Ludar, he stood at the bottom, while I, with half the troop growling at my back, was stuck midway. Yet we all reached the bottom in time; and as we did so, the boom of a gun from the rocks above us told that our men were already before the castle knocking for entrance.

Then we waded and scrambled in the darkness at the water's edge, till we came to the base of the great black rock on which the fortress stood. Often we were wading waist-deep in the pools, and often on hands and knees drawing ourselves over the surf-swept ledges. Ludar seemed to know every step of the way, despite the years that had passed since as a boy he hunted there for sea-birds, nor was he in the humour now to slacken speed for us who knew not when we put out one foot, where we should land with the other.

Above us, the noise of the guns was already lost in the thunder of the waves as they echoed in the cave under the castle rock. It seemed, as we stood there and looked up, that not a foot further could we go. The great angry cliff beetled over our heads, and on its very edge, far above, we might discern against the gloomy sky the dim corner of a buttress.

A PERILOUS VENTURE

But it was not here that Ludar meant us to ascend. "Now, my men," said he, "put your powder in your bonnets and follow me."

Whereupon he took a step up to his neck in the deep water, and started to swim. One by one we followed him, armed and clad as we were, into the angry surf. 'Twas a perilous voyage, and had not the tide been full and high above the rocks, we should not have come out of it, some of us, sound in limb or wind. Once or twice as I was flung upwards with a swirl almost upon the jagged cliff, I thought my last hour was come, and wondered whose eye would be dim at the news of my end. Then, when, with a like swirl I was heaved back into the safety of deep water, I thought what a big venture was this, and who would not follow when Ludar led?

So, I scarce know how, we rounded the mouth of that resounding cave and stood panting on the narrow ledge on the far side. I say, we stood—yet not all. Of the twenty-two men who had plunged, only nineteen foregathered at the far side.

"'Twas bravely swum," said Ludar, "and though it has cost M'Donnell three brave sons, it has won him Dunluce. I promise you, we shall go back by land."

I asked him, where next? and he pointed up to what seemed a rock as sheer and threatening as ever we had met on the other side. Nay, on this side, the castle itself seemed to hang clean over the edge.

"There is a path, I remember," said he, "by which in old days the M'Quillans came down to the cave. I went up it myself as a boy. See here."

And he led us a few steps round, as if back towards the cave; where was an iron spike driven into the smooth rock a little above the edge of the water.

He reached forward at this, and swung himself out over the water till his feet rested on a narrow ledge beyond, scarce the width of his boot, at the water's edge. Above this was a jutting nose of rock by which he raised himself on to the peg itself, and from that, by a long stride, on to a safer ledge above.

"Follow me," he cried, "and look not back."

Painfully and clumsily I achieved the perilous stride, and found myself at the entrance of a crack in the rock, into which the waves below dashed and thundered, and then, beaten back, shot up in an angry column high over our heads, descending with a whirl that all but swept us headlong from our perch.

Up this rift I watched Ludar clamber, losing him now and again in the shooting foam, and now and again, as the spray cleared off, seeing him safe, and ever a foot higher than before. How I followed him 'twould be hard to say. Yet the rock seemed riven into cracks which gave us a tolerable foothold, the better as we got higher up; and had it not been for the constant dash of the water, and the darkness, it might have been accounted passable enough. As it was, but for Ludar's strong arm above me, I should have lost my feet twice, and in my fall, perchance, might have carried away one or more of those who followed.

When we reached the top of the rift, a still worse peril awaited. For now we had to crawl painfully for some distance along a narrow edge on the face of the naked rock, with little hold for our hands, and, since the ledge slanted downward and was wet and slippery with the spray, still less for our feet. Even Ludar, I could see, was at a loss. But to halt now was useless; to turn back impossible. So, gripping as best he might at the rugged rock, he stepped boldly on to the ledge. I could but follow. Yet, at the first step, my feet slid from under me, and but that my hands held firm I should have been headlong. Inch by inch hugging the cliff, with our backs to the sea, we crawled over that treacherous ledge, sometimes slipping to our knees, sometimes hanging sheer by our hands.

Once, in a moment of weakness, I looked back to see how our men were faring. As I did so, a youth, next after me, a tall, brave youth who had been foremost in all the peril, suddenly staggered and slipped. For a moment he hung by hand and knee to the ledge; the next with a loud groan he fell backwards into the darkness. I heard the crash of his body on the rocks below, and, in my horror, my own grip for an instant relaxed, and I felt myself following. But a strong hand caught me and held me up, and Ludar said:

"Humphrey, are you a fool? Look up, man, or you are lost."

After that I had eyes for naught but the cliff before me. And although, before that terrible passage was ended, I heard

A HARD CLIMB

five more groans and as many more crashes on the rocks below, I managed to keep my own footing, till at last, with my head in a whirl, I stood beside Ludar on a broader, straighter ledge, within a dozen feet of the cliff-top.

Ludar was pale, and his breath came and went hard, as he made room for me beside him. He too had heard those terrible crashes.

"That path," said he, "is easier passed by a boy than a man. Had I known what it would cost us—— Yet, come on now!"

There was indeed no time to tarry, for the men behind—all that were left of them—came up, and we must perforce move forward to make them room.

Now, once more we heard the guns above, and a mighty shouting on the far side of the Castle. But, towards us, all frowned black and solitary.

The short distance yet to climb compared with what we had passed, was easy. For, steep as it was and often overhanging the sea, the rock here was rough and dry, and our feet held fast. Just as we came to the top, Ludar turned.

"Follow close, my men; shout, and discharge your pieces if you can," called he, "and once entered, make for the drawbridge."

Almost as he spoke, we heard a shout above us, and the report of a musket discharged into the darkness. A sentinel had heard our voices, and this was his greeting.

Next moment I saw Ludar on the top, struggling with a man. It was too dark to discern which was which; but a moment later, one of the two staggered a step backwards to the edge. There was a yell, a shower of loose earth; then, as I stood below clinging to the rock, a dark mass fell betwixt me and the sky, brushing me as it passed, and bounding from the ledge below with a hideous crash out into the deepness.

I stood there an instant as cold and pulseless as the stone against which I leaned. What if this were Ludar who had fallen?

A voice from above restored me to life.

"Quick there, come up, and the place is ours!"

In a moment I stood beside him on the narrow edge of grass between the castle wall and the brink. We could hear the shouts and firing away at the gate, but not a soul was left here to bar our passage. Even the sentinel's shot had passed unheeded. There was a low window leading to one of the offices of the castle, through which we clambered. Next moment we found ourselves standing within the walls of Dunluce.

"*Froach Eilan!*" shouted Ludar, drawing his dirk and waving on his men.

"*Froach Eilan! Ludar!*" shouted we, some of us discharging our pieces to add to the uproar, while one man exploded a swivel gun which stood on the seaward battlement.

The effect was magical. There was a sudden pause in the fighting at the bridge. Then rose a mighty answering cry from our M'Donnells outside; while the garrison, caught thus between the two fires, looked this way and that, not knowing against which foe to turn.

Though we were but thirteen—nay, only twelve, for the English sentinel in his fall had swept yet another of our brave fellows from the ledge—it was hard for any one to say in the darkness how many we were or how many were yet behind; and the thirty defenders to the place, when once the panic had spread, were in no mood for waiting to see. Many of them laid down their arms at once. Some, still more terrified, attempted to descend the rocks, and so perished; others plunged boldly into the gulf, and there was an end of them.

Ludar meanwhile rushed to the bridge. Many a brave fellow to-night had met his fate on that narrow way. For so far, no assault from our men without had been able to shake the strong portcullis, or make an opening on the grim face of the fortress. Indeed, it seemed to me, a single child in the place might have defied an army, so unassailable did it appear. Our men had carried easily the outer courtyard across the moat, driving the slender garrison back, with only time to lower the gate and shut themselves within before the assault began. But, though they thundered with shot and rock, all was of no avail. The guns of the besieged swept the narrow bridge on either side, and scarce a man who ventured across it returned alive.

Now, all was suddenly changed. Ludar, with a wild shout, fell on the keepers of the gate within and drove them from their post. So sudden was his onslaught, that none had time to ask whence he came or how many followed him.

DUNLUCE FOR M'DONNELL

Only a handful of soldiers withstood us. Among these was the gay English fellow whom we had let go an hour or so back ; and who now, true to his word, rushed sword in hand at Ludar. I wondered to see what Ludar would do, for kill the fellow I knew he would not. He met the Englishman's sword with a tremendous blow from his own sheathed weapon, which shivered it. Then with his fist he felled him to the ground, and, thus stunned, lifted him and laid him high on a parapet of the wall till he should come to.

Ere this was done, I and the rest of our men were at it, hand to hand with the few fighting men of the garrison that remained. It did not take long, for there were but half-a-dozen of them, and valiantly as they fought, we were too many and strong for them. One by one they fell or yielded, all except one stout man, the constable of the place, Peter Cary by name, who fought as long as he could stand, and then, before our eyes, flung first his sword, then himself, headlong from the cliff.

That ended the matter. Next moment, the English flag —alas! that I should say it—tumbled from the battlements ; and with shouts of " *Ludar! Froach Eilan!* " the portcullis swung open, and Dunluce belonged once more to the M'Donnells.

Leaving us to guard the tower where most of the enemy had shut themselves, Ludar stalked off to a remote corner of the castle ; whence in a short time he returned and called me.

" Humphrey," said he, " the maiden is safe, thank God. Go to her and see what she and the old nurse may need. I have other work to do. Friend," added he, " is this all a dream ? Is this indeed the castle of my fathers ? and when Sorley Boy comes, shall it be I who will give it into his hands ? "

" You and no other," said I, " for the place is yours."

" Alas! " he said, " at what cost! When I heard my brave men fall from the cliff like sheep, Humphrey, I was minded not to stay there myself. But adieu now. To the maiden! Keep her safe for me."

He waved his hand and stalked to the gate, where I watched him, erect, amid his cheering clansmen, with a joyous smile on his face such as I had rarely seen there before, and which I knew belonged in part to the noble chieftain, his father, and in part to his true love, the maiden.

SIR LUDAR

Alas! 'twas many a long day before I was to see him smile again like that, as you shall hear.

For the present, I went light at heart to the maiden, whom I found pale, indeed (for she had been ill), but serene and happy. The old nurse, who, I thought, ill liked my intrusion, forbade me to weary her young mistress with talk or questions.

"A plague on every man of you," growled the old woman. "You're only matched by the women, who be worse. Did I not tell you, Humphrey Dexter, my Lady Cantire would be no friend to my sweet mistress? 'Twas in vain the silly child tried to wheedle her over. Wheedle the Tether Stake! My lady bade her be civil to the Captain, if she would please her step-dame. And when the maiden put down her little foot at that, she was clapped within walls like a rogue, and fed on bread and water. Little harm that would have done, had not the captain himself served her as jailer, and every day thrust his evil presence into our company. I tell thee, Humphrey, that maiden hath fought as well as you or any of them; and shame on your sex, say I, that this devil should be one of you! Ill? No wonder if she was ill; with not a soul to pity her save a poor old body like me. Where's her father, to leave her thus? Eh, you mug-faced champion, you?"

"Indeed, Judy," said I, taken aback, "'tis a terrible case; but you cannot blame me."

"Not blame you! when instead of playing soldier you might have ridden to Toome and brought Turlogh to help us? Take shame on yourself; and, when you see the maiden weak and white, thank God her death be not on your head. For dead she would have been, like the brave maid she is, before ever she would have looked at this fellow-countryman of yours. He thought he had her safe, forsooth, when he whipped her off here and took the key with him. Fiend! Little wonder if she hates the name of you English!"

I grew angry at this, and told her she was a churlish old woman and had best leave me in peace till her temper was better. So we parted ill friends; I to guard the door, she to carry her waspish tongue where she list.

CHAPTER XVI

How Sorley Boy M'Donnell came Home to his own

I WAS not left for long to a solitary watch at the maiden's tower. For, just as dawn began to break, and my head, after the labours of the night, began to nod, I was roused with a thwack betwixt my jaw and my ear which sent me backwards to the ground. When I picked myself up, I found it was the English fellow whom Ludar had put snugly to roost on the parapet an hour or two since. He had come to in no very merry frame of mind; and, finding the castle in the hands of the besiegers, and his own life not worth an hour's purchase, was minded to hit out a bit for his Queen before giving up the ghost.

More than that, I suspect, he was a little jealous to find me on guard at the maiden's tower, where, till now, he had stood sentinel. Anyhow he caught me a crack which I have scarce forgotten yet, and which might have left me lying on my back to this day, but for the blow which Ludar had dealt him first.

He was unarmed, so that I could not make an end of him as shortly as I was minded. Nor had I sword to offer him to cross with mine; so I had him by the leg and the collar and walked him to the cliff's edge.

"You will do less harm down there," said I, "than here. So say your prayers."

"As you please, comrade," said he. "I should have sooner have had breakfast first. As for the blow I gave you, I thought you saw me come at you, else I would have woke you up first, and knocked you down next."

I set him down at that.

SIR LUDAR

"If that be so," said I, "you are not the cur I took you for; for I had no business to be nodding. Stay here, and I will fetch you a sword, and you shall die like an Englishman."

"I ask nothing better," said he, "even if it be at the hands of an Englishman turned traitor."

That took the spirit clean out of me. Was it not true? Was not this fellow a truer servant of her Majesty than I, who for months had done naught but break her laws, assault her mayors, fire on her flag, and slay her soldiers? Yet, how could I help it?

The fellow's gibe made me so miserable that instead of fetching him a sword, I gave him mine, and bade him do to me as I deserved.

He laughed.

"By my soul, no!" said he. "If you be a servant of her Majesty, 'tis not for me to touch you. If you be not, the sword belongs to you, and I call it no shame to die by it. Yet, if you are minded to fetch me a weapon, I warrant you I shall not run away till you come again."

So I went and fetched him a sword. And we fought there a half-hour by the clock, till our breath failed us, and never a blow could we get home on one another. I had no stomach for the business; and yet, when I found him so stubborn a swordsman, my blood got up, and I think I should have run him through if I could. But he had no mind to let me, and put me to it hard to keep my own skin whole.

So we halted to fetch breath, and before we could go to it again, the maiden came out of her lodging and stood betwixt us.

"Put by your swords," said she, "I command you both. What is your quarrel? and have you no work for your captain, that you thus bring civil war into his castle?"

"By your leave, fair maiden," said the Englishman, "no man here is my captain. This brave lad is an enemy to my Queen; therefore it is my duty to slay him."

"If so," said the maiden, "I too must be slain, for I love not your Queen."

"But you be no traitor like this——"

Here I whipped out my sword, and we were at it again, ere the maiden, with flashing eyes, could step once more between us.

AN INTERRUPTED DUEL

"Humphrey Dexter!" cried she in a voice I hope I may not hear from her lips again, "give me your sword, sir."

I obeyed meekly. 'Twould have been impossible to do aught else.

"And you, sir," said she, turning to the Englishman, "give me yours."

"Marry! 'tis yours already," said he, handing it up. "Mine was shivered by a blow from the young M'Donnell, and I am his prisoner. But, by your leave," added he, looking hard at me, "did you call this honest lad Humphrey Dexter? Why, may I perish if it is not the same swashbuckling ruffler I once knew in London town! I thought I had seen his gallows face before! Why, Humphrey, my lad, dost thou remember how I cracked thy skull at quarterstaff a year since in Finsbury Fields, and how thy Jack 'prentices groaned to see thee bite the dust? I liked thee none the less for it, though I beat thee. For 'twas a fair fight! Come, since 'tis thou, give us thy hand, and tell me how thou comest here amongst the enemies——"

"Aye, aye, I'll tell you," said I, not wanting to hear the end of the sentence.

Sure enough, this was a brawling soldier lad I had once met in the fields—Jack Gedge, by name—with whom I had had a bout at the quarterstaff. But he lied vilely when he said he beat me thereat; for, although he felled me once, I had him down three times, and the last time so that he had to be carried from the place by his legs and arms.

Howbeit, 'twas strange enough to see him here; and when, after the maiden had left us (having restored us our swords under promise of peace), I told him my story, he took my hand, and said, had he been in my shoes, he had been a traitor too. Yet he thanked his God he stood in his own.

And now, it may have been ten o'clock, there came a great shouting and noise of guns from the outer walls, and presently Ludar came into the hold, sword in hand, and told us that Captain Merriman and his soldiers had arrived from Castleroe, and were preparing to assault the place.

"Humphrey," said he, "whate'er betide, I commit the maiden to your care, till this fighting be over. This prisoner of mine," added he, pointing to the soldier, "will also stand by you, unless I mistake him."

SIR LUDAR

"Marry! so will I," said the man; "for a maiden in distress is no alien to a true servant of the maiden Queen. Count on me for so much, Captain."

"I do. Humphrey, I must go out and meet my enemy. He is in force, and must be scattered before he can blockade our ill-provisioned hold. Capture it he cannot; but he may starve it."

"Go then," said I. "Yet, will you not see the maiden first? She would be sorry not to bid you godspeed."

He seemed for a moment as though he would refuse. Then a look of great longing came into his face as he glanced up at the turret window.

While he debated, a messenger arrived with news that Alexander M'Donnell and his men were at hand, and that the English—seeing their constable hang from the walls on one side (for we had found his body, and displayed it thus as a signal of our triumph), and hearing the shouts of the M'Donnells on the other—were falling back, and making ready to turn tail.

It was even so. While he spoke, we could see on the cliffs eastward the M'Donnell standard, and hear the shouts of Alexander's company as they bore down upon the English, who for a moment ceased their assault on the castle, and turned doubtfully to face them.

Ludar laughed.

"If Alexander be there," said he, "our minds may be easy. Call in our men, and keep them within the walls. For he who yielded me the glory of taking Dunluce, shall not be robbed by me of the glory of sending these knaves packing. It needs not two M'Donnells to do that. Humphrey see to this, keep a watch how the battle goes, and come again presently. You know where to find me."

And he went, with a light heart, into the maiden's tower.

I know not why, I grudged to see him go in. 'Twas not jealousy—I was beyond that now. Nor was it that his help was needed without. For Alexander, I guessed, would have easy work with the foe; and 'twas like Ludar's nobleness to leave this new glory to his brother. 'Twas not that he did not deserve the rest and comfort, for he had worked like a lion that night, and denied himself till now the greeting the maiden owed to her preserver. Yet, for all that, I know not

A CHALLENGE

why, I had sooner he had remained, sword in hand, on the walls with us.

I scorned myself for my silly qualms, and hastened to call in our men, and bid them give fair field to Alexander and his company. They obeyed with difficulty; yet, when they heard that it was Ludar's order that no man should baulk his brother, they came in, and lined the walls to view the combat.

The M'Donnells on the cliff, when they saw the constable hang over the castle walls, and perceived the great bunch of heather on our topmost tower, stopped a moment to cheer and wave their bonnets. Then Alexander shouted to them in a voice we could hear half-a-mile away, and they broke into a run.

Meanwhile, Captain Merriman's party was, as I said, taken aback by this new danger, and threatened to draw off. But when they saw our party retire into the castle, and understood that the battle was between them and Alexander only, they stood their ground again, and wheeled round to meet him. They were some five hundred men against the M'Donnells' three hundred, and contained not a few of O'Neill's men in their number.

From where we stood we could see but little of the fight, except that within a few yards of the enemy Alexander halted his men, and then, stepping forward sword in hand, boldly dared the English leader, whoever he might be, to single combat. I marvelled to see if Captain Merriman would accept the challenge. For a while, amid the shouting and threatening on either side, I could not discern what followed, but presently, as Alexander, brandishing his sword, stepped up and repeated his challenge, there sprang out upon him, without warning, a huge gallowglass of the O'Neill's men, who with a club smote the young chief to the earth. The blow was so sudden and unexpected (for Alexander was not even looking that way) that the M'Donnell was reeling back in the arms of his men before friend or foe knew what had happened. Then, with a terrible yell, the Scots seized their weapons and closed on the enemy.

But Alexander, staggering to his feet, his head streaming blood, called to them once more to halt, as he leapt forward, half stunned, on his assailant. The duel was short and swift.

SIR LUDAR

For at the first onset the great gallowglass, amazed to see his man yet living, and ashamed, perchance, of his foul stroke, missed his mark and tumbled in a heap upon his foeman's sword. Then with a mighty shout (for all thought this was the English leader slain) the two bands closed in, and a deadly fight began.

But I kept my eye on Alexander, whom, despite his prowess, I could see to be wounded hard. Gradually, as his men fell on the enemy and the battle roared off eastward, he himself drooped, and drew out of the fray. I could see him stand a moment, waving his sword, but his body swayed like that of a drunken man, and he leaned at last against a rock to keep from falling.

Then it was, before I could determine whether to warn Ludar of this accident or no, that a horrible deed was done.

For I was not the only one who had kept his eyes on the wounded chief. While he stood there fainting, yet still shouting his men forward, Captain Merriman (an Englishman!), who had lagged behind his host, crept stealthily round the hill to where he stood, and suddenly fronting him, dared the dying man to single combat! From where I stood I could mark the curl of scorn on the young chief's lips, as he drew himself up and strove to lift his drooping arm. Next moment the English captain's weapon flashed between, and as Alexander fell the coward's blade plunged through him twice.

Instantly a mighty cry went up from the enemy, for Captain Merriman, waving his bloody sword above his head, ran through the ranks yelling, "Victory! M'Donnell is slain!" and the M'Donnells, when they heard the shout, reeled under it in a panic and were slain by the score.

As for me, I had stood there like a lump of stone, not able to stir or shout. But at last, by a huge effort, I sprang to the ground, and with a cry of horror rushed to find Ludar.

I found him standing on the cliff-edge, grave and happy, with the maiden beside him, looking down at the great Atlantic waves as they flung their eternal surge up at the castle rock. His sword lay on the ground at her feet. She was fixing a tuft of flowers in his cap, singing softly as she did so. And he, as he gazed now at her, now at the sea below, looked as if cloud could never come more between the sun and his noble face.

THE M'DONNELLS IN RETREAT

Alack! that I myself must bring the cloud.

"Ludar to the front! Something is wrong. Your brother—— "

May I never hear again the cry with which he snatched up his sword and rushed to the gate!

I followed close to his heels, only bidding the maiden get to her tower whither I would send her English squire to guard her. But Ludar, as we reached the gate, turned and ordered me back.

"Stay," said he, hoarsely, and white as a sheet, "stay here!"

Then, as he waited for the portcullis to open, I hastily told him what I had witnessed, and where he would find his brother.

"My brother!" he groaned, "my brother! Humphrey, if I ever return here it shall be with this dog's blood on my sword. Farewell."

And in a moment he had passed the bridge and was rushing headlong on the foe. My heart sank as I saw him go thus; and, whether it vexed him or not, I shouted aloud:

"Who follows Ludar? Follow! follow!"

Instantly a hundred M'Donnells started at the call, and leapt over the bridge. Then with my own hand I let down the gate, and bade the rest, in their chief's name, stand and guard the walls.

Alexander's party were already in retreat, half-a-mile away, for they had no leader; and the English, flushed with victory, and strong in numbers, were pushing them back at the sword's point. Nor did this new company help them much, for Ludar, when he saw who followed him, angrily ordered them to stand, while he went alone to the place I had told him of, in search of his brother.

But brother there was none. I could see my friend from where I stood stalk round the place, now deserted of friend and foe, shouting and calling like a man possessed. Perhaps the murderer had taken off the body as a trophy; or perhaps —perhaps Alexander yet lived, and was safe. But sign of him there was none. For a weary hour Ludar called and searched; then, weary and sick at heart, I saw him call his men, and march off in pursuit of the enemy.

Thus all that day we stood and waited in Dunluce, and

SIR LUDAR

not a man spoke to his fellow. For the joy of our victory was turned into mourning. The Clan had lost one hero; and who should say whether the Banshee's warning was not to be fulfilled on another?

The only man who kept up heart was the Englishman.

"These M'Donnells," said he, "have the lives of cats. You shall see your lordling back yet. He oweth me a bout, and is too honest a man to rob even an enemy. But, Humphrey lad," added he, "I pray you see to these women. There is sore distress in their camp, and I durst not put in my head. Besides, I know not if they have so much as a crust of bread to eat."

The honest fellow was right. When I went in, the maiden was in strange woe, pacing up and down her chamber with pale face and heaving breast.

"Humphrey," said she, and her voice was dry and hoarse, "this is my fault, my fault! He will love me no more! I tempted him to stay when he should have been at his brother's side. I, for my own comfort, made a woman of him, who should have helped make him a hero."

"Nay," said I, "you are wrong, maiden. Had he been there he could not have helped this. It was in nature he should——"

"Humphrey!" she exclaimed, in a voice which staggered me, "talk not like a fool. I have forfeited his love. He did well to leave me without a word! I have been worse to him than his worst enemy. I dare not see him again, for he will loathe me. You must take me hence, or, truly, I will go without leave."

"Maiden," said I, "have patience. This is the act of God, not of man; and Ludar when he returns may need your comfort sorely."

She laughed bitterly.

"I know Ludar," she said; "you know him not. Think you the sight of me will not drive him mad when he comes back, brotherless?"

"At least," said I, "be content to wait here till to-morrow. I should be a traitor to him and myself were I to let you depart unattended; and I may not leave here till he or the old chief comes."

"Will Sorley Boy be here to-morrow?" asked she.

HOME!

"He will; he has said so."

"Then," said she, "I stay on this condition. Tell him naught of me but that I am an O'Neill, a prisoner here, who demand to be restored to my father, Turlogh Luinech O'Neill. Ludar will not return yet. When he does, he shall find me gone. Go back to the wall, Humphrey. No man shall say again I stood between him and his duty."

I returned sadly enough to my post; and all that night we kept weary watch on the walls, straining our ears for Ludar's call or news of the battle.

But neither Ludar nor news of him came.

At daybreak, however, as the sun rose over the headlands, there came a noise of pipes and shouting, and a flutter of pennons on the hill tops. Then we knew Sorley Boy had come.

Before him fled scattered parties of the enemy, yet far enough beyond our range; nor, when they sped away into the hills westward, did the chief allow his men to continue the chase. The M'Donnells gave a wild, mighty cheer, when they saw the heather of the clan flying aloft on their ancient castle; and in the silence that followed I could see the old chief stand a moment to pass his hand across his eyes, as if to make sure he saw aright.

Then, erect, with a proud step, he advanced at the head of his men and crossed the bridge. Our men, waving their hats aloft, answered back the cheers, and, as the gate swung up to let them in, all else seemed forgotten in the triumph of this home-coming of the grand old chief.

But when, a moment after, he halted and looked round him, the shouting suddenly ceased and there fell a dead silence.

"My sons," said he, "where are they?"

No one seemed ready to answer, so that I was fain to step forward.

"Sir," said I, saluting, "Sir Ludar, your son, renders you your castle, which he won by his own arm two nights ago. He is not here to salute himself, as he is tending his brother who was traitorously wounded in the battle yesterday."

The old man said nothing, but blazed on me with his eyes as though he would blast me where I stood. Had I been the murderer myself, I could not have trembled more. At length:

SIR LUDAR

"Alexander, where is he?" he demanded in a hollow voice.

I said I had seen him last near the hill, but that Ludar, not finding him there, had gone to seek him, I know not whither.

Then the old man handed his great sword to his esquire, and flinging off his cloak, walked into the hall of the castle, where none durst follow him. I longed to ask his permission to follow Ludar, besides making the maiden's petition. But his look that day was too terrible to be faced. So we stood to our guard, as we had stood all day long.

When at evening no sign came yet of Ludar, I braced myself up with a great courage, and entered the hall.

The old warrior was sitting at the head of the empty table, immovable, like a man stunned, looking straight before him. But when he saw me, he seemed to recover himself and said:

"What news?"

"None," said I, "but as his servant, I pray you let me go and seek Sir Ludar."

"You shall not go," said he. And there was naught left to say after that.

"I obey you, sire," said I. "There is, by your leave, a maiden in this castle, a prisoner, and daughter to the O'Neill. She craves your permission to return to her father; and hath bidden me ask it of you."

He nodded his head, as if the petition were too trifling to be heeded; and, having got what I was in need of, I withdrew, thankful.

Next day, at daybreak, the maiden, white as a sheet, and with lips close-pressed to hinder their trembling, walked slowly across the bridge to the castle gate. I had got her two horses, one for her and one for the old nurse; and a trusty escort of six M'Donnells and the English soldier to conduct her to Toome.

At parting she held out her hand.

"Humphrey," said she, "tell him of this; and may she who loves you never lose you as I have lost him."

"All is not lost," said I, "we shall meet again, and all will be happy yet." And I lifted her to her horse.

"Now, sirrah," said the old nurse, as I did the like service

NO NEWS

for her, " be happy for a year and a day! You have broken a sweet heart among you, and what matters it to you, so you be rid of us? Mark my word; some heads shall ache for this! What is to become of us, do you suppose, in this O'Neill's house? Little trouble to you to send us from one cruel fate to a worse! Be proud that you, a soldier, forsooth, and calling yourself an honest man, thus betray my poor maiden to her stepdame and your English Captain."

" He is dead by now," said I.

" Not he," said she. " What is to become of us, dost thou hear? Who is to help us now? "

" Dame," said I, " is there no God in heaven that you chide thus? Farewell, we shall meet again, I think, in a happier season."

Then I stepped once more to the maiden and said:

" Lady, that maiden's name we spoke of is young Mistress Walgrave, the printer's daughter in London. Should chance bring you thither, she will be your friend for my sake. If it be possible, pray send us word presently of your welfare by this English fellow."

Thus that maiden left Dunluce; and still the days passed and no tidings of Ludar.

But one evening, as I watched at the gate, a haggard figure crossed the bridge, scarce dragging one foot after another for weariness.

" Ludar! " said I, as I admitted him. " What news? "

" No news! " said he between his teeth, and he flung his sword with what little strength was left him to the earth. Then he himself fell beside it; and, when we carried him within, he was in a fever and raving.

CHAPTER XVII

How a Dog's Head was set on Dublin Gate

THREE months after, as the February snow lay deep on roof and road, Ludar and I walked in a strange procession through the streets of Dublin. In front went three trumpeters on horseback, with the pennon of England drooping from their trumpets. Behind them rode a picked troop of English horse, gaily caparisoned and very brave with ribbons and trappings. Then, alone, went Sir John Perrott, the Lord Deputy, a smirking man who seemed to doubt the whole business. He was mounted too, and at his tail rode three officers of his house, and after them more trumpeters and troopers. Then came the strange part of the procession, for at the heels of these English cavaliers stalked fifty huge redshanks with the M'Donnell's heather in their bonnets, and their hands on their sword hilts.

Yet still stranger was what came next. For, unarmed, with long, slow strides, walked a noble figure of commanding stature, whose eyes flashed now and again on the shouting rabble, and whose white hair, escaped from his cap, waved tempestuously in the winter wind. There walked Sorley Boy, upright, sullen, disdainful; and behind him came Ludar, with tight-pressed lips and thunderous brow, his fingers twitching nervously on his belt, and his feet at every step kicking the snow impatiently from his path. I followed my master as in duty bound, and behind us stalked fifty more silent Scots.

Such was the procession which conducted Sorley Boy M'Donnell at the end of his stormy career to do homage to the English Queen. How it all came to pass I know not. But once possessed of Dunluce, with his favourite son gone

LUDAR'S LOYALTY TO HIS FATHER

from his side, the old man broke down, and sighed for peace. 'Twas said the English paid a good price for his alliance, in territory for himself, and lands and title for his elder sons. Be that as it may. He sheathed his sword, and called in his fighting men all round. He heeded not Ludar's demand for vengeance on his brother's murderers; and, indeed, forbade any man to mention Sir Alexander's name in his hearing. Yet day by day the empty chair stood beside his in the castle hall; and day by day, at the muster call, the young chief's riderless horse fell into its place betwixt that of the father and the second son, Sir Randal.

As for Ludar, when after many weeks the fever left him and he rose from his bed, his father and he met rarely, and spoke less. For the old man (sad to tell), from the day that he came into his own, had changed towards his youngest son, and, blaming him for the ill that had befallen the house, ceased not to reproach and scorn him for his brother's fate.

Never did I see Ludar so noble a man as during those gloomy months. Never once did he waver in his loyalty to his father; never once did he suffer a word to be said to rebuke the old man's harshness; never once did he complain if more than a common soldier's hardships, with a common soldier's fare, fell to his lot; never once would he allow the men, who were ready to die for him, raise a shout when he came among them, or even salute him in his father's presence. He took his punishment as beseemed a hero; and it was the hard work and stern discipline of those few months, I think, which braced him up once again into his former manhood and brought back the glow into his cheeks and the fire into his eyes.

Concerning the maiden he spake not a word; nor would he suffer me to speak of her. Only when the English fellow returned who had escorted her to her father did Ludar order him back, charging him to look to her safety as he valued his own life; which charge the faithful fellow cheerfully accepted, and departed.

Of all his trials, this journey of submission to Dublin was the bitterest to Ludar; and I, as I walked at his heels that day in Dublin city, could see that every step was a pang. The old man chose to bring Ludar and not his elder brothers for this very reason ; and never a duty taxed the lad's courage and loyalty more.

So to me the pleasure of marching once again under the royal flag of my Queen was tempered by the concern I felt for my master.

A vast rabble lined the roads to see the doughty Sorley Boy—the hero of the North, against whose arms England had fought in vain—march thus, to the tune of English trumpets, to her Majesty's Castle. But if any looked to see a hanging head or a meek demeanour they were sore mistaken. For, as the procession moved on and the shouts grew louder, the spirit seemed to come back into the old warrior, and he walked rather as one who marches to war than to peace. Perhaps, had the way been a mile longer, or had the smirking Lord Deputy looked round oftener, this notable treaty would never have come about ; for, by the time Sorley Boy reached the Castle gate, he was glaring round him defiantly, and the hilt of his sword was an inch out of the scabbard.

At the gate the Deputy stood and bade him enter. The old fox gave a suspicious look round, like one that suspects a trap, and then beckoned to Ludar.

"Stay here with the men. Let your squire follow me."

So Ludar stayed with the M'Donnells at the gate, while I followed Sorley Boy, amid shouts and flourish of trumpets, into the Castle. All was prepared to do the old Chief honour. Attendants bowed, guards saluted, and my Lord Deputy's womenkind waved handkerchiefs from the windows. Sir John Perrott himself, all smiles, chatted affably. But never a word spake Sorley Boy.

He stalked on at a pace which made the Deputy trot at his side, and, heedless of lackeys, guards, ladies and all else, flung into the great hall.

I followed as in duty bound ; and beside me no man but Sir John and Sir John's secretary.

Then followed a strange scene.

"Sir Sorley Boy," began the Deputy, motioning his guest to a high chair on the daïs, "this is a happy occasion ; and I would her Majesty had a Deputy more——"

"Enough of this," said the Chieftain impatiently. "I came not from Dunluce to make speeches or bandy words

AN HUMBLE SUBMISSION

with you. I owe *you* naught—or if I do, 'tis a debt you had rather I paid not."

"I," said Sir John, pulling himself up, "as representing her gracious Majesty——"

Here Sorley Boy stalked off to where a miniature picture of her Majesty hung on the wall.

"Is this Elizabeth ?" demanded he.

"That is a presentment, far short in splendour, of her Majesty's admirable presence," said the Deputy.

Sorley Boy took the picture in his hand and mused on it in silence. At length:

"Pray heaven she be no worse favoured in the flesh! Yet, being a woman, I do her homage."

And, like an old gallant, he doffed his hat, and raised the picture to his lips.

Thus it was the M'Donnell made his peace with the Sassenach. He handed the picture to me gloomily to replace; which I did after humbly doing it obeisance on bended knee. Then he summoned me to follow him from the hall.

Sir John witnessed this strange scene in bewilderment and displeasure. He had reckoned on the satisfaction of hearing his old foe renounce his enmity and sue for terms; and it vexed him to find the ceremony thus taken out of his hands and curtly disposed of by the proud old Scot. Yet he knew enough of Sorley Boy to take what he could get, and must needs pocket his pride. Only he made one effort to save his own dignity.

"Sir Sorley, in her Majesty's name I accept your dutiful homage. It remains for you to sign this written document of fealty, in return for which I am bidden hand you her Majesty's gracious permission to you and your heirs to enjoy your territories without let or hindrance."

The old man laughed scornfully.

"My lands are my own. Let who dares come and take them. Keep your papers, John Perrott. Come, squire; out into the fresh air."

And he stalked out, followed angrily by the Deputy.

At the Castle gate we found a tumult afoot. For the hot-headed Scots who waited there face to face with their old enemies had not been able to restrain their impatience; and, goaded alike by the jeers of the rabble and the taunts of the

SIR LUDAR

Englishmen, had answered threat by threat and gibe by blow. Ludar himself, already exasperated, had said not a word to hold them back; and, as the old chief and I came out the gate, the street was full of war, and dead men lay strewn on either hand.

A shout from Sorley Boy restored order among the redshanks in a moment; and, without waiting for further parley with the Deputy, he stalked to the head of his men, and with the single order " To Dunluce ! " turned his back on her Majesty's Castle at Dublin.

But Sir John, fearful, perhaps, of an outbreak in the city, or in pursuit of a still deeper design, mounted his horse and bade his men form again the procession to conduct the Queen's new ally to the city gate. He himself rode forward at a hand's pace beside the old chief, who heeded him no more than if he had been me or Ludar.

We had come to the gate at the bridge, and the English troops were halting to let us go out. The strange ceremony of the day was near ending, and the free country beyond shone in the winter sun, when the Deputy, suddenly bending level with the old man's ear, said :

" Look up. Behold your son's head ! "

Sorley Boy, stood, as did we, and looked up. There on a pole, rocking in the breeze, above the city gate, looked down upon us a head, livid and scarred, with eyes set and tawny locks streaming in the wind. 'Twas a terrible ghastly sight! for, battered as it was, even I could recognize the once noble features of Alexander M'Donnell, as I had seen him last, reeling under the cowardly blow of that foul Englishman.

The old chief uttered a cry scarcely less terrible to hear than the head was to see. Then, suddenly commanding himself, he blazed round on the Deputy and hissed through his teeth :

" My son hath many heads ! "

I never saw a man change colour as did Sir John Perrott when he met that look and heard those bitter words. Men say he went home that afternoon with that look burned into his breast, and those words dinging in his ears. Nor, go where he would, could he escape the one or the other. They possessed him waking and sleeping, in council and in war, at home and abroad. And, when at last he died, some say

A PARTING OF WAYS

he was found crouched in a corner of his room with his fingers over his eyes and his thumbs on his ears.

Nor, after what I saw, did I find it in my heart to pity him.

As for Sorley Boy, he walked out of Dublin like a man in a dream. None of us durst speak to him, or say so much as a word in his hearing. Nor had we the heart to do it. Ludar with his clenched teeth looked straight before him; and the Scots who followed, only half comprehending what had happened, dropped into sullen silence, and gave no sound but the dull beat of their steps on the road.

About an hour beyond Dublin, Sorley Boy halted and turned to Ludar.

"Ludar M'Donnell," said he, sternly, "we part here. I have no son—no son. Farewell."

And he and the soldiers marched on without another word, leaving Ludar and me looking after them, and marvelling if all this were what it seemed or some horrid vision.

Ludar recovered himself sooner than I.

"Come," said he; "why stand you here, Humphrey, when all the world, except Dunluce, is before us? Let us back to the city."

I knew why he wished to go back. He was thinking not of Sorley Boy or Dunluce, but of that cruel trophy above the city gate. And in my heart I pitied the keepers, should they chance to withstand him in his purpose.

'Twas dark when we crossed the bridge and found ourselves once more within the walls. The streets were empty, for the night was bleak, and the troops had long since been called into their quarters. Only a few sentinels stood about the gate, who, to keep away the cold and cheer their stomachs, huddled together in a sheltered nook and discussed the news of the day over ale and sack. Little heeded they the creaking pole with its horrible burden, as it rocked and swung in the winter wind above them!

While we waited the snow began to fall and drove the tipplers further into the shelter of the guard-room, where was a merry fire. Now was our chance. Ludar led me round to where, over some tumbled stones, we were able to scramble on to the wall, and thence back towards the gate. So thick fell the snow that, as we crawled along, we were as white as

SIR LUDAR

the ramparts we passed over, and not a soul could have heard or seen us had any been there. It was easy to get from the wall on to the gate, and all might have gone well had not a wolf-hound, imprisoned in the tower, or left there to do the watching which the sentinel neglected, sprung out to meet us as we stepped on to the battlement with a mighty howl.

So sudden was his leap that he had Ludar by the throat before we knew what had happened; and ere I had drawn my sword and saved my master from so savage a death there was a noise, with shouting and lights, in the road below.

"Quick!" cried Ludar, springing to his feet and running to the pole.

In a minute he had scaled it and robbed it of its fearful burden. Already I could tell by the shouts below that we were pursued, but Ludar, as he stood there, panting, with his precious burden held to his breast, heeded nothing.

"Come," said I; "we are followed."

He laughed bitterly.

"Humphrey," said he, "as you love me, cut me this hound's head off and put it there, where my brother's head stood. Quick!"

I did as he bade me, though it cost us precious moments. Nor would he budge till the grim exchange was made. Then suddenly he descended on the far side of the gateway. It was well he did so, for there being no regular way on to the wall that side, our pursuers had mounted by the other, leaving only a couple of stupid sentinels to watch below. Happily for us, the snow lay thick and soft; for more than once we fell as we scaled the ramparts, and might have broken our limbs. Our pursuers behind, having come to the gate top and finding no one there, liked not to follow us the way we had gone, and contented themselves with discharging their pieces into the darkness our way. But we were out of their reach. For, once on the wall, 'twas easy going, and instead of descending we made a quarter of the way round The city, till, somewhere near the north-eastern tower, we slid down by a drift of snow into the deserted street.

Then, Ludar leading, we returned some distance along by the foot of the very wall on whose top we had lately crept, to where stood a church, with a graveyard verging on the wall. Here my comrade halted, and reverently set down his burden,

A SOLEMN BURIAL

and between us, as we knelt in the snow, we digged a grave to shelter it. Our swords served us for spades, nor, alack! did it need many inches of kind mother earth to hold all that remained of Alexander M'Donnell. With a prayer each, Ludar in his way, I in mine, we buried that dear relic. Then, beside the place, Ludar drove his sword deep into the earth, till the hilt stood up like an iron cross to mark the spot. We stood in silence while the pure snow fell and laid its white shroud upon the grave. Then, when all was done, he took my arm, and we walked sadly away.

As we passed down a street not far off, the glow of a tavern fire and the sound of voices within brought us to a halt. For we were cold and famished and weary, and the good cheer of the place tempted us. Within was mine host, a merry Irishman, who loved every man that drank his ale. Round his great fire sat half-a-dozen guests, two wayfarers like ourselves, a soldier, a merchant, a sailor, and one who seemed by his look a private gentleman.

They gave us little enough heed as we entered. Even when mine host, catching sight of us, came to take our orders, they went on with their carouse and pulled their benches closer round the fire, with scarcely a blink our way.

As we sat apart, thawing our frozen limbs in the warmth of the room, and reviving our inner man with food and drink —we had staked nearly all we had on this meal—we could not forbear hearing some of the talk that went on at the fireside.

"By my valour," said the soldier, "I was there and saw it with my own eyes. The old dotard turned the colour of my teeth when he looked up and spied it."

"Aye, aye," said the merchant, "I know it was he. I saw the lad in Cantire once, and a fine lad he was."

"They tell me," said mine host, "a woman was at the bottom of it, as usual. This Captain Merriman (who oweth me a pretty score for entertainment in this house) and this lad had a quarrel over a wench, and 'twas for that he pursued him as he did. Why, sirs, for six weeks the lad lay hidden in a cave, and for a week more lay quick in a grave, before Sir Captain, who had never ceased to hunt him, caught him, and sent up his head to the Deputy here. And now, they say, the wench, who is particular, not fancying a headless trunk, hath struck her colours and said yea to the next best man. Poor lass! who's to blame her?"

"Not I," said the soldier, "albeit you are all wrong, mine host, about this quarrel, for I heard of it from Tom Price, the Captain's man. It was this headless chief's brother the lass doated on. But it's like enough she thinks the head was her sweetheart's."

"There was a son of old Sorley's in the pageant to-day; a plaguey ill-favoured hound, who walked with his father," said the landlord, "with a face sour enough to curdle all the milk in Dublin."

"That was Sir Ludar," said one of the strangers. "I had it from one of the redshanks."

"Ludar?" said the soldier; "the very man. 'Tis his wench the Captain hath run away with. She thinketh him gibbeted, and——"

Here the door was flung open suddenly, and in rushed another soldier.

"Have you heard the news?" he cried.

"News?" cried the others, turning round to look at him.

"Why, yes. Her Majesty hath been robbed of a jewel. The traitor's head that grinned on the gate hath been stolen, I tell you, and there sticketh a dog's head in its place. 'Tis true."

"Who has done it?"

"That's the point," said the messenger, who was plainly proud to have so much news to tell. "That's the point. For we were all on guard, I tell you. Not a soul passed us. 'Tis said 'twas some spirit." Here he doffed his cap. "We stood below, I tell you, when there came a blast of wind in our faces with a smell of brimstone in it. I smelt it. Then something curled up past us, like a white shroud, and shrieked as it went up. And, before we could look in one another's faces, a great howl of devilish laughter broke over our heads, and drops of blood! Yes. I felt them. Here's one on my sleeve—it burns like fire, I tell you. That was all. We fetched lights and went aloft (who is to be afraid of a spirit or two?), but we saw naught. Not a footstep in the snow, or a sign of man or fiend either—except only a headless dog. Aye, you may stare, but I saw it—it smoked brimstone,

A WONDERFUL STORY

neighbours, and the snow all around it was redhot! And what was most horrible of all, when we cast up our lights, I tell you, the Scot's head had changed to the head of a dog, which grinned and leered at us, with eyes like coals and tongue all ablaze, till we could scarce stay where we were. That's all. And ere I go back to that gate, neighbours, may I turn Pope and Spaniard! Give me a drink, host, for, by my soul, I know not which end of me is uppermost."

By this time the company had left their benches and were scattered about the room, gossiping over this last great news and questioning the fellow more. Some came to the table where Ludar and I sat; and the soldier, looking hard at me, exclaimed:

"Where saw I that gallows face before? Who be you, sirrah?"

"A printer," said I.

"You lie," said he, "for I saw you to-day accompany the old Scotsman to the Castle. And, by my body, that slouching dog there should be—— Hillo! comrades," cried he, amazed at his discovery, "more ghosts! May I perish if there have not been sitting in this very room while we talked of him this same sour-faced, love-sick clown, Master Ludar, and one of his merry men. Marry come up! The very man, skulking here, while his light-of-love is on her honeymoon, and the old dotard, his father, with his pockets full of English gold——"

He said no more. Ludar had no sword, but the blow he gave him silenced his foul tongue for a week. Instantly the room was turned into a shambles. 'Twas no time to mince words or blows, and we did neither. Nor were we two left alone to withstand all the rest; for the gentleman of the party (whom I have mentioned) sided with us, as did also the sea captain, who owed mine host a long score, and saw a good way to cry quits without shortening his purse. Among us, we made so good an account of ourselves, that when at length we took our leave, not a man bade us stay.

"Come," said the captain, "my ship lies at the bridge. To-morrow we shall see England."

CHAPTER XVIII

How I found myself again in London

THREE days later, as our ship laboured up the gulf of the Solway, Ludar came to me, as I stood on the poop, and said :
"Humphrey, I have news."
"Good or bad ? " I asked.
"Neither," said he, " for it means we must part."
"I call that bad news. How is it, Ludar ? "
"Our fellow-voyager," said he, and I could see he spoke nervously like one who doubts his listener, " is in the service of my Queen, Mary of Scotland. There ! fly not out, Humphrey ; I never said she was your Queen."
"Heaven forbid ! " said I. "And as for this stranger, I mistrusted him all along. How calls he himself ? "
"He is one Captain Fortescue, and hath a commission to engage loyal men to the Queen's service. And, indeed, she needs it ; for she lies in prison, watched and solitary, with scarce a face about her that is not an enemy's. What would you do, Humphrey, were your Queen in such a plight ? "
"Were my Queen a traitor—— " I began, and stopped.
"I cannot help myself," said he. " I owe her my life. Only one woman else could claim it, and her I have lost."
"But," said I, " are you sure of this man ? May this not be some trap to your ruin ? What if he be a spy and no more ? "
Ludar laughed.
"If so," said he, " he would have better sport on foot than to practise on an outlaw like me. No, Humphrey, he is a loyal man, as, pray heaven, so am I. And he commands me in a name I cannot resist."

THE TWO QUEENS

"Then," said I, sadly, "we part. I would have served you, Ludar, on any other service. But I, too, have a Queen, who owns me."

"So be it," said he. "I expected it; and naught else could part me from you. Be sure we shall meet again, Humphrey, when all is over."

"Who knows but it may be on the field of battle?" said I, sadly. "Yet, tell me where I shall hear of you; and take note where you shall hear of me. For I will back to London——"

"To your love," said he, with a sigh. "So be it. You shall hear of me there, Humphrey."

"And, before we part," said I, taking his great hand, "swear me an oath, Ludar, that you will not forget me."

He flung my hand away impatiently.

"Do you take me for a knave, brother? I swear to you, that next to my Queen, my father, and the memory of her who once loved me, you have the chiefest right to say, 'Ludar, help me,' and if I forget you, 'twill be that I have forgotten I am a man."

That comforted me vastly, and I too made my vow.

"Next to my Queen," said I, "and no one besides, you are still my master; and my life goes for nothing, so it shall serve you and her you love, who, I am sure, is true to you still, and waits for you somewhere, whatever men say."

He gripped my hand hard at that; and, sorrowful as it was, we loved one another the more at that parting than ever before.

Next day we landed. Captain Fortescue, suspecting me to be no friend to him or his cause, was in haste to reach Carlisle, and shortened our leave-taking in consequence. We had but time to renew our vows, when the boat which was to carry my friend and his new master from me came alongside and severed us. I watched him till the envious hills came in between; and, as I saw him last, standing and waving his hat, methought a great piece had gone out of my life, and that there was left of me but half the man I once was.

. . . .

And now must my story hasten on by strides, such as never the laggard months took after I had said farewell to Ludar. For 'tis of him, not of Humphrey Dexter, that I

SIR LUDAR

am the chronicler, and till my history meet him once more my reader is without his hero.

Yet there are one or two scenes awanting to fill up the gap; which, even though they concern chiefly me, I must relate in their proper place.

Two months had gone by, and in the budding woods the spring birds were wakening the earth out of her winter sleep, when I stood once more, footsore and friendless, in the streets of London. How I had got so far it matters not, nor how like a vagabond I begged and worked my way; staying now here for a few days ploughing, now there to break in a colt; held in bondage in one town because I lacked the money to pay my score, and chivied from the next for a rogue, which I was not. Not a few men I fought by the way—for I clung to my sword through all—and not a few constables I laid by the heels (Heaven forgive me!) in mine own defence. Be all that as it may, I stood again in London town, whence, it seemed, I had been absent not nine months but nine years. With tattered hose and doublet, with coat that scarce held together at my back, with no cap to my head, and scarce one shoe to divide betwixt my two feet, 'twas little wonder if no man but the watch heeded me, still less suspected me to be the once famous captain of the clubs without Temple Bar.

My way into the city led by Finsbury Fields, where were many 'prentices at their sports, and citizens taking their sweethearts to sniff the sweet spring air. No one wanted me there. The lads bade me make way for my betters, and the maids held back their skirts as they swept by. So I left them and wandered citywards.

I marvelled to see all so little changed, forgetting how short a time I had been away. There stood Stationers' Hall, as lordly as ever, and Timothy Ryder, the beadle, taking his fees at the compter. There, too, was the great Cathedral with its crowd of loungers, and Fleet Street full of swaggering 'prentices, and the River sparkling in the sun.

Then, as I came near Temple Bar, my heart fell a thumping. Not that I forgot the place was deserted and the old home broken; but because it reminded me of what once was before all these troubles began. I crawled at a snail's pace, wishing to put off the pang as long as possible. In fancy I was at my

LONDON ONCE MORE

case, as I had been a year ago, clicking the letters into my stick, in time to the chirping of my little mistress who sang at her work within. At my side I could hear the dull groaning of the heavy press, and not far off the whining of Peter Stoupe's everlasting psalm-tune. All was as if——

Was I dreaming? or was this the self-same psalm-tune come again to life, and, to accompany it, the dull grinding of the self-same press? Strange, that the bar was off the door, and, as I came to it, a fellow with a ream on his back laboured out. I had expected naught but the desolation and silence which I last remembered in the place, and it staggered me to find all going on as before. No doubt here was some upstart printer, standing in my late master's shoes and working at his forfeited press!

In no pleasant mood I walked, ragged and travel-stained as I was, into the shop. Sure enough, it was Peter Stoupe, my late fellow-apprentice, who was whining, and beside him a new journeyman lugged at the press.

Peter knew me not at first, so changed and unkempt was I with my long journeyings.

"Come," said he, surlily, "bustle hence, thou varlet. We keep nought here but sticks for rogues like thee to taste. Get you gone!"

And he advanced on me with the stick.

Just to remind him of old days, I whipped it from his hand and gave him a crack on the skull, which brought him to himself at once.

"Why," said he, dropping his jaw, and gaping at me as if I had been a ghost, "if it be not Humphrey Dexter, as I'm a sinner!"

"As certain as thou art a sinner," said I, "it is none other. What of that, Peter Stoupe?"

"Why," said he, "I warn thee to pack hence. For Master Walgrave hath had enough of thee, I warrant; and there is none else here wanteth thee."

"Then Master Walgrave is out of gaol?" I asked.

"No thanks to thee; he hath made his peace with the Company, and is restored to his own."

"And my mistress, and Jeannette, and the lad?" I asked.

"They are naught to thee," answered he, curtly.

"Are they here?" I asked again.

SIR LUDAR

"I tell thee that is naught to thee, Humphrey Dexter. I marvel, after what is past, you dare name them."

"By heavens, you shall have something to marvel at," said I, laying hold of him by the collar, and shaking him till his bones rattled. "Answer me, are they here?"

"To be sure, to be sure," gasped he. "I pray you unhand me, Humphrey; my old friend, you are too rough."

I flung him off, to the mirth of the new journeyman (who, it was plain, loved him no more than I), and walked through the shop to the parlour behind.

There in a nook beside the window, which was open to let in the sweet scent of the spring and the merry chirping of the birds, sat my sweet young mistress, Jeannette, reading out of a book to the little sister who sat on her knee; and ever and anon looking out at the swift, shining river, as it washed past the garden wall.

I remember the very words she was reading as I entered unheeded.

"'So it fell, that knight returned, and none knew him; 'no, not even the dog in the outer court. But when he 'spake, there was a certain little maid knew his voice, whom, 'as a child, he was wont to make sport with. But now, 'because she was grown from child to woman, and her mirth 'was turned to love, did she say never a word when he 'appeared, but ran away and hid herself.'"

"And do tall knights and ladies play at hide-and-go-seek, like boys and girls?" asked the little sister.

Jeannette laughed at the question, and as she did so, she looked up and saw me standing there.

She, at least, knew me!

For a moment the colour left her cheeks, in fear and doubt. Next, it rushed back in a crimson flood; then she uttered my name, and hid her face in the bosom of the little child.

I was but a plain 'prentice with no more than my share of brains. Yet, I had need to be slow-witted indeed, not to read a long, wonderful story in what I saw then.

"Aye," said I, stepping forward, and answering the little's one's question, "and sometimes they find one another too."

And, as in the old days, I kissed them both, and was very happy.

BACK AT MASTER WALGRAVE'S

When, presently, Master Walgrave returned and saw me there, he seemed not too well pleased. Yet, I suspected he was not altogether discontented to see me back, for he counted me a proper workman and handy at my craft. And when I set to and told them a plain tale of what had befallen me, and how ill I had been slandered by my fellow 'prentice, and how ready I was to serve them now, he grew less sullen, and bade me abide where I was till he considered the matter.

From my mistress in turn I learned something of their doings since I saw them last in the street of Kingston. The minister, she said, had pinched himself to shelter them for many a week, while they worked for him among the harvesters and in the dairy, in return. But at last when Autumn came, and they could do no more to serve him, they departed, and petitioned the Company to admit them back to the printing house; which, after much ado, was granted, and so they continued with much labour to subsist. But Peter, I was told afterwards, made himself master of everything, and, in return for his services, exacted all the profit, little as it was, they made by the printing. At last, after lying six months in gaol, Master Walgrave grew weary, and permitted his wife to sue for him to the Bishop; which she did, and so prettily, that his Grace allowed the prisoner to go free, on his submission. Since then, all had fared well. Peter Stoupe, who could hardly be parted with, was put back to his place and a new journeyman obtained. Business came back, winter went, springtime returned, and roses blossomed once more in sweet Jeannette's cheeks; and all went merrily.

As for Mistress Jeannette's cheeks, it seemed to me, as I sat and watched her that evening, that the roses had not done blossoming yet. But I said little to her, for I guessed she would not talk. Only, when bed-time came, and I went, as of old, to carry her up the steep stairs, she looked up brightly and said:

"I can walk now, Humphrey; *violà*. That was one good thing your going did for me."

"I would it had been any other good," said I, "for it was pleasant to help you. But, see, you still want some help."

"Well, sometimes I walk better. But to-night—no, I am not a baby, truly," said she, laughing as I offered to take her up. "Give me your arm, Humphrey; that is enough."

SIR LUDAR

So I helped her up the stairs, and at the top she thanked me, and said she was glad I was come back, for her father's sake—meaning Master Walgrave, her stepfather.

I asked was she glad for no reason else? and she said, perhaps for my sake 'twas good to be at work once more.

"Anyone's sake besides?"

"*Peut-être*," said she in her French jargon, vanishing into her chamber. I was a better scholar than I once was, and could translate the words in a way that made my heart beat.

So I left her and came down to supper.

There I found Peter Stoupe, very black in the face, awaiting me. He tried to look civil as I came to the table, but 'twas plain he had little stomach for his meal.

"My master telleth me," said he, "he is content to give thee another trial, Humphrey. Pray heaven he may never hear how much it is he forgiveth thee. As for me, this folly of his is like to cost him my service, as I told him."

"When are you going?" I asked.

"That concerns myself," said Peter. "But since we be alone, Humphrey Dexter, let me say to you one thing. Whether I go or stay, know that I desire you hold no converse with my mistress' daughter, and that for a very sufficient reason. She is promised to me."

I laughed at this.

"Since when?" I asked.

"That too concerneth me," said Peter, who liked not my mirth. "I shall wed her anon; and till then I would have her kept clear of your company."

"Pass the mug, Peter Stoupe, and cease your funning. The day sweet Jeannette weds with you, I will saddle the horse shall carry you to church. Till then, if I catch so much as her name on your foul lips, I will drop you, feet uppermost, in the mud of Fleet Ditch. So make a bargain of it."

He turned green at that, for he guessed I meant what I said.

"What?" began he; "you who ruined my master, and robbed——"

Here I sprang to my feet, and he stopped short.

"Robbed whom?" demanded I.

"Enough," said he, motioning me to sit down. "I

PETER STOUPE IN A NEW LIGHT

resolved, when you came, to hold no parley with you, and I repent me I have done so. Henceforth, Humphrey Dexter, we are strangers."

"Be what you will," said I, "only keep a civil tongue in your head."

And I went up to bed.

Now this was yet another trial to Peter, who had been used to lie alone while I was absent, and now loathed that I should rob him thus of half his kicking room. But he durst say naught. Only he lay at the far edge, and, instead of saying his prayers, cursed me between his teeth.

It was in my heart to pity Peter Stoupe that night. For it was plain I had come in an evil hour for him. Master Walgrave had been hoodwinked by his smooth manners and lying tongue, and was fain to believe he owed him more for the duty he had done while his master was in gaol than in truth he did. Nor durst my mistress thwart him over much for the same cause. As for Jeannette — if she humoured him and endured his civilities, 'twas because she was ever kind. So all was going well with Peter when I chanced home, who knew him for his worth and promised to spoil his sport. Little wonder, then, if he hated to see me, and kept at the far edge of the bed.

However, I had more to think of than him; and, finding him deaf, even when I tried to be civil, I busied myself with other thoughts, and fell asleep, to dream a jumbled dream of Ludar, and Jeannette, and the captain of the *Miséricorde.*

I remember I dreamed that Ludar and Jeannette were keeping the watch on deck while I slept below; and that my hour being come, the captain had come down to fetch me, and was standing over me; when I awoke suddenly, and, in the dim moonlight, saw a real figure at the bedside. It was Peter Stoupe, and, though I could scarce see his face, I knew he was glowering on me, while in his hand he slowly lifted a knife above my heart. I was motionless, not with terror—for his hand trembled so it could scarce have dealt a deadly blow—but with horror to find such a man at such a deed. So, though my eyes were open, he saw not that I was awake, and with a gasp brought down his hand.

Mine was out in time to catch him by the wrist.

"Peter Stoupe!" I cried; "are you gone mad?"

SIR LUDAR

'Twas pitiful to see him then drop on his knees, his face as white as the sheets, and with quaking lips beg for mercy.

"Oh, Humphrey!" he gasped; "forgive—I knew not what I was—— Yes, I was mad—forgive this once——"

"Forgive!" said I, "you ask the wrong person. You are on your knees; ask Him who is above to forgive you! 'Tis Him you have wronged, more than me. And when you have done, come back to bed, for I am weary."

I know not if he prayed, or what he did. But presently, when he came back to bed, he lay very still and cold, and when we rose in the morning never a word spake either of us of what had passed that night.

But, as I expected, we were none the better friends for all that. For though he durst never lift his voice in my hearing again, he scowled at me under his brows, and, as I suppose, wished he had done what he tried to do that night. I found it best to let him be, even when he made up to Jeannette, which happened but seldom, and then little to his comfort. But when, after a month or more, his articles being ended, he took his hat and left the shop for good, I was not surprised, nor were my master or mistress over-much cast down.

As for me, I had a shrewd guess Peter Stoupe had not yet done with me.

All went happily, then, in the house without Temple Bar. Only my little mistress held me off more than she had been wont, and was graver with me. Yet it was happiness to see she counted somewhat on my company, and scorned not to ask my arm whenever she needed its help.

Often and often she made me tell her of my journeyings, and of Ludar and the maiden. And her bright eyes would glisten as she heard how they were parted and what they had suffered for one another. And she longed to see both, and was ever wondering where they were and how they fared. But the spring wore into summer, and the summer grew towards autumn, before a word of news came.

Then one Sunday, Will Peake, my old adversary, walked into the shop with a monstrous letter in his hand, tied round with blue silk and sealed black at either end.

I had seen Will often since I came back to London, but had always forgotten to tell him, that when I was put to it

A LETTER

to advise Ludar where he might hear of me, I had told him to send to my brother 'prentice on London Bridge, who, if any, might be counted on to know where I was to be found.

So now, when a letter was come, Will was vastly wroth that he should be mixed up in the matter, and needed much satisfying that 'twas a sign of friendship and nothing else that made me give his name, he being—as I told him—the only trusty man of my acquaintance in London.

"I like it not, Humphrey Dexter," said he, tossing down the letter. "The air is full of treason. Only to-day there is talk in the city of some new conspiracy in the North, and 'tis not safe to get a missive from so much as your lady-love. There, take it. I am rid of it; and, hark you, let no man know I had it in my fingers. Farewell."

The letter was in a great and notable hand, which, I was sure, did not belong to Ludar. Yet it was addressed:

"*To the worthy 'prentice Humphrey Dexter, by the hand of one Will Peake, a mercer's man on London Bridge, give these——*"

With beating heart, I took the letter to where Jeannette sat in the garden, and bade her break the seal.

CHAPTER XIX

How I was concerned in Treason and Love

THE first words of the letter left me in no doubt as to who the writer might be.

"To a certain Hollander, once my servant, and honoured still to live in my memory. Know, my son of Neptune, fledgeling of the Nymphs, and half-brother to the Tritons, that he whom thou knewest once in Parnassus' grove (whither he himself led thy halting feet) respireth still in sighs for beauty and exhalations of sweet verse. Know, too, that he hath of late composed a notable and admirable epic in praise of the Sun, which, if it please Heaven to bring him, ere the year fall, to London, thou mayest have the high honour of setting in print, thereby assisting at the birth of an immortal.

"Know further, that after many buffetings from the jade Fortune, and tossing, such as ships ne'er endured on thy brawling element, my Hollander, I am here in Chester, beloved of the Muse, yet ill-beholden to the men of the place, who, as the Mantuans their Maro, clapped me in ward because forsooth I stirred the rabble with my moving measures. The moon hath not kissed the golden locks of Galatea four times since I was let out. Now is no zephyr freer than I—or emptier. Yet hath heaven need of her needy sons, and the meanest of Olympus, denizens hath his part to play amidst the earthlings. Know, then, that on the second day after I had ceased to eat my bread at her Majesty's cost, I met, in eager haste, a certain Irish Achilles who knoweth more of war than verse, and whose arm is more terrible with the sword than is my hand with the pen. This Sir Ludar—such is gratitude and reverence !—*O tempora ! O mores !*—would have given me the go-by, had I not stood boldly in his way, that he

A GRIM POSTSCRIPT

might at least see how great an honour he avoided. When he saw me, to be brief, my Hollander, he honoured himself by seeing in me the god Mercury, who beareth messages to the dim regions of the earth. He bade me tell thee, by a means the receipt hereof will apprise thee, that the cause goeth perilously. What cause, I know not; but, be it what it may, it taketh him hence, on what, perchance, may be his last journey. He biddeth you remember your oath, and would have me advertise you that one Merriman hath been heard of in these parts, travelling for London, with a party, of whom one is the lady of the castle on the river, with her ward. He is a dark mysterious man, this Irish wolf-hound of thine, my Hollander, and, did I not suspect him to have a secret tooth for the olives of Parnassus, I had not thus condescended to act as go between you. When I enquired of him concerning her, that incomparable swan, that bright and shining star, that white snowflake, that Cupid's elder sister, my lady-love —to serve whom I counted as nought the perils of a certain fell voyage you wot of—when I enquired him of her, he asked me back, Did I desire to flounder in the castle moat? By which talk it appeared to me much care hath weakened his mind, and I misdoubt me his present journey bodes no good. My Hollander, I beg not any man's bread, yet am I hard put to it to show the world that heaven doth not desert her favourites. If the pity of a 'prentice can reach from you to Chester, lend it me, I pray you, as I sit here gazing into the empyrean for my next meal. If I may, I shall shorten the space betwixt us. Meanwhile, count for thyself a lodging in at least one poetic breast, which is that of thy patron and friend, THOMAS GRAVES.

"*Post Scriptum:* I have overtook my messenger—a poor country carrier—to tell thee strange news. This Ludar hath returned suddenly from his journey in the custody of a troop. I saw him marched through the streets but just now, amid cries of ' Treason ! ' ' Away with him ! ' ' Hang him ! ' sad to hear. The talk runneth that he is party in some great conspiracy against her glorious Majesty, whose foes may Heaven confound! If it be true, then is our Achilles wounded in the heel, and is like enough to journey from here to Tyburn free of charges. Farewell, from thy well-wisher."

This letter cast me into terrible woe; for it was plain

SIR LUDAR

by it that Ludar was in mortal peril, and without a friend to help him. I could do naught, for I knew not where he was taken, or if I did, what could I, outside a stone wall, do for him within? Besides, the message about the maiden put a service on me I was bound to fulfil. Yet what could I do?

Jeannette saw my trouble and shared it; and, being a shrewd lass, advised me to go to Will Peake and hear what was this news of a new-discovered treason, and who were in it?

So I went and found the Bridge (Sunday as it was) in a flutter. Will Peake I could not see, but from another gossip I heard that news was come of a terrible plot to murder her sacred Majesty and place on her throne, with the help of Spanish rogues, the upstart Mary of Scotland. Many wild stories were afloat concerning the business. One, that not a few of her Majesty's trusted advisers were mixed in it; others, that the Scotchwoman herself was prime mover; another, that it was the work of the Spanish king, whose armies were on the coast waiting the signal to land.

But as we stood, there came a mighty shouting from the Tower Hill, and, running thither, we saw a man in a cart being conducted by twenty horsemen to the prison. He was clad as a papist priest—yet, when I looked at him, I seemed to know his face.

"Who goes there?" I asked of one who stood near.

"The head and front of it all," said he; "a renegade priest, Ballard by name."

"Who hath travelled," said another, "on this accursed business in the garb of a soldier by the name of Captain Fortescue."

"Fortescue!" cried I. "Why, to be sure, it was he! I knew I had seen him."

"You saw him, where? what know you of this?" asked several persons round, suspiciously. "If you be a friend of his, get you up on the cart beside him."

I had a mind to make a rush that way, if haply I might get a single word with the traitor as to where Ludar was. But I might as soon have tried to get within hail of the Scotch Queen herself, so closely was he fenced in.

"He is no friend," growled I, "but a vile enemy and

A DEVILISH CONSPIRACY

traitor, whom I would to God I had run through the body when I had the chance at Carlisle, months since."

Then to avoid more questions and get away from the rabble, I hastened back and told all to Jeannette.

She was very grave. "What think you now?" she asked.

"I can think nothing," said I, "save that, whatever has befallen Ludar, he could not knowingly be guilty of plotting against the life of a woman, even if she be the Queen herself. Jeannette," said I, "I could no more believe that than I would believe you to be unkind or untrue."

She smiled at that and said she, too, could not think so ill of this Ludar of mine.

As the days passed, news came in thick and fast. The plot, we heard, was a devilish one to murder the Queen and her ministers, and give England up to the heretic Spaniard. Men stood aghast as they heard of it. Presently came word that the worst of the traitors were in hiding in London, being mostly young gentlemen of the Court, who had fed at the table of the very Lady they plotted to slay. Try all I would, I could hear nothing of Ludar. Nor durst I name him to my comrades, for fear I should bring him mischief thereby.

One day in the middle of August it was, a man came into our shop in hot haste to tell Master Walgrave that the company had been taken, hidden in a barn in Harrow. Never shall I forget the joy of the City as the news spread like wildfire through the wards. No work did we 'prentices do that day. We marched shouting through the streets, calling for vengeance on the Queen's enemies, and waiting till they should be brought in, on their way to the Tower.

As for me, my joy was mingled with strange trouble; for, if Ludar should be among them—

"The leader of them is one Babington," said Will Peake, "and besides him are half-a-dozen dogs as foul—English, all of them."

"Save one," said another, "who I hear is Irish."

"Irish!" cried I, as white as paper. "What is his name?"

"Not Dexter," said the fellow, looking at me in amaze. "Why, man, what ails you?"

"Tell me his name, as you love me," said I.

"How should I know the name of every cowardly hound that walks the streets? Go and ask them that can tell you."

SIR LUDAR

I walked away miserable, and waited at the Aldersgate to see the prisoners come by.

When at last the cry was raised, I scarcely durst look up, for fear that among them should tower the form of Ludar. But when I lifted my eyes and saw only six hang-dog men, who held their hands to their ears to keep out the yelling of the mob, and shrunk closer to their guards to save them from a worse fate than the hangman's, the beating of my heart eased. For *he* was not amongst them. So joyful was I that I could even lend my voice for a while to the general cry, and, when night fell, bring my torch to the flaming barrels that blazed on Finsbury Fields.

Yet I came home that night ill at ease. Fresh news had arrived already that other men had been taken in the country—amongst them, certain who had been in attendance on the Scotch Queen. Yet, ask all I would, never once could I hear of Ludar by name, or of any man resembling him.

A month later we 'prentices had another holiday, this time to witness the end of that terrible business on Tyburn Hill. 'Twas a horrible sight—I would I could forget it—to see those traitors die, foul as their crime had been. Yet what sickened me the most was to think that Ludar perchance might presently follow to the same fate, if indeed he had not already shared it.

But no news came. The weeks slipped by. Men ceased to talk of Babington, and spoke rather of the coming trial of the Scotch Queen for her life. And presently a time came when they even ceased to speak of that. And all the while, never a whisper came to me of Ludar.

Now you are not to think that all this time I had forgot the message contained in the poet's letter concerning Captain Merriman and the maiden. Far from it. I haunted Whitehall after work hours in the hope of seeing or hearing something of them. But all in vain. It would have been easier to hear of Ludar, I think, than to get any news of an Irish maiden and her step-dame at Court, or of a swaggering captain.

"What is that to thee?" said most whom I asked; and others pricked me out of their company with their swords.

But late in the year, chance put in my way what all my pains had failed to procure.

I remember, it was that same day that the news came

BONFIRES IN MOORFIELDS

to town that Mary Queen of Scots was condemned to die. London went mad with joy at the news. For our pity of the woman was swallowed up in joy that the evil destiny of our country was mastered, and that our gracious Queen was to be freed at one stroke from all her enemies. Be that as it may, we burned bonfires that night in Moorfields, and I had my mistress' leave to take Jeannette with me to see the sport. For by this time the sweet maid's lameness was nearly cured, and, like a prisoner newly uncaged, she loved to spread her wings a bit and go abroad.

Had the arm she leaned on been that of Peter Stoupe instead of mine, I wondered if she would have mended as fast as she did? I was a vain coxcomb those days, and thought, no. Yet, for anything she said to me or I to her, we were still 'prentice and young mistress. Only, the duty I owed her was my great joy; and the service she had a right to claim of me, she sometimes prettily asked as a gift.

'Twas a wild, weird scene—those hundreds of citizens lit up by the fierce glare of the bonfires, whose roar mingled with the shoutings, and whose heat was less than the loyal fires which blazed in our bosoms. I could feel Jeannette's hand tighten on my arm as the rabble surged closer round; and presently, seeing her tired and frightened, I made a way for her through the crowd.

As we reached the skirts there reeled against us a drunken man who, had I not caught him in my arm, would have fallen against my young mistress and done her some hurt. He was not so drunk but that, when I set him on his feet and gave him a kick or two, he was able to stand upright and talk. And at the first word he uttered, I recognised the voice of my old acquaintance, Tom Price, the Captain's man; whom I had seen last with his master the day Alexander M'Donnell fell outside Dunluce.

So dark was it away from the fire, that but for his voice I might not have known him. Certainly he, as he then was, could hardly know me.

"Patience," whispered I to Jeannette, "here is a man can give us some news. He shall not hurt you; only I must speak with him. Hold close to me."

And to guard her better, I put an arm around her, while I parleyed with the sergeant.

SIR LUDAR

"Come, comrade," said I, concealing my voice as best I could, " 'tis time you were in quarters. The Captain will be calling for thee."

"Captain me no captains. Stand thee still, steady—when came he—ugh ? "

"He'll be here to look for thee I warrant, an thou go not home."

"Got back ? what for ? when came—— Harkee, comrade—keep it snug—he'll not find her—he, he ! he'll not find her."

"Not he," said I, making a guess. "We know where she is, though. Eh, Tom ? "

"He, he ! do we ! So doth that other varlet. But, keep it mum, comrade—the wall is none too high, but my Captain may climb it."

"Aye," said I, "but he must needs find it first. Eh ? That will trouble him, eh ? honest Tom."

"Honest ! thou art right, comrade. Ere he learn where she be I'll—I'll—harkee, friend I like not that other varlet. What needs she with two of us? Am not I man enough? eh ? thou and I, without him ? By my soul, comrade, I will slay him."

"So, he is there, too, where she is ? "

"Ho, ho ! Jack Gedge in a convent ? ho, ho ! Ne'er such luck for him, or thee, or me ; eh ? ho, ho ! Jack in a convent ? No, but, comrade," here he took my arm and whispered, "he ne'er quitteth the city, and no man can get at her but he knows it. 'Tis a very bulldog. Hang him, comrade, hang him, I say."

"Aye, I am with you there," said I. "What right hath he to stand betwixt her and honest folk like you and me ? "

"Harkee, friend. This varlet, they say, was appointed to the service by one—hang the name of him—an Irish knave that made eyes at her. You know him—— "

"Aye, aye," said I. "Lubin, or Ludar, or some such name."

"Thou hast it. Ludar. Well, as I told thee, this varlet is appointed to the charge by this Lu—— Say it again, comrade."

"Ludar," said I.

"Aye, Ludar. Well, this varlet, as I—— "

TOM PRICE HEEDS NOT HIS TONGUE

"And where is the villain now?"

"Why, as I told thee, dullard, he lurks in Canterbury city hard by the convent—and though 'twas I helped her there—I or thou, I forget if thou didst assist—I say, though 'twas I—or I or thou—or I and thou—helped her there, this dog now keepeth guard like a very bulldog."

"Well," said I, trembling to have so much news, "may be he doeth no harm. The lady oweth more to thee than him."

"Aye—'twas a deft trick, spiriting her thither—and the Captain little knows 'twas honest Tom Price baulked him. Not but—harkee"—here he whispered again—"not but the lady did not make it worth the while, eh? I have a noble of it left still, comrade. As I told thee, the Captain knoweth naught. Ho! ho! he hath followed her hither and thither. But, mercy on us, he'd as soon look in the Fleet Ditch as in Canterbury. Harkee, comrade, that other varlet is a knave. Hang him, I say. 'Twas thou and I helped her there—he knew naught till—how a plague found he us out? Honest friend, I pray thee slay me this dog."

"Where in Canterbury shall I find him?" said I.

"Thou knowest a certain tavern, or inn, or hostel by the sign of the Oriflame, neighbour. Well, 'tis but a stone's-throw from the convent; and I warrant the sot will be not far away. Fetch me his head, comrade; and I vow thou shalt share my noble. Get thee gone."

That moment Jeannette gripped my arm and pointed to a figure which slouched away from us towards the fire. I got but one glimpse of him. He may have been anyone; for the crowd was spreading fast. Yet Jeannette and I both fancied the form was like that of Peter Stoupe, whom we had already seen once in the crowd that evening.

"Poor Peter," said I, "no doubt he envies me my charge of you, Jeannette."

She disengaged herself from my arm, and put her hand on my sleeve.

"Let us begone," said she, uneasily. "I am sorry I came here."

So I left Tom Price sitting on the grass, singing to himself; and full of my great news, yet troubled at Jeannette's speech I walked with her silently homewards.

SIR LUDAR

As we neared Temple Bar, I could not refrain from questioning her.

"You are silent, Jeannette?" said I.

"The better company for you," said she.

"Are you tired?"

"Yes."

"And vexed?"

"Yes."

"Because Peter—if it was Peter—saw me with my arm around thee?"

"He would not know that it was only because I feared the drunken man," said she.

"He would suspect me, instead, of being thy sweetheart?" asked I.

"Aye," said she, "Peter hath a long tongue."

"What if he suspect me aright, Jeannette?"

I felt the hand on my arm give a little start, as she dropped her eyes, and quickened her flagging steps.

She said nothing. But you might have heard the beating of my heart, as I looked down at her, and laid my hand on hers.

"If Peter guessed aright," repeated I, "what then, Jeannette?"

This time her hand lay very quiet, and her footsteps grew slower, till at last they stood still.

Then she lifted her head and looked me in the face.

"Then, Humphrey, I should not mind what anybody said."

So all was peace betwixt us two; and we were sorry when our walk was ended.

CHAPTER XX

How there came Visitors to Master Walgrave's House

SO occupied was I with my new joy, that for a day or two what I had heard from drunken Tom Price in Moorfields slipped me. Or, if I thought of it, it seemed all was well. For I gathered from his wild talk that the maiden—left no doubt by her harsh step-dame to fight her own battles—had fled from the Captain's persecutions with the help of Tom, to Canterbury, where (as I knew) was the convent school in which she had been brought up. Here she was safe from his clutches, even if he knew where she was, which Tom took care he should not. And, to make all surer, there was that English soldier—Ludar's prisoner, whom he had charged to protect her—hovering near, true to his trust and ready to defend her from all and every foe that should assail her.

Therefore, I felt easy in my mind to leave her thus secure, and set myself to win my mistress' and master's good-will for my match with the sweet Jeannette.

'Twas no easy task. For my mistress said the child was over young; and my master told me I had somewhat else to think of than such tomfoolery. Howbeit, when I told them that, say what they pleased, Jeannette was mine, and that so soon as my time was up two years hence I should take her to myself with leave or without, they thought better of it, and yielded somewhat.

My mistress said, two years hence we should all be grown older, and if we were then of the same mind perchance she might be of another. My master, too, counting to retain me in his service as a son-in-law, said there was time enough betwixt now and then. And thus it came to pass Jeannette

SIR LUDAR

and I were left to our hopes, and needed no sweeter comfort to make the weeks fly.

But, one day early in February, as I walked on my master's business near Charing, I saw a sight which made me uneasy on another's behalf. For there, at the road corner as you go to Whitehall, I perceived a man who pulled out a purse and gave it to another; and when I looked closer, I saw that he who gave was Captain Merriman, and he who received was my old fellow-apprentice, Peter Stoupe.

Instantly, although I heard not a word, and there might have been a hundred other considerations, I took it into my head that this business meant mischief to Ludar. And, cudgelling my brains further, I called to mind how, that memorable night in Moorfields, while I talked with the drunken sergeant, Peter had sneaked past us, and put my sweet little mistress in a flutter.

What if, instead of heeding us, he had been listening to what the soldier said? He knew or guessed enough of the maiden's story—having heard me tell it often—to put two and two together. What if he, as well as I, had learned the soldier's secret; and, to despite me and profit himself, had sold it to the one man from whom it was by all means to be kept?

I cursed my wickedness, who, lapped in my own happy fortune, had thus neglected my absent master's interest and let this knave get beforehand with me. For, be Ludar alive or dead, I owed it to him to save the maiden from the Captain, even if it cost me my life.

So, as I say, this vision of the passing of the purse woke me out of my dream, and warned me that there was danger in the wind.

That afternoon, the same Providence which gave me the alarm put into my way a means of acting upon it.

My master I found in a sore state of vexation because a certain book he was printing, from which he expected some profit, was refused a licence by the Stationers' Company. They liked it not, said the clerk, and had sent it on to his Grace, who had other matters to think of, and was, besides, away in Canterbury on a visitation.

At this my ears pricked.

"By your leave, Master Walgrave," said I, "here is a

A JOURNEY TO CANTERBURY

matter that presses. If we get not his Grace's licence now, the occasion for the book will be gone by. How if you let me go to Canterbury, to wait upon him?"

Master Walgrave shrugged his shoulders.

"Have you forgot your last journey for me?" said he. "For if you have, I have not."

"Oh," said I, rather sheepish, "I am older than that now. Besides, I know what I go for this time, and have not my business sewn up in my cloak's lining."

"'Tis bad weather for so long a journey," said my mistress.

"I heed not that," said I, like a hypocrite, "so I get my master his licence."

"Beside," said Jeannette, who knew what was afoot, "Humphrey likes to travel, and he pines, I know, to be freed a day or so from my apron strings."

I vowed she wronged me there; but between us all, my master yielded and said I should start next day to see his Grace.

"Nay," said I, "I will start to-night. There is no time to lose."

But they would not hear of that, and for fear of betraying myself, I forbore to press it, and went betimes to bed, promising to be away before daybreak on the morrow.

Early as I was next morning, Jeannette was astir to bid me God-speed and give me my breakfast.

"Humphrey, *mon ami*," said she. "I should not grudge to see thee go on so good an errand. Yet, I shall be glad to see thee home."

"Perhaps," said I, "it is all for nothing, and Ludar's maiden may be safe from harm. Yet, something tells me she needs my help."

"You may tell that maiden," said Jeannette, "that I lend you to her; and if she need shelter, she shall have it here."

I thanked her for that brave speech, and tore myself away. By dint of hard walking—for I had no nag to carry me this time—I arrived late that night at Rochester, where I was glad enough to turn into the first inn I met, and sleep.

I know not how it was. I dreamed all night that Ludar was calling to me to turn back, while the maiden was bidding

SIR LUDAR

me go forward; and betwixt them I was torn in two, and lay kicking all night, listening to the clatter of hoofs that went past, and fancying that while I tarried there, his Grace of Canterbury was carrying off my sweet Jeannette, I know not whither. It must have been towards morning when at last I shook off my nightmares and fell asleep. And thus it happened that, instead of being far on my road, at ten of the clock I still lay snoring, with all my day's work before me to reach Canterbury that night.

As it fell out, I did not even do that. For close by Feversham I met a parcel of knaves who laid hold of me and rifled me of all I had, save one noble that I had hid in my hat. And because I showed fight, and ran two of them through, they wanted to hang me at the roadside and so end my travelling days for aye. But as they must needs find a tall tree, which was not to be had at the roadside, they hauled me away to the wood to make an end of me there. And since I walked meekly with my head hung down, they slackened their guard of me, so that presently I was able to make a dash away from them, and hide myself in the forest.

I escaped them, but it cost me a whole afternoon. For I lost myself among the trees; and daring not to show myself, must needs lie low while the hue and cry lasted, and afterwards find my road under shelter of night as best I could.

You may guess if I chafed not under this delay; specially as the way from there to Canterbury was too hard to be walked in the dark. Halt where I was, I must; but I did it, feeling that I might be too late, and that each moment lost to me was a gain to that foul Captain.

At early dawn I was afoot, and before mid-day stood in the city of Canterbury. As in duty bound, I asked my way first of all to his Grace's palace (which was hard by the great Church) where I longed to have my master's business disposed of.

Alack! his Grace was not to be seen, being away on a visitation; and his Grace's secretary had other matters to attend to, and sent word to me to enquire again to-morrow about the same time. So I was forced to let the business wait, much to my sorrow, and meanwhile seek to hear some news of Ludar's maiden.

NEWS OF JACK GEDGE

I remembered what Tom Price in his drunken speech had said of the nunnery, hard by which was a certain tavern by name of the "Oriflame," where I was like to hear of the English soldier, Jack Gedge. Thither, accordingly, I went, being told I should find it outside the walls on the Dover road.

'Twas a low, mean house, with little accommodation for man or beast, being, indeed, as much farmhouse as hostel, with naught but the flaming sign to tell me I might wade through the muck and litter to the door and there call for refreshment.

The host was a civil, stupid fellow, who eyed me like one from whom he suspected mischief, and seemed impatient till I had drained my pot and was gone.

But I had no thought of going, and bade him, since business kept me that night in Canterbury, get me a bed.

He declared he had none to spare, and that I might get better quarters in the town. But I replied I wanted no better quarters than the "Oriflame," and if it came to a lack of beds, he and I could do with one betwixt us.

"Or," said I, "if, as I am told, my old friend and comrade Jack Gedge, once a soldier, lodgeth here, he and I will not quarrel over our share of a crib."

At that he looked uneasy and said Jack Gedge was not there. He would have me believe at first he knew no man of the name; but I wormed it out of him that a month back a fellow had come and taken service with him as drawer and labourer, calling himself plain Gedge. But only a week ago, as this same fellow was bringing in the pigs, a handful of men had set upon him, with a magistrate's warrant, and arrested him as a deserted soldier, skulking to avoid her Majesty's service, and had carried him away to Rochester gaol. I questioned him as to who his captors were, but he said he knew them not, but supposed them to be men in the company of the Captain whose colours the fellow had abandoned.

Knowing what I did, I guessed this was so, and that it had been part of a plan against the maiden thus to get one of her protectors out of the way.

"And have you had much company here of late," I asked, "that your house is so full?"

He looked queerly at me, for he knew as well as I there was no guest but myself beneath the roof.

SIR LUDAR

"By your leave," said he, "I am ill prepared to make any guest welcome, and pray you do me the favour to seek entertainment elsewhere."

"Nay," said I, "I like the place. And if you suspect me, let me tell you I am a plain London printer's 'prentice, come to seek my Grace's licence for a book, which I hope to receive to-morrow."

"I hope you say true," said he, "for I have had trouble enough with guests here lately, not as honest as you. Why, sir," said he, filling my mug, "only yesterday there came here such a surly-faced varlet as you never saw, who whined and sang psalms as he drank my ale; and then when the time came to pay, told me to score it to one Captain Merriman, in whose service he was, and who would come and pay it presently. I ask you, sir, how would you like that at your inn?"

"Thank Heaven I have no inn; but tell me, landlord, this varlet, was he a long pale fellow, with straight hair, and eyes half shut; and was this the tune he whined?" And I hummed Peter's favourite tune.

"The very man," said my landlord, rising to his feet with a start. "You have hit him to a point. And be you then this Captain Merriman that is to pay my score?"

"Not so," said I, laughing, "and you may bid farewell to your money if you are to look for it to him. I know the villain, landlord, and if I saw him here, I warrant you this sword of mine would not be lying thus in its sheath. But tell me. This surly-faced rogue, what did he do? What was his business?"

"Indeed, I know not. Save to ogle all the women that came this way, not sparing the Popish nuns in yonder convent."

And he pointed to a plain building close at hand, peeping from among the trees, and walled all round with a high wall.

"He asked so many questions of the place, and was so curious to see the sisters and their scholars walk abroad, that had I a daughter in keeping there, I would be glad to get her safe back under my roof."

"And did he see them?"

"I warrant you, yes. For while he was questioning me the bell sounded, and they walked across to the Popish Chapel

TWO MEN HABITED AS PRIESTS

in the wood. And there was my gentleman, turned Papist all of a sudden, and must needs go and worship images too."

"And where has he gone now?" I asked.

"I know not, neither do I care, so I am rid of him. But come, guest, if you must stay, get you to bed; for we be early folk here."

I slept not a wink that night, and before daylight was astir and out of doors. For I, too, was curious concerning this nunnery and its inmates; and was minded to turn Catholic too for occasion, and see if, amongst the ladies, might appear the stately form of her whose fate had been so oddly woven with mine own.

But ill fortune attended me. For early as I was, matins had been sung an hour ago; nor was there another service till noon, and that only for the sisters. I must wait till evensong, to satisfy myself, and, with much misgiving at the delay, dragged myself back to the "Oriflame."

Just as I turned off from the Dover road, there passed me in haste two men habited as priests, travel-stained, as coming off a long journey, yet apparently familiar enough with the path which led to the friendly shelter of the convent. I saw neither of their faces, for both were bent over the books they read; but I marked that one of them was tall and lean, while the other, who walked with more of a swagger, was shorter and better fed. I doubt if either of them saw me. But somehow I liked not the sight of them, or the path they took. It seemed to me to bode ill to the maiden; and I longed to have my business with his Grace ended that I might return and be near the place where she was.

For three mortal hours, that forenoon, was I kept kicking my heels in his Grace's ante-chamber; and in the end was told curtly his Grace had no leisure at present for such business, and that I must come again on the morrow. I own I spake disrespectfully of his Grace when they gave me this message, and was fain, on that account, to retreat from the precincts more hastily than most suitors are wont to do. Here was another day wasted, and who was to say that the same put-off did not await me to-morrow?

It was late in the afternoon when I found myself again at the "Oriflame," and there I found mine host in a monstrous

SIR LUDAR

flutter, thinking I, too, had given him the slip without paying my account. I made him happy on that score with the moiety of my gold piece, and thereby bound him to me for ever and a day. For he seemed a man whose wont it was never to get his due.

I was solacing my impatience as I waited for vespers, by pacing to and fro in the wood which divided the road to Dover from the convent wall ; when I was startled to come suddenly upon a horse, saddled and bridled, tied up in a covert. It had a pillion on its back ; and seemed like the beast on which a farmer and his wife might ride together to market. So, indeed, I thought it to be, when, looking about me, I perceived in the saddle-bow a knife, the hilt of which I had seen before. It was, in fact, a knife I had myself given to Peter, one day two years ago, when I had won a new one at Finsbury Fields, and when my fellow 'prentice and I were better friends than we became later on.

The sight of this knife suddenly brought the blood to my head with a mighty rush. For it showed that this horse waited here for Peter ; and if for Peter, for what lady was the pillion provided ? I had wit enough, without a moment's delay, to hide myself among the trees ; assured that whatever mischief was in the air, it would come at length to this trysting place. And so it fell out.

I heard the chapel bell begin to toll ere long, and pictured in my mind the sisters and their wards crossing devoutly from the convent garden to the little chapel in the wood. No doubt the sleek Peter would be there to eye them as they glided in ; and when the service was done, perchance, he would seek to make his wicked swoop on that poor, unsuspecting lamb, and carry her off to his foul paymaster. In an hour——

What was that ? I suddenly heard close to me staggering footsteps and a stifled groan, accompanied by the hard panting of a man who laboured with a heavy load. That they were coming my way was evident by the crackling of the under-wood and the impatience of the horse. What a year did those two minutes seem as I waited there, sword in hand !

Then there broke into the covert a man, dragging on his arm the fainting form of her whom, though I had not seen her for a long year, I knew in a moment to be Rose O'Neill, my master Ludar's maiden. But what amazed me most was

I RESCUE THE MAIDEN

the man who carried her. I had looked for Peter Stoupe to a certainty; but instead of him I saw the taller of the two priests whom I had passed only that morning on the way to the convent. The delusion lasted only a moment. For as he turned his head, I saw beneath the cowl the well-known, cadaverous, hungry visage of my masquerading 'prentice, and knew that I was right after all.

He flung his senseless burden to the ground with a curse, and was turning to the horse, when I stepped out, sword in hand, and faced him. I gave him no time for parley or excuse. I heeded not the yell he sent up as he saw who I was, and felt nothing of the one savage blow he aimed at me with his knife. Time was short. At any moment that other masquerading priest, whose name I guessed shrewdly enough now, might be here on the top of us. So I had at him and ran him through the carcase, and without waiting to look twice to see if he lived or no, or to restore his fainting victim, I lifted her on to the horse in front of me, and dashed, in the gathering night, through the forest roads.

Two days later, as the snow fell thick in the London streets, I stood with the maiden at my master's door without Temple Bar. There were crowds in the Strand, I remember, talking over some notable news which had just come in; and so full was every one of the same, that we passed unheeded, and not a man had time to recognise me or wonder who was my companion. Even my master and mistress were abroad gossiping; so that, to my vast relief, when I opened the door and walked in, there was Jeannette to meet us and no one else.

"Thee art welcome, dear Humphrey," said she, coming forward; "and so is this lady."

And she dropped a curtsey as she turned to my companion. But seeing her pale face and sad looks, she went to her and, taking her hand, kissed her on the cheek. I think that sisterly welcome put new life into the maiden, for the colour came again to her face, and a smile to her lips, as she said—

"We are not strangers, sweet Jeannette. It does me good to see thee now."

And somehow I was overlooked in the talk that ensued betwixt those two, and so left them and went out to the street to hear what this great news might be.

SIR LUDAR

It was indeed great news. Yesterday, in the early morning, the Scotch Queen had paid the penalty of her grievous treasons, and had been beheaded at Fotheringay Castle. Men seemed half dazed by the news. To many it had seemed that the dangers of which she was the author were to trouble England's peace for ever ; and now that, by a single blow, the cloud had been lifted, some of us fetched a great sigh of relief and had time to pity the fate of the fair woman, whose name we had so lately hated. So there was not much shouting or burning of bonfires. But every one felt something wonderful had happened, and rubbed their eyes, like those awakened out of some long drawn nightmare.

When I returned my master and mistress were still abroad. Jeannette, I found, had carried the maiden to her own bed, and having left her there to rest—and indeed she needed it, for we had travelled hard two days by long and tiresome roads —awaited me with a grave face.

"All this is passing strange," said she, "and I love this maiden. But, my Humphrey, I have sad news to tell you since you left. 'Twas the evening of the very day you went ; as I was helping the father draw his charges, there came suddenly into the shop a man, tall, haggard, but noble to look at, and seeming like a hunted lion. He looked round him wildly, and then asked, was this the printer's house outside Temple Bar ? The father answered shortly, yes. ' Then,' said he ' is there one here, Humphrey Dexter by name ? ' ' No,' said the father, who, I thought, mistrusted the fellow's looks, and wanted to be rid of him. Without a word, then, he turned and left us ; before I could so much as cry to him that you would be back anon. Where he went I know not, but that this was Sir Ludar, and that he goes in peril of his life I am as sure as that I speak now to thee."

Now, I understood why, as I lay dreaming that night at Rochester, I had heard my master's voice calling me back, while that of the maiden urged me forward. To think he had been here, in this very spot, calling for me, and I not at hand to answer ! It was too bitter a cup ; and late as it was, I rushed out once again into the street, in the foolish hope of seeing or hearing of him. But it was all too late !

CHAPTER XXI

How a Certain Man was hanged at Tyburn

MONTHS passed, and the Irish maiden became one of Master Walgrave's ordinary household. And she and my Jeannette were as sisters.

It was not without a struggle that my master and mistress were prevailed upon to open their home to the fair stranger. At first, my master, being sorely wroth with the miscarriage of my errand to his Grace, vowed so roundly that he would turn both me and my papist wench—so he called her—out of doors, that it seemed likely there would be broken heads as well as hearts over this business. For it was hard to keep my temper even with Jeannette's stepfather, when he talked like that.

But I deemed it wise to leave the management of the matter to daintier hands than mine; and when Jeannette, clinging to her father's knees, besought him with tears at least to let the maiden stay a few days till she could find a shelter, he surlily yielded so much, provided she stayed in a chamber by herself, and brought not her papist blasphemy within earshot of any in the house. Then, when a day after, my mistress, being won over by her sweet daughter, saw how ill and withal how gentle the maiden was, it was even permitted her to walk in the garden and exchange civilities with the two ladies of the house. Soon after, yet another event served to put my master in humour. For a message came from his Grace's secretary permitting the printing of the book. And that evening, as I observed, Master Walgrave even condescended to speak to the maiden himself. And last of all, when she told him prettily that she was rich enough to recompense him for his hospitality, and begged him take charge of her purse so long as she lodged with him, he had no more to say, but let her go in and out as she pleased, pledging her only to speak not a word of her religion to Jeannette or anyone else in his house.

It was not much I saw of her; for, despite her liberty, she never strayed beyond the little garden, and many a day kept close to her chamber. Yet often I heard of her from Jeannette, and now and again she herself enquired for me, and asked me to walk with her.

I soon learned what little she had to tell of her own adventures. After leaving Dunluce she had been kept close prisoner in Toome Castle by her old step-dame, despite her father's protest, who had no more voice in his own house than a dog and was not sorry to escape from it to Castleroe. The English soldier who had been sent to guard her was not admitted within the walls, but paced—faithful fellow—outside, within sight of her window, the only reminder she had of the happiness she had lost. Presently rumours came that Ludar had been slain in battle; and after a while Captain Merriman came on a visit. Happily, this time, he returned not to the violence with which he had persecuted her at Castleroe, but tried to win her by civilities which were scarcely less loathsome to her than his old rudenesses. Amongst other things, he told her Ludar had cursed her for being his brother's murderess; and that he believed it was true, as had been reported, that the young M'Donnell was slain. And two days after, to confirm this, an officer came to the Castle with news that Ludar's head was set on a pole above the gate at the Bridge of Dublin.

After that, the maiden said, she wished no longer to live. For she knew not what to believe; or how much was a wicked plot to deceive her into yielding to the Captain. Presently her father came home, and she begged him on her knees to send her to England. He consented; but when my Lady heard of it, she took the whim to go to Court too, and invited the Captain to be their escort. So nothing was gained by that move—or nothing would have been gained, had not Providence directed that Captain Merriman and my Lady should grievously fall out on the journey about some act of disrespect to herself, such as the neglecting to see her lifted to her horse before he assisted the maiden. Whatever the cause was, it saved the maiden much trouble during the journey;

THE MAIDEN'S PERILS

for the Captain was kept thereby at arm's length and never permitted to come near. And, to add to her comfort, she had espied among the men who formed the escort the same English fellow who had escorted her from Dunluce to Toome, and who, it was clear, was still true to his trust.

But as they neared London, my Lady, feeling in need of some little pomp to make good her entry, took the Captain back once more into favour; and with that the maiden's troubles began again. For the Captain bargained, as a price of his good-will, that he should wed the maiden so soon as they reached town. To this my Lady seemed to consent, and told her step-daughter, sternly enough, to prepare herself for what was no longer to be avoided.

Thus made desperate, on a certain morning about a day's ride from London, the maiden made some pretence of her saddle being broken, and beckoned to the English fellow to come and attend to it. But instead of him, for his head was turned, came Tom Price the Captain's sergeant. And while he made good the straps she took heart of grace and begged him, for pity's sake, help her, and slipped into his hand some gold pieces. And he, having no liking to see his master married and himself, perhaps, cast out of service, willingly offered to help her when the time came. So she bade him be ready with a horse at midnight of the very day they reached London, and to bring the other English fellow, if needs be, also.

The rest of the story I knew. How Tom Price had carried her to her old nunnery school at Canterbury; and how the fellow Gedge (though Tom had no mind to share the reward with him) discovered what was afoot and went to Canterbury too. And how Peter Stoupe, having heard the secret from the drunken sergeant, had found out the Captain, and sold the same to him; and, finally, after getting the honest watchdog out of the way, how, disguised as priests, those two villains had invaded the convent and, but for the Providence which took me thither, might have had her across seas and at their mercy long since.

"So, my good Humphrey," said the maiden, "once more I owe you more than my life. I cannot repay you, but Heaven will. Nay it is doing so already, in giving you this sweetest little Jeannette to love you."

And then, as her eyes grew dim, and her bosom heaved,

SIR LUDAR

I could guess whither her thoughts had flown, and how my happy lot contrasted with her own.

I had told her all I knew of Ludar, up to the time of the poet's letter. But for a long time I durst not tell her of his visit to my master's house that evening while I was at Canterbury. At last, however, I summoned up courage, with Jeannette's help, to tell her that; and it was pitiful to see how it moved her.

"Talk of it no more," said she. "He will not return; or if he does, the sight of me—to whom he owes all these troubles, who tempted him to desert his duty and ruined his life—will drive him hence. Jeannette," said she, taking my little mistress' hand in hers, "why must one live when it would be so happy to die?"

"Maiden," said Jeannette, boldly, "you do wrong to talk so, and I shall love you less if you say it again. Of course he will come, and of course he loves you, and of course all will be happy yet. Is the God you pray to less kind and strong than ours?"

The maiden said nothing, but her cheeks flushed as she lifted Jeannette's little hand to her lips. And after that we seldom spoke together of Ludar. Yet he was in all our thoughts.

As for me, I wandered about the town night by night for many a week, hoping to hear of him. But never a word could I hear. And in time people ceased even to talk of the Scotch Queen and all the troublous times which had ended at her death. And a leaden weight was falling on my heart, as I wondered if I was never again to hold my friend's hand in mine; when one day I chanced to stumble on news of him in the strangest way.

It was near midsummer that a journeyman came urgently one day to my master from Master Barker's, her Majesty's printer, desiring his aid in the setting up in type of certain matter which was to be printed forthwith, but which Master Barker (being crowded with other work) must needs hire out to be done. My master, who desired by all means to keep the good graces of the Queen's printer, undertook to give the help asked for, and handed to me the paper to put in type.

I opened it, and found it headed thus:—

"A List of Persons who in these late grievous times have

"ONE, LUDAR, AN IRISHMAN"

"suffered punishment for treasonable acts against the state "and person of her Most Gracious Majesty. To wit—— "

Then followed a goodly list of names of persons suffering death in the ill cause ; headed by that of the Scotch Queen herself. Afterwards came the names of certain persons imprisoned, together with a note of the place where each was imprisoned, and the term of his punishment.

Amongst these, towards the end, was a line which made my blood suddenly run cold, and set the stick a trembling in my hand. It ran thus :—

"*One,* LUDAR, *an Irishman, who carried certain Letters abroad. He lieth in ye Tower of London, waiting Her Maties pleasure.*"

.   .   .   .

The summer passed, and each week the maiden's cheek grew paler. She had said little when Jeannette showed her the name on the proof which I had kept. But she quietly took the paper and hid it in her bosom, and for a day kept herself to her chamber.

After that she rarely mentioned Ludar's name, and when we spoke of him to her, she always changed the talk to something else. Once or twice, in the late summer evenings, I took her and Jeannette to row on the river. And on each occasion we dropped on the tide to below London Bridge, where standing out in the gloom of twilight we could see the great frowning Tower which held still, as we hoped, a life dear to us all.

But as the weeks sped by, with one consent we let go even that hope ; and on the last evening, when we rowed, the maiden said—

" Humphrey, row us some other way to-night."

And as she spoke, her face looked to me scarcely less white than the shivering moonbeams on the water.

About the middle of the autumn, I met Will Peake one day, who told me that there had been of late not a few men hanged at Tyburn and elsewhere ; some for recent treasons, and others whose sentence had been overhanging ever since the conspiracies concerning the Scotch Queen.

When I pressed him closer, he said he had been present at one hanging at Tyburn, but that was of a debaser of coins. But a friend of his, said he, had seen four traitors hanged, drawn, and quartered; of whom he knew the names of three. But the other, thought to be a Scotchman or Irishman, no one knew his name.

I begged Will to take me to his friend that I might hear more, and plainly told him my reason. Whereat he drew a very long face, and said he thought better of me than to consort with such vile carrion as these traitors to her Majesty. Nevertheless he took me to his friend to hear what he had to say.

His friend sickened me with a long story of the horrible death of these men, whereby he thought to entertain me as he had entertained not a few other idle fellows during the past month.

"Oh," said he, "pity on us you saw not the fourth rogue dangle—be hanged to him that he had no name! I tell you, Master Dexter, it almost made me creep to see all they did to make an end of him. First of all——"

"Hold thy peace, beast!" roared I. "Keep it to thyself. But tell me, what was he like?"

"If I be a beast," said he, mightily offended, "thou art like to hear that better from anyone else."

"Your pardon," said I, "but my imagination is quick, and your horrible story well-nigh made me ill."

He took this as a mighty compliment, and smoothed down forthwith.

"Aye, aye," said he, "some stomachs are squeamish, but I thought you one of the stout ones. This fourth fellow, say you? Marry, by the build of him he might be a brother of yours, for his feet dangled a foot nearer the ground than the others; and when it came to——"

"Was he dark or fair?" I asked hurriedly, frightened lest he should turn again to his horrible relation.

"Why, he had a shock of hair as like straw for colour as anything I saw. I tell you no man knew his name. Some said he was a Highlander. And he looked it, though I never saw one. But a wilder, more bold-face, shameless villain I ne'er set eyes on. Aye, and he kept it up to the end, too; after the hanging and when they——"

"Have done!" cried I, angrily, "no more of that. But tell me one last thing. Said he anything, before he died?"

"Never a word. But there was a curl on his lip as if it

SECRET PRINTING

were we who had the rope round our necks and not he ; and when the chaplain came to exhort him, he swung round on his heel and pulls me out his papist crucifix and kisses it before all the people. What think you of that for a stubborn dog ? The others died with their tails betwixt their legs, I tell you ; but this notable ruffler, from the moment he swung aloft to the moment—— "

I could stand him no more, and left him telling his horrible story to the church steeple ; while I crawled back, scarce daring to think, to my master's house.

I told this news neither to Jeannette nor the maiden. For it might be false, as former panics had been. And if it were not false, what good could it do to break that gentle heart a day sooner than Heaven ordained ?

So the year ended miserably, in doubt and gloomy foreboding ; and Jeannette and I, as we looked at the maiden's white cheek and suffering brow, dare scarcely claim as our own the happiness which came of the love that grew daily betwixt us.

· · · · · · · ·

Now, I grieve to say that early in the new year, my master, who had of late seemed docile and obedient to the orders of the worshipful the Stationers' Company, fell once more into his evil practices of secret printing. I know not how or why it was, but more than once he was absent visiting the minister at Kingston ; and once, that same Welshman, Master Penry, whom I had met in Oxford, came to our house and had a long conference there, and left behind him certain papers which my master carefully locked away.

And one night, after I had been late out, when I came back, I spied a light in the cellar below, and heard the rumble of a press there, and knew that, cost what it would, my master was once more risking his liberty and fortune at the bidding of his bishop-hating employers.

"Master," said I, boldly marching below, to where he stood busily working his press, " since I am to be your son-in-law, I may as well share your peril. Have I your leave ? "

He looked half-vexed and half-contented ; and declared that what he did, though it might be against the rules, was yet a righteous thing, and he wanted not my help unless I thought the same. This tract, said he, could it but get abroad, would save God's Church from much evil that threatened her; and to that end he was willing to risk his liberty in printing it.

Now, whether he was right or wrong, I was not scholar enough to understand all the tract said concerning the state of the Church. But since no one wished to see the Church improved more than I, I was ready to believe my master's cause a righteous one, and told him as much.

And having once lent myself to the work, it suited my humour to carry it on without question, though not without sundry misgivings as to how far it sorted with my loyalty to my Queen to be thus flying in the face of a decree of her honourable Star Chamber.

But before this labour was done, a new task fell into my hands. For one day, as I worked at my case, I heard a voice at the door say:

"Is it here I find my Hollander, like Pegasus clipped of his wings, yet giving wings to the thoughts of the wise, so that they may fly abroad, as, in sooth, shall presently mine own burning numbers? Salute me, my once servant, now honoured to be called my friend, and the goal of my muse-sped wanderings."

It was the poet. But how changed from the gay popinjay I knew on the *Miséricorde!*

He was so lean that the skin scarce held together over his bones; his face was shrunk and nipped with hunger; a ragged beard hung from his chin. His attire was the same as he had worn when last I saw him, but so tattered and dirty and threadbare that it was a marvel to me it did not fall to pieces before my eyes. The great ruff drooped brown and dank upon his shoulders. The gay shirt and doublet hung like grey sackcloth on his limbs. His shoes flapped in fragments about his feet, and the empty scabbard at his belt swung like the shreds of a worn rope beteeen his legs.

He was a sorry spectacle in truth, and but for his unchanged speech I might have looked at him long ere I knew him.

"I am come," said he, when I had greeted him and bidden him sit and rest, "like a dove from the ends of the earth, yet with not so much as an olive leaf to fill my mouth withal. My Hollander, even the poet, friend of the immortals, can eat. Even the honey on Mount Athos satisfieth not; and nectar leaveth its void. As a sign of peace and good-will,

A SORRY SPECTACLE

my humble comrade, I will eat whatsoever bread and meat you may place before me ; for in truth my teeth have lost their cunning, and he who late warbled elegiacs hath almost forgot how to swallow a cup of vulgar sack."

'Twas not long before with Jeannette's aid I set before him a meal the very sight of which filled his eyes with tears, and set his hand a trembling. It seemed kinder not to stand by while he devoured it ; yet even in the adjoining room we could hear him, betwixt his mouthfuls, talk of Hebe and Ganymede, and utter brave speeches about Venus who ever haunted his wandering steps, and in mortal guise waited on her favoured servant. By which I understood he was struck with the beauty of my sweet Jeannette ; for the which I forgave him much.

But when, after a little, we returned to see how he fared, he was fallen forward on the table in a deep sleep, from which it never even roused him when I lifted him in my arms and laid him on a clean straw bed in the corner of the office. And for twenty hours by the clock did he sleep there, never turning a limb, till it seemed a charity to rouse him and give him more food.

Then when he found himself refreshed and filled, he gave us his news ; which, shorn of all its flourishes, was shortly this.

After he had written his letter from Chester, he was detained many a week in custody as a vagabond and a lunatic. And at last, shaking the dust of that city from his feet, he tramped to the next, where a like fate awaited him. And so, tossed about, like a drift log on the unpitying ocean, he had found himself cast up at last in London ; where, remembering me, he had with many a rebuff sought me out, and here he was.

When he discovered that the maiden—his once mistress and incomparable swan—was of our househid, he fell into strange raptures concerning the indulgences of the gods towards their favourites—meaning himself. And the sight of her, and her goodness to him—for with her own purse she found him a lodging not far off—called up from him many a burst of poetic fire, such as it grieves me to think cannot now be recovered. More than that, he told us a little of Ludar, whom, as has been said, he encountered at Chester.

More yet, he had one piece of news which was of no little import to the maiden and us all, as you shall hear.

CHAPTER XXII

How Master Walgrave fell short of Type

WHAT the poet had to tell might never have been known had he not chanced to hear me speak to the maiden one day of Turlogh Luinech O'Neill, her father, and the Lady Cantire, her step-dame. He pricked up his ears at the names.

"Hath Fortuna then reserved it to her mortal favourite to discover in my mistress, my paragon of all virtue, the Lady Rose O'Neill?· My Hollander, why this churlish secrecy? why told ye not as much before?"

"Why," said I, "I supposed you knew the name of the lady you call your mistress."

"Groundling!" said he, "a poet needeth no name but Love and Beauty. But had I known this lady was she you say, I had relieved my mind of a notable piece of news for her ear."

"Say on, Sir Poet," said the maiden, who had approached and heard these last words.

"Now then, mistress mine," said he, "and thank not this voiceless dabbler in ink for the mercy, that travelling not a week before I reached London, I chanced into the company of a stranger, who fell captive to my wit, and displayed so lively a tooth for the sweets of Parnassus—to wit, my poesy—that, hearing I was about to issue the same imprint, prayed me enrich him with a copy. The which I condescended to promise him. Being thus established in a brotherhood of poetic kinship, we opened our hearts one to another. And in our talk he confessed to me that he was an Irish gentleman in the service of one Turlogh Luinech O'Neill, a notable chieftain in the Isle of the Saints; and that he travelled to London on an errand to no less a man

THE POET'S PIECE OF NEWS

than her Majesty's Secretary of State to report to him the death and burial of one Lady Cantire, an aged servant of her Majesty, and sometime wife to the said Turlogh."

This was news indeed; and the maiden's face flushed with many mingled emotions as she heard it.

"Can it be true?" said she. "Sir Poet, tell me briefly what else this gentleman had to tell of my father?"

"Nay, mistress mine, I can remember little else; for I was thinking not of his master, but his poetic tooth; not of his defunct mistress, but of my living muse. Yet, stay, he told me the old man was desolate, his sons being all established elsewhere, and his one daughter lost. By which I take it, he spoke of thy celestial self. And strange indeed if the loss of such a one were not as blindness itself to one who hath looked in they resplendent face."

"Humphrey," said the maiden, turning from the poet to me, and taking Jeannette's little hand in hers, "this news means much to me. If it be true, I must to my father."

A cloud that sweeps over the April sun could scarce have cast the gloom which did this little speech on us who heard it. For the maiden, lady as she was, had become a sister to us.

Yet she was resolved; and hearing that the poet had remembered where he might hear of this gentleman in London, to deliver to him his poem, she begged me to go with the man of verse and find him out, and if possible bring him to her.

Which I did with no great difficulty. For the Irishman—who seemed a sort of steward of Turlogh's household—was still in his lodgings, waiting an audience with the Secretary's secretary. And when he heard who it was had sent me, he fell on his knees and thanked the saints for vouchsafing his master this great mercy; and, never looking twice at the poet, he came with me joyfully to the maiden.

It was all as the poet had reported. And the fellow had somewhat more to say. Which was that when the lady Cantire, now six months ago, had returned home to die, she had confessed to her lord her wickedness with respect to the maiden, whom she fully believed, despite her flight, to be in the clutches of the wicked English captain, who had vowed to move heaven and earth to find her, and (as had been reported) had been as good as his word. Turlogh found it hard to forgive his lady this great wrong, and, since her death, had longed for his child as he had never longed before. Furthermore, being now old and past fighting, he and his old foe, Sorley Boy, had become friends, and all was quiet in the country of the Glynns.

There was naught to be said to all this, and the maiden, though the tears stood in her eyes as she spoke, told us she must leave us and go home to her father.

It went hard with me then. For my duty to Ludar seemed to demand that I should see the maiden safe to her journey's end. Yet, while a shred of hope remained that he still lived, how dare I quit the place I was in? Besides, my master every day had more need of my service for his secret printing, and was indeed so restless and nervous concerning the work, that he even grudged my walking out of an evening, or stealing an hour now and again in the company of my sweet Jeannette.

But one day the maiden called me to her, and said—

"Humphrey, you have been a friend and a brother to me. I have two things to ask of you now. One I even command, the other I beg as a precious boon."

"Before you ask," said I, "I will obey the command, for you have a right to command anything; and I will grant the boon, for nothing I can give you can come up to what I would fain give you."

She smiled gently at that and said—

"Wait till you hear, Humphrey. My command is that you quit not London at present."

"I understand," said I, "and had already resolved that only your command should move me hence."

"That makes me happier," said she, with a sigh of relief. "Now for the boon. What if I asked you to spare me Jeannette for a season?"

I think I looked so taken aback by that, that she had it on her lips to take back the request. But I recovered myself in time. "What says she?" I asked.

"I have not asked her," said she.

"I will ask her then," said I, and we went together to where Jeannette sat waiting for us.

"Jeannette," said I, "this maiden asks me to lend her the most precious thing I possess. Say, shall I do so?"

"Yea, Humphrey, and with a willing heart."

OUR HOUSE WAS LEFT DESOLATE

"Then, sweetheart," said I, kissing her, "I will even lend her thee."

. . . . . .

It surprised me that when it came to asking my master and mistress they gave their leave after but a short parley. For the two maids were so bound together, and the lot of the one was so pitiful and desolate, that it seemed, after all, not too great a boon to ask. And when Jeannette herself seconded the request, and I encouraged it, they yielded.

In truth, my master was just then so full of his work and of the peril he ran, that I think he was all the better disposed to see one of his family thus provided for. Besides, he might safely reckon on the more work from me, when I should have naught to tempt me nightly from my case. As for my mistress, she was already making ready to take her younger children to visit a gossip of hers, one Mistress Crane; and it eased her of some little difficulty to find her party lightened by one for a season.

So all fell out well for the maiden, and sorrowfully for me. Yet, when she reproached herself for her selfishness in robbing me of my sweetheart, I had not the heart to show her all I felt. In sooth, this maiden needed a friend and comforter sorely; and how was she to fare on that long troublesome journey with no comrade but a rough man, and perchance a half-witted poet? For the poet, vowing that Aphrodite should never need for a gallant, nor a maiden in distress for a knight, begged so hard to go too, that she was fain to yield and admit him of the party.

'Twas late in March when our house was left desolate. On the last evening before they went, she asked me to row her and Jeannette once again on the river. I guessed why she asked, and needed no telling which course to take.

And as our boat lay on the oars beneath the shadow of that gloomy tower, she looked up long and wistfully, as one who takes a long farewell. Then with a sigh she motioned to me to turn the boat's head and row home.

Not a word did any of us say during that sad voyage. Only, when we reached home and I handed her from the boat, she said—

"Humphrey, I am glad you are staying near him."

SIR LUDAR

So, then, I discovered, she believed him living still and that I should see him again.

That night, as Jeannette and I stood in the garden watching the moonbeams play on the water, and feeling our hearts very heavy at the parting that was to come, we heard the splashing of an oar at the river side, and presently a man stepped up the bank and stood before us, saluting. At first I was so startled that my hand went to my belt, and I had out my sword in a twinkling. But I sent it home again directly I heard his voice, and recognised not an enemy but that same Jack Gedge whom Ludar had charged long ago at Dunluce to see to the maiden.

Only two days since, he told us, had he been let out of Rochester gaol; when he had gone forthwith to Canterbury and heard from mine host at the "Oriflame" that a certain printer's 'prentice by name Dexter, if any one, could tell him what had befallen the nunnery maiden. Whereupon he had travelled all the way to London in a day, and had not been able to hear of me. But, spying us just now in a boat, as he stood near London Bridge, he had taken craft and followed us, and here he was, ready to take up his charge, and, whether we willed it or no, look after the maiden.

This was a great joy to us all, not least of all to the maiden herself, to whom it seemed like a message from an absent one.

So it came to pass, when on the morrow the travellers started westward, there were five of them. And methought if any harm came to those two fair women with such champions to guard them, it would indeed go hard with all.

They had not been gone three days, and the desolate house, occupied only by me and my master, seemed as void and dull as ever, when one afternoon who should step into the shop but a fine gentleman whom I had never seen before, but whom I guessed to be no friend, as soon as I saw him.

"I am told," said he, "that an honest 'prentice, one Dexter, dwelleth here."

"You be told very right," said I, affecting to be as simple as he wished me. "I am he."

"To be sure, honest fellow," said he, "we have met before."

"Where might that be?" asked I.

"No matter where," said he, "but I remember you for a fine honest fellow. And, indeed, 'tis for that reason I am

QUESTIONS FOR A SIMPLETON

come. I have but lately lost my servant, a drunken scoundrel whom I am well rid of. And hearing from more than one a likely report of you, and knowing you myself that you are the sort of fellow I need—honest, strong in the arm, and quick of wit—I resolved to offer you the service. And as for wage, if you will come, marry I value a good servant so well that there shall be no question betwixt us on that score. Here is a purse for thy first month's service; and if you be the man I take you for, you shall have the like each month you serve me."

"I am mightily beholden to you," said I, gaping at the money and smelling villainy in it all. "And by your leave, Sir Captain, what may be your service?"

"Easy enough for a lad of thy mettle. Indeed, whether you take my service or no, you shall keep that purse, provided you tell me where a certain maiden, ward to the Lady Cantire and daughter to the O'Neill, is now?"

Now I guessed whose messenger I talked with, and what his business might be with me.

It surprised me that he came to the point so quickly. But the greedy way I fingered his money deceived him, and he supposed me won already.

"And how should I know aught of her?" said I.

"Come now," said he, "'tis I am here to ask you questions, not you me. If you want not the money you need not answer. There be others whose tongues it can loosen. So hand it back."

Hereupon I feigned to be in a monstrous panic and said—

"Nay, sir Captain, I said not that I did not know of her. But why do you ask? I desire not any harm to the maiden; for she hath been good to me."

"Harm?" said he. "What do you take me for? I am commanded to deliver her a jewel, bequeathed by her stepdame, and if you refuse to answer me, it is not I but you who do her harm."

"Your pardon," said I, "but there be so many evil disposed persons in the world, and the maiden is so very fair."

"Come," said he, getting impatient, "where is she?"

"Alas!" said I, "she is not here. I heard of her indeed not long since in Kent."

"Yes, and where?" he asked, getting excited.

SIR LUDAR

" 'Twas in Canterbury, where she hid from a villain, one Captain Merriman."

He looked at me hard; but I looked so simple, and fingered the money so greedily, he suspected naught.

" Where is she now ? " he asked again.

" Look you, Captain," said I, getting close with him, " if you truly mean well by this maiden, I shall tell you where to look for her. Only you must keep it secret, and, above all things, tell it not to this Captain Merriman, who is a very devil, and whom I would like to split with my sword, could I catch him."

" Yes, yes," said he, eagerly, " I know him not—where is she ? "

" In faith," whispered I, " if you seek her, you must be quick, for a week hence she may be flown."

" Where is it ? " he asked, impatiently.

" 'Tis—but the name slips me. Yet, your patience, Captain, I have a paper I will fetch."

And I left him and wrote hurriedly on a paper.

" *Pont-Marie, at Calais in France.*"

" Look you, Captain," said I, " you are to go to the place named here. 'Tis across seas, in France. I can tell you no better than this paper. I pray you breathe not to the maiden, if you see her, that 'twas I told you where to look for her; for she would be vexed, as would others I know of. And to prove I am honest, here, take thy purse; for I will never touch it till you tell me you have found her and given her the jewel. As for thy service, I will think of that betwixt now and the day I see you again. Therefore, I pray you, appoint no servant meanwhile. And remember, not a word to the maiden how you came to find her."

He took me for a simple fool, and went off very content with the paper in his pocket, and leaving the purse with me. So I knew I was rid of him and his fellow dog, Merriman, for well-nigh two weeks; and by that time the maiden and her party would be beyond all reach. As to what would happen when they returned from their trip,—well, I had two hands and a sword as well as others.

But whether they came back or not, I know not; for weeks went by, and I forgot all about them, when one night, as my master and I worked secretly, with closed door, at the press,

THE WOLFE PROWLETH O' NIGHTS

I feeling very desolate to know that the whole house was empty, and that were I to open the parlour door, there would meet me no merry note of singing from a sweet voice within—while we worked thus, I say, there came a rustling at the threshold, and presently a piece of paper was thrust under the door. By the dim rush light we took and read it. It said simply this—

Have a care, Walgrave! The Wolfe prowleth o' nights.

"What make you of that?" asked I of my master.

"It comes from a friend," said he, "with evil news. For ever since this greedy John Wolfe was appointed beadle of the Company in room of Timothy Ryder, he hath had a jealous eye on me; and being an old offender himself, he is like to have no terms with others who do as he once did. Humphrey, our hands are too far gone in this business to pull back now; therefore, Wolfe or no Wolfe, we must end it."

"And how?" said I; "since he will be here to-morrow, and find two presses where there should be but one; and the libels hanging here yet damp from the printing?"

"He must find neither," said my master. "We have time yet to give him the slip."

Then he told me how it was arranged, should this mischance befall, which he had expected long since, that the secret press and stuff pertaining to it, should be removed to Mistress Crane's house near the Dowgate (where Mistress Walgrave now lodged), and thence taken secretly to her country house at Moulsey. And since there was no time to lose, we set-to then and there to take the press to pieces and bestow it and the printed sheets in barrels, which, when all was done, my master bade me trundle to the river's edge and place on a wherry, and so convey to Dowgate.

The which, with much sweat and labour, I accomplished, and about eight of the clock next morning delivered them at Mistress Crane's house, who asked no question, but gave me a sixpence for my pains, and bade me return at once the way I came.

Now, you must know, so soon as I was back in my boat, I pitched that sixpence into the Thames. For although, to please Jeannette's step-father, and because I wished well to my Church, I had lent myself to this business, I liked it not, and remembered it each day in my prayers as a thing to be

SIR LUDAR

forgiven. So that I could not take Mistress Crane's sixpence, and hoped the throwing of it away would stand somewhat to my favour when all was reckoned up.

I had not been an hour at work that morning, when in comes John Wolfe with hungry maw, and demands to search the house. Which my master craftily tried to put him off; thereby making John the more sure that he was on a right scent. At last Master Walgrave yielded and bade him take his will. So after overlooking the usual room, and finding naught there disorderly, he walks me with a smack of his lips to where the reams stood piled on the secret door. And with great labour and puffing he and his men set-to to move them, with no help from us. And the door being thus uncovered, he calls for a light and goes below.

Now, my master, whether of purpose or by chance, so soon as the cellar had been cleared the night before, had let run some water over the floor, which, by standing there, had made a pretty slough in the place. And Master Wolfe, not knowing as well as we did that the bottom step of the ladder was awanting, and being encumbered with his candle, fell flat on his face into the mire, and lay there spitting and kicking a round five minutes before we above had the good fortune to hear him.

I went below to help him up—and it was sad to see so great a man in so brave a livery so befouled! Instead of thanking me for my pains he vowed this was a trick put on him, and that some he knew of should smart for it. But for all that he found neither press, nor forme, nor printed sheet contrary to regulation, no, not by searching the whole house over, even to my sweet Jeannette's deserted chamber.

When he inquired where Mistress Walgrave and the children were gone, my master bade him go packing, and concern himself with his own business and not hinder honest men in theirs. So John Wolfe and we parted not too good friends; he threatening to be even with us yet; and we bidding him go wash his face and get a change of raiment.

" 'Twas in good time we were warned," said my master, after he was gone. " Yet still am I in a great strait. For what can a press and paper do, if we have no type? I durst not use this I have here, for it will be known. And from no one else can I borrow it, for those that be not jealous of me

NONE CAN PRINT WITHOUT TYPE

are too timid of his Grace to lend letter for such a cause. Humphrey, type I must have, if not from at home from abroad."

"What!" said I. "From whom abroad will you get any?"

"My wife hath kinsmen in the town of Rochelle, who be printers. I have had type of them already, but not enough."

"But how will you get it now?" I asked. "Who will fetch it?"

"I think you will, Humphrey," said he.

"I!" I cried. "No, master. I would serve you in much, but I cannot in this; for I am bound to stay here, by an oath I would not break if I could. Master, cost what it may, I will not go this errand."

Little knew I how soon I was to change my mind!

CHAPTER XXIII

How the *Miséricorde* sailed for Rochelle

MY master was very surly with me when I refused to go his errand abroad; yet he had too much need of my service in the business he was engaged on to fall out with me as he would have liked. And seeing me resolved to abide where I was, he bade me stay and look to the place while he himself saw after the removing of the stuff from Mistress Crane's house to Moulsey.

"As to the type," said he, "we will speak of that again. But mark me, Humphrey, a 'prentice who is not good enough to do an errand like this is not good enough to be my son-in-law."

And he went off in dudgeon, leaving me very lonely and miserable. And, to tell the truth, at any other season I should have hailed this voyage; and when next day I saw lying near London Bridge the *Miséricorde* herself, and hailing the captain (who was that same shipmate who had steered us into Leith Roads) heard from him that in a week he should sail for France, I wished I could divide myself in two and go half with him and half remain at my post in London.

A day or two later, being evening, I had locked up the printing house and was wandering to take the air towards Smithfield. I had passed under Temple Bar and was making my way down Fleet Street, when there knocked up against me a great carter fellow, whom, by his gait, I took to be more than half drunk. Being a 'prentice, and not in the humour for knocks of that kind, I swung round on the fellow to kick him for his clumsiness, when he looked me suddenly in the face and uttered my name.

It was Ludar.

It was my turn now to reel like a drunken man; and so

LUDAR IS FOUND

mighty a knock did my heart give against my ribs that I believe I should have fallen had he not roughly caught my arm and muttered—

"Not a word, but lead on." And he staggered away, smacking his whip and calling to his horse to go forward.

I walked on in a dream, knowing by the crack of the whip behind that he followed at a distance, yet never daring to turn my head. At last, as we came near Smithfield, I looked back. He lay on the top of a load of hay in his cart, singing aloud noisily and cracking his whip, and seeming no more concerned in me or any one else than the patient horse he drove.

The market place was full of carts, amidst which he was presently able to leave his own and come near where I stood with a crowd looking at some bulls just brought in. He had left his whip behind, by which I guessed he had done with his cart and was free to follow me on foot. So presently I edged out and wandered slowly back citywards. It was already dusk, and by the time I got back to my master's door and unlocked it, night had fallen. I durst not look back as I entered, and indeed made a great noise as of fastening bolts and bars within. Then I stood and waited in a fever.

Had I been wrong after all? An hour passed and never a footfall on the pavement. Then the watch marched by, and as their slow tramp died away in the distance the door quietly opened and there stood Ludar, very pale, but as cool and unconcerned as the day I first met him near Oxford.

"Are you alone?" said he.

"Yes."

"Is there any food in the house?"

I flew to get him some, while he slowly took off his faded carter's cloak, and flung himself wearily on a chair.

He kept me waiting while he ate, nor had I the words to question him. But when his hunger was appeased, he said:

"Six days I have waited and thought you lost. Yet I knew I should find you at last, and I did."

"You escaped?" I asked, the words coming slowly and charily.

"Yes, Humphrey, my friend. After six months, with great labour, and by the help of a nail, I filed my wrist chain

SIR LUDAR

and freed my hands. Then when my warder came one evening later than usual, I flew on him and felled him. He was but stunned, and lay still scarce long enough for me to strip him and put him in my clothes. Then I left him and walked out, jingling the keys. In the dark, no one looked twice at me, even when at the porter's lodge I went to hang up my keys. 'You be late in your rounds to-night," said the porter, who dozed at the fire. I grunted in reply, and sat beside him till he was well asleep. Then I slipped the great key from his belt, and bade him good-night, to which he muttered something. At the great gate stood a young sentry, who, seeing me to be a warder, asked me where I went at that hour. I told him a state prisoner was very sick and I was bidden by the leech go to the druggist for a plaster. 'A pretty errand to send an honest fellow,' said I, 'who has work enough of his own without being waiting gentleman to every knave in the place who has a fit of the colic.' The soldier laughed and said, 'twas a pity they did not keep a supply of plasters in the place. To which I agreed, and unlocking the gate, bade him guard the key while I was out, as 'twas a risk to carry it beyond the precincts. 'But I pray you, comrade,' said I, 'be at hand to admit me when I return.' 'Aye, aye,' said he, with a grin. 'There be some in here who would not tap hard to get in again.' So we parted good friends, and out I got. After that I went down to the river, where all was dark, and being anxious to part with my warder's clothes which might tell tales, I stripped, and filling the pockets with stones, dropped them into the tide. Then I set out to swim to the other shore, and you may guess if it was not brave to feel free once more. 'Twas a long swim, and the tide carried me far down to Rotherhithe, where, as luck would have it, as I neared shore I struck against something floating on the stream. At first I thought it a log, but as I laid my arms upon it, I found it, to my horror, to be a corpse of a man drowned. I was going to cast off again, when I bethought me, here was a man whose clothes were no use to him or any one else, while I went naked. So I dragged him to a desolate part of the shore. He seemed to be a carrier, and having no wound or sign of violence on him, I concluded him to have fallen in the water either by accident or of his own accord. These garments I wear are his."

A TALE TOLD IN THE DARK

I shuddered as I looked at them. They seemed scarce dry yet.

"That was a month ago," said he, "since then——"

"A month," cried I, "and I only find you now?"

"I have hidden here and there, and worked for my livelihood across the water; not daring to show myself this side; till two weeks ago, I was sent to Smithfield with hay, and after that came daily. But till yesterday I never saw you; nor expected it then. But you have news for me, Humphrey," said he, "tell it, for I can hear it."

Then I told him all that had happened since I saw him last, and much the story moved him. And when I came to speak of the maiden, this great, strong man's hand trembled like a leaf as he stretched it across the table, and put out the light which burned there.

"We can talk as well in the dark," said he, hoarsely.

So, in the dark, never seeing his face, yet guessing every look upon it, I told him how the maiden had gone often by boat and gazed up at the great Tower; and how, when she left, she had said to me, "Stay near him"; and how hardly she had torn herself away to return to her father.

He heard me, and said not a word, nor moved a muscle; and, when there was no more to be told, he sat on in the dark, breathing hard, until I supposed he had fallen asleep.

But when, after a while, the early dawn struggled through the casement, it found him still awake, with a look on his face half hope, half bewilderment, and a light in his eyes such as I had seen there only once before—on that day we crossed from Cantire to the Bann with the maiden.

But the sight of day roused him.

"Humphrey, I dare not be seen here," said he, "there is a hue and cry after me. Where shall I hide?"

That was a question had been troubling me all night. For stay where he was he could not. And, if he fled, was I to lose him thus, the moment I found him?

Almost as he spoke there came a step without, and a loud tap on the outer door, at sound of which Ludar started to his feet, and his hand went by instinct to his belt.

"Hush," whispered I, "'tis only my master, the printer. Here, follow me," said I, leading him up the narrow stairs, "here is a room where you should be safe," and I put him

SIR LUDAR

into the chamber that was once the maiden's. "Presently I will return. Meanwhile give yourself to guessing who once called this little room hers."

Then I went down drowsily, and admitted my master.

"Humphrey," said he, "the stuff is safely removed to Moulsey; but without type we can do nothing. As it is, I must take what we have here till I can get more. I have no one I can send but you. Once again, are you willing to go? or must I lose a 'prentice and Jeannette a husband?"

While he spoke, a thought had flashed on me, and, presently I replied, humbly enough:

"Master, I am bound to obey you. When you asked me a week since, I answered you like a fool. I have thought better of it, and if you will yet trust me, I am ready to start to-night."

At that he gripped my hand, and said he knew I was a good lad all along, and was content to forgive me. And he told me what grief my disobedience had caused him and my mistress, and read me a long sermon on the sinfulness of my course.

"As to thy voyage," said he, "I hear there sails a ship from the pool for Rochelle to-morrow at dawn. Make ready to start, therefore, and meanwhile I will write you your letters for my kinsfolk there."

It seemed he would stay all day; and presently he sent me a message to a stationer on Ludgate Hill, which I must needs take, and so leave him and Ludar alone in the house.

While out, I got a great fright. For the watch were abroad in search of the notable villain who had late escaped from her Majesty's Tower, and who was reported to have been seen lurking in the disguise of a carter, not many days since, near Newgate. And it was said, I heard, that he had been seen even later than that—to wit, yesterday—at Smithfield, where he had suddenly left his cart and disappeared. And some said it was known he had a confederate in the city, who was giving him shelter, and of whose name the watch had a pretty shrewd guess. Whereupon, ill at ease, I said, "Pray Heaven they may find both the rogues," and so hastened back as fast as my legs would carry me to Temple Bar.

There I found my master ready to leave.

HUE AND CRY

"Here are the letters," said he, "and money. While you are gone I must hire a man to see to the printing here, since my duties will take me elsewhere. Should aught befal me, Humphrey, you must keep the work going for the sake of your mistress and the children. For it is like enough my head is none too safe on my shoulders, or if it is, it may chance I must hold it up a while across the seas. My lad, God hath chosen you to assist in a mighty work, which, whether it succeed or fail, will be a thing to pride in some day hence. Farewell, my son, see you get good type for the money, and bring it quickly. So, Heaven speed you."

When he was gone I went up and found Ludar mad with hunger and impatience.

"What news?" said he, "and speak not to me unless it be to say, dinner is served."

He looked pale and harassed, and I think, although the little room had a bed and a chair, he had stood upright in it all day, touching nothing.

But when I had him down to dinner, he touched a good deal, and told me, in explanation, that the meal I gave him last night had been the first for three days, and that, then, he was too eager for news to take all he might.

When I told him of the hue and cry, and how near the watch was on the scent, he turned to me and said:

"Where shall we go, Humphrey?"

Which meant, that wherever he went, he counted on me to follow. So I told him of my errand to Rochelle, and of the *Miséricorde*, which lay below the Bridge. Then his face brightened.

"That is well," said he. "It matters not whether we go to France or the Pole, so I breathe some freer air than this of England. Let us start now. We must not go together. I will take the wherry while you go by land."

"First," said I, "put on this cast-off suit of mine, which I thought to give away to a beggar man, once; but thank Heaven I did not."

"You give it to a beggar now," said he, "and I thank you, Humphrey, for a gift I never expected to take from you."

Then we hid the dead carter's clothes in the river; and, not long after, a skiff put out from shore with a big 'prentice lad in it, who rowed lazily Bridgewards.

SIR LUDAR

I stood watching him, when, suddenly, the outer door opened, and a company of the watch trooped in.

"Good e'en to you, Master Dexter," said the leader of them, whose head I had once chanced to break, and who had been monstrous civil to me ever since. "We must search this house, by your leave."

"What for?" I asked.

"For villains and lurchers," said he, "and if you keep any such in hiding, you had best speak and save trouble."

"Wert thou not on a good service," said I, blustering, "I would knock some of your heads together for supposing I harboured villains. The only villains in this place are some of you, sirs. What do you take me for?"

"Nevertheless," said the leader, "we must look round. And, if there be naught to find, there is naught for thee to fear, Master Humphrey."

"You must bring twice your number before I shake in my shoes at you," said I. "Come, look where you will, and, when you have found them, I pray you let me have a sight of the rogues." And I went on with my printing.

Of course they found naught. But I, as I stood at the press, could see from the window far down the river a boat lolling on the stream, and thanked Heaven all this had not fallen an hour earlier.

They searched upstairs and downstairs, in the wet cellar, and in the maiden's chamber. They peeped in the cupboards, and up the chimneys, and put their heads out on the roof. Then, when they were satisfied, I asked would they like to spy in my pockets, whereat they departed somewhat ruffled, and left me to breathe again.

Late that night I stood on board the *Miséricorde*. The captain was on the look out for me.

"By your leave," said he, "you be none too early, comrade. Your fellow 'prentice"—here he gave me a knowing look—"hath been here this hour, and is in his berth."

So I went below, and there lay Ludar sound asleep in a hammock, in the very cabin where he and I had lain once before.

About midnight I could hear the grinding of the anchor chain at the bows, which was music to my ears, as was the heavy trampling on deck, and the shouting, and the

THE FREE OCEAN

dabbling of the water at the ports. Amidst it all, I too fell asleep; and when I woke and stood next day on deck, I could see on our right the sullen forts on the Medway, and, behind, the long, low, green line of the Essex mud banks.

Ludar was there before me, pacing restlessly with troubled brow. The joy of his freedom had vanished before the sad memories which crowded the ship.

"Humphrey," said he, presently, "when and where is all this to end? How does it bring us nearer to our heart's desires?"

"Indeed," said I, with a sigh, "'tis a long way round. Yet, patience; the farther East the nearer West."

He looked at me, as much as to say he knew I was not such a fool as my words showed me.

"And after Rochelle," said he, "what then?"

"Time enough when we are there," said I.

Time enough, indeed!

CHAPTER XXIV

How the Invincible Armada came into British Waters

WE had scarce got our head round the South Foreland, when there met us a gale of wind, such as boded ill enough for our quick voyage to Rochelle. June as it was, it was as cold as March, and along with the rain came sleet and hail, which tempted us to wonder if winter were not suddenly come instead of summer.

I feared good man Petrie, the captain, would run for shelter into Dover or some English port where (who knows ?) Ludar might be seen and taken. But instead of that he stood out stoutly for the French coast, and after a week's battle with the waves put in, battered and leaking, at Dieppe. There we waited some two weeks, mending our cracks, and hoping for a change of weather. But the gale roared on, defying us to get our nose out of port, and sending in on us wrecks and castaways which promised us a hot welcome from the open channel.

But after about two weeks the wind slackened and shifted a point from the seaward. So, although the waves still ran high, we put out, and with short sail laboured towards Cherbourg.

This storm suited Ludar's humour, and while all of us whistled for fair weather, his spirits rose as he turned his face to windward, and watched the good ship stagger through the waves. Of his own accord he volunteered to help among the seamen, and ordered me to do the same. And the captain was very glad of the aid ; for it was all the crew could do to keep the *Miséricorde* taut and straight in her course.

When we came off Cherbourg we resolved to lose no more time by putting in ; and finding our timbers sound and our canvas well in the wind, we stood out for Ushant.

THE *MISÉRICORDE'S* LAST PLUNGE

But Master Petrie repented, a day out, that he had been so hardy. For the nearer we struggled to the open ocean, the greater grew the seas, which presently broke across our bows with a force that made every timber creak, and laid us over almost on our beam-ends. It was soon more than we could do to carry any but a reefed foresail; and all day long some of us were hard at work at the pumps.

How long we laboured thus I can hardly say. It must have been three weeks or more before we breasted Ushant; and by that time the water was gaining on us in the hold, and our victuals had fallen short. Whether we liked it or not, we must try to make Brest, and Heaven would need to work a miracle on our behalf if we were to do that.

Our captain, brave man as he was, lost courage when he found the water coming higher in the hold, and saw the *Miséricorde* labour harder with every new wave and ship more water each time than the last. As for the men, they gave up the labour at the pumps in despair, and took to what liquor they could find to drown their terrors.

But Ludar alone never lost heart or head. He took charge of the deserted helm, and bade the seamen cut away spars and throw over cargo. And they obeyed him, as they would their captain, and plucked up a little spirit at sight of his courage.

"Humphrey," said he, on a night when, although the gale was slackening fast, it was plain, even to him, the end of this voyage was near, "your master will need to wait for his type. Come and stand by me here, for there is nothing else to be done for the brave ship now. I would have liked to save her for the sake of one who once stood at this very helm. But it seems to me we are near our last plunge."

"Perhaps," said I, "God has not done with us yet, and those who pray for us pray not in vain."

Here the *Miséricorde* reeled upwards on a huge wave. For a moment she hung quivering on the top, and then plunged into the trough.

I felt Ludar's hand on my arm, and caught sight of his face, steady and stern, with a flash in his eyes as he looked ahead. He was right. It was the *Miséricorde's* last plunge; for, instead of righting herself, she seemed entangled in the water, and, like one who writhes to get free, heeled half over on her side. Then, before she could recover, up came the next wave,

SIR LUDAR

towering high over our heads, and fell like a mountain upon us.

The next thing I was aware of was that I was clinging to a spar in the water, with a strong arm around me, and a voice in my ear:

"Hold on, hold on!"

Then, when I opened my eyes, I saw Ludar and some floating timbers, and nothing more.

But towards one of these timbers he was striking out desperately, which proved to be a small boat, bottom uppermost, which had lain on the deck, and which having been wrenched from its cords, had floated free of the wreck. Between us we reached it, and, with much labour, turned it over. It had neither oars nor sail. Yet, as we clung to it, we could see it was sound of bottom, and would at least hold the two of us.

How we got in, I know not; yet, I think, between two waves, Ludar steadied it while I got in, and then between the next two, I hauled him in. At first, it seemed, in this cockleshell, we were little better off than clinging to the spar, for every wave threatened to swamp it. Yet by God's mercy it carried us somehow.

Not a sign could we see of any of our late shipmates. Only once, a body, clutching at a board, even in death, crossed us. And when we reached out and hauled it to, it was one of the sailors, not drowned, but with his skull broken.

Presently, as I said, the waves grew less, and drifted us we knew not whither, save that it was far from where we had gone down, with no land or sun in view, nothing but a howling waste of waves, and we two at its mercy.

Ludar and I looked at one another grimly. It was no time for talking or wondering what next. For nearly two days we had not tasted food or moistened our lips; and here we were, perhaps a week or a month from land, in a bare boat on a hungry sea. Might we not as well have gone down with the *Miséricorde*?

The daylight went, and presently it was too dark even to see my comrade across the little boat. The last I saw of him he had closed his eyes, and seemed to be composing himself for sleep. But I guessed it was the sleep, not of weariness, but of hunger. The night went on; and presently I could hear him

A TERRIBLE NIGHT

mutter in his sleep. He fancied himself still in the Tower with his warder, whom he charged with messages to me and the maiden. And sometimes he was in the presence of the Scotch Queen, and sometimes in Dunluce with his father. It was all a fevered jumble of talk, which made the night seem weird and horrible to me, and full of dread for the day that was to come.

When it dawned, which it did early, the sea was tumbling wearily, shrouded in a thick mist, which chilled me where I sat, and blotted out everything beyond a little space around the boat. Ludar by this time was awake, but still wandering in his mind with hunger and fever; while I, after my sleepless night, felt my eyelids grow heavy.

How long I slept I know not; but I know I dreamt I was at the foot of the great rock of Dunluce, and looking up could just spy a light on the battlements, and hear a gun and the shout of battle on the top; when suddenly I woke and found it was more than a dream.

High above my head in the mist there loomed a light, and from beyond it there sounded the tolling of a bell, and, as I thought, a clash of arms. I looked across at Ludar, and saw him, too, looking up, but too weak to speak or move. Then the light seemed to plunge downwards, towards us, showing us a huge black outline of a ship, within a few yards of where we drifted.

Instantly I sprang to my feet and shouted, and called to Ludar to do the same. For a moment it seemed we were unheeded. The light swung once more upwards, and after it the great ship, carrying a swirl of water with it, and throwing off a whirlpool of little eddies, in which our boat spun and shook like a leaf in a torrent. Again we shouted, frantically. And then it seemed the bell ceased tolling, and instead there came a call; after that something sharp struck me on the cheek, and flinging up my hand I caught a cord, and felt the boat's keel grind sharply against the side of the great ship.

What I next remember was standing bewildered on the deck, amidst a crowd of soldiers, many of whom wore bright steel armour, and who exercised on the heaving planks wellnigh as steadily as on dry ground. The deck was ablaze with pennons and scutcheons. Somewhere near, the noise of trumpets rose above the roar of the waves. The sun, as it struggled through the mist, flashed on the brass of guns, and

SIR LUDAR

the jewels of sword-hilts. The poop behind rose like a stately house, illumined with its swinging lanthorns. Now and again there flitted past me a long-robed priest, to whom all bowed, and after him boys with swaying censers. There was a neighing of horses amidships, and a tolling of bells in the forecastle. The great bellying sails glittered with painted dragons and eagles and sun-bursts. And the men who lined the crosstrees and crowded the tops shouted and answered in a tongue that was new to me. Above all, higher than the helmsman's house or the standard on the poop, shone out a gilded cross, which looked over all the ship.

Little wonder if, as I slowly looked round me and rubbed my eyes, I knew not where I was.

But Ludar, standing near me, steadying himself with the cordage, called me to myself.

"This must be a Spaniard," said he, faintly.

"A Spaniard!" gasped I, "an enemy to our Queen and——"

"Look yonder," said he, stopping me and pointing seaward, where the mist was lifting apace.

There I could discern, as far as my eyes could reach, a great curved line of vessels, many of them like that on which I stood; some larger and grander, some smaller and propelled by oars; all with flags flying and signals waving, and their course pointed all one way.

Not even I, landsman as I was, could mistake what I saw. This could be naught else but the great fleet of the Spanish King, of whose coming we had heard rumours for a year past, but in which I for one had not really believed till thus suddenly I found myself standing on the deck of one of its greatest galleons.

In the horror of the discovery, my first impulse was to fling myself back into the waves from which I had been saved; my second was to seize my sword and fly at the first man I saw, and so die for my country then and there.

But, alas! I was too weak to do either. When I took a step it was to fall in a heap on the deck, faint with hunger, wrath, and shame.

When I came to, I lay in a dark cabin, and Ludar, scarcely less pallid than I, sat beside me.

"Come on deck," said he, "this place is stifling. If the

SPANIARDS!

Dons mean to make an end of us, they may as well do it at once."

So, bracing himself up to lend me an arm, he made for the deck.

A sentinel stood at the gangway, whom Ludar, brushing past, bade, in round English, give us food, and lead us to the captain.

The man stared in surprise, and muttered something in Spanish, which, as luck would have it, Ludar, mindful of his smattering of Spanish, learned at Oxford, understood to mean we were to remain below.

Whereupon he pulled me forward, and defied the fellow to put us back.

We might possibly have been run through then and there, had not a soldier, who had overheard our parley, come up.

" Are you English ? " said he, in our own tongue.

" My comrade is English, I am Irish," said Ludar, " and unless we have food forthwith, we are not even that."

" I am an Irishman myself," said the soldier, who, by his trappings, was an officer, " therefore come and have some food."

I know I felt then hard put to it, whether, despite my famine, I could eat food in such a place and from such hands. But I persuaded myself, if I was to die so soon, I might as well meet death with a full stomach as an empty.

While we ate, the Irishman questioned Ludar as to his name and the part of Ireland he lived in. He himself was the son of a southern chief—one Desmond ; and, after living some years in Spain, was now attached to the enemy's forces. He was close enough as to the movements of the fleet, and so soon as he had seen us fed, he bade us come with him to the Don.

The deck was as crowded as Fleet Street, and, as we passed to the poop, very few of these gay Spaniards took the trouble to look after us, or wonder how we came there. Only, when Ludar, as we reached the commander's door, suddenly took his sword and flung it out to sea, did a few of them stare. I followed my comrade's example. The sea had as much right to my weapon as a Spaniard, and I was thankful to see that Ludar, in this respect, was of the same mind with me.

In the cabin was a tall, elderly, slightly built man, clad in a fine black steel breastplate, with a crested helmet on the table before him. He stood bending over a chart, which several of

SIR LUDAR

his officers were also examining ; and as he looked quickly up at our entry, I was surprised at the fairness of his complexion and the grave mildness of his demeanour.

Our Irish guide briefly explained who we were and how we came on board. Don Alonzo—for that was his name—eyed us keenly ; and addressing Ludar, said in a broken English :

" You are Irish. Your name ? "

" Ludar M'Sorley M'Donnell of Dunluce and the Glynns," said Ludar.

The commander said something to one of his officers, who presently laid a map of Ireland on the table, and placed his finger on the spot where Dunluce was situated.

" Señor has no sword. Your calling ? "

" My sword is in the sea. It belonged to my father, my mistress, and myself," said Ludar, shortly.

The Spaniard inclined his head, with a faint smile.

" His Majesty is unfortunate not to be a fourth in so honourable a company," said he.

Ludar looked confused, and his brow clouded. He was no match for any man when it came to compliments.

" Sir," said he, " I am indebted to your watch for my life, and to his Majesty, your King, for my dinner. I am sorry it is so, but I cannot help it. If you command it, I am bound to make payment ; and, since I have no money, you have a right to the service of my hands till we be quits."

Don Alonzo looked him from head to foot and smiled again.

" Sir Ludar is his Majesty's guest on this ship," said he, with a fine motion of the head. " Any service he may render I shall be honoured to accept. I refer him to Captain Desmond, here, for further intelligence."

" And you, Señor," said he, addressing me with somewhat less ceremony, " you are English ? "

" I thank Heaven, yea," said I, " a humble servant to her Majesty Queen Elizabeth, and a foe to her enemies."

" And your estate ? " demanded he, coldly ignoring my tone.

" I have no estate. I am a plain London 'prentice."

" We shall have the honour of restoring you to London shortly," said he. " Meanwhile Sir Ludar shall not be deprived of the service of his squire."

Then turning to his officers, he occupied himself again

CAPTAIN DESMOND

with the chart, and left Captain Desmond to conduct us from the cabin.

Neither Ludar nor I was much elated by this interview, but it relieved us, at least, of any immediate prospect of execution, and, unless the Don were jesting, consigned us to no very intolerable service on board his ship. From Captain Desmond, who was not a little impressed by the commander's reception of Ludar, we learned rather more of the expedition and its prospects than before.

"If all go well," said he, "we shall be in English waters to-morrow, and a week later should have dealt with the enemy's fleet and be landed at Dover. This Don Alonzo, it is said, will be appointed governor of London, till the King arrive. He is a prime favourite at the Spanish Court, in proof whereof the *Rata* carries a crew of the noblest youth of Spain, committed to his care for this great venture. They are hungry for battle, but, alack! I fear we shall none of us get more than will whet our appetite. As for you and me, M'Donnell, this business is like to settle scores between our houses and the vixen—— "

"Stay, Captain Desmond," said Ludar, interposing suddenly betwixt me and this blasphemer. "My comrade here is a servant of Elizabeth, and has no sword. As for me, my queen is dead—dead on the scaffold. I hate the English Queen as you do; but, if I fight against her, it shall be in my own quarrel, and no man else's. Therefore appoint us a duty whereby we may repay the Spanish King his hospitality, without fighting his battles."

The Irishman shrugged his shoulders.

"I understand not these subtleties," said he: "whom I hate I slay. However, as you will. This voyage will soon be over; but if you choose, while it lasts, to keep the forecastle deck clean, none shall interfere with you; and perchance, when we get into action, you may find it an honourable and even a perilous post."

So we were installed in our ignoble office on board the *Rata*, and since Captain Desmond's duties never brought him before the foremast, and since Don Alonzo, whenever he went his rounds, never looked at us, and since not a man on the forecastle comprehended a word of English, or could speak a Spanish which Ludar was able to follow, we were left pretty much to ourselves, except that the sentry kept a close eye on our movements.

All day long the soldiers paraded, the trumpets played, the pennons waved, and the blazoned sails swelled with the favouring breeze, so that towards afternoon Ushant was far behind, and every eye was strained forward for the first glimpse of the English shore. The other vessels of the fleet, which had spread out somewhat in the mist, now gradually closed in at nearer distance, and passed signals which I could not understand. Some were so near we could hear their trumpets and bells, and see the glitter of the sun on the muzzles of their guns. Then about sundown, with great ceremony, a priest came forward, and recited what I took to be a mass; and after him, at the sound of three bells, the whole company trooped to the middle deck, where at the main-mast the purser read aloud a long proclamation in Spanish, at the end of which huzzahs were given for the King, and the lanthorns lit for the night.

I confess I turned in to my berth that night uneasy in my mind. For I never saw ships such as these; no, not even in the Medway. What could our small craft do against these floating towers? and what sort of hole could our guns make in these four-foot walls? And when it came to grappling, what could our slender crews do against this army of picked men, who, even if half of them fell, would yet be a match for any force our English ships could hold?

So I turned in with many forbodings, and all night long I could hear the laugh and song of coming victory, mingled now and again with the fanfar of the trumpets, and the distant boom of the admiral's signal-gun.

Next morning, when we looked out, there was land in sight ahead.

CHAPTER XXV

How the Dons sailed up Channel

FOR a long while we could discern only a blue haze on the horizon. Then, towards noon, when the sun stood higher, and the wind behind us freshened, there appeared a grey line through the mist, and above that a gleam of green.

The sight was hailed by the gay young Spaniards who crowded the deck with a mighty shout and a defiant blare of the trumpets. And, ere the noise died away, we caught a faint answering echo from the vessels nearest us. Then, acting on some arranged signal, the whole fleet seemed to gather itself together, and closing into a great crescent, at about cable distance, advanced with sails full of wind—a majestic sight, and, to me, who gazed with dismay from end to end of the magnificent line, fraught with doom to my poor country.

The *Rata* held a post near to the left of the line, and was thus a league, or thereabouts, nearer to the coast than the ships of the other flank. Already out of the mist the black headlands were rising grim and frowning to front us; and already, betwixt us and them, a keen eye might detect the gleam of the afternoon sun on a little white sail here and there. But except for a fishing-boat or two which cruised along our line, taking a good eyeful of us, and then darting ahead before the galleasses could give chase, we saw no sign of the Queen's ships anywhere.

Towards dusk we opened a great break in the coast, which we knew presently to be Plymouth Sound. The Dons, as they stood fully armed on the decks and gangways, laughed at the sight, and all eyes turned to the Duke-Admiral's vessel ahead, to see if he would sail straight in on the unprotected

SIR LUDAR

Sound, and so take possession of the coveted land before supper that night. It looked at first as if this were his purpose, when suddenly there was a stir among the onlookers, and Ludar, taking my arm, pointed down the coast to our rear, where, from behind a high headland, peeped out a small cluster of sails.

"There are your ships," said he, "lying in wait, and with the wind of the Don, too."

My heart lept up at the words. For till now I had supposed our poor fellows cooped up by the wind in Plymouth Water, unable to get out and waiting like sheep for the slaughter. I was tempted to cheer in the Spaniard's face, when I saw them thus clear, on the right side of the wind, and ready to show fight for their Queen and country.

The sails were seen by other eyes than ours; and presently up flung a light from the Duke's ship; and with that we hove to, and dropped anchor where we lay for the night.

Great was the discontent of the grandees on the *Rata* to be thus put about by the sight of a parcel of herring-boats—as they chose to call them. But it came as a little comfort to them when a message went round for the men to be under arms and ready for battle at daybreak. And with a proud laugh they went off to their quarters for the night. As for Ludar and me, we sat on the forecastle with our eyes straining westward, and full of a strange excitement.

"Humphrey," said Ludar, "if it be any comfort to you, I like not these Dons."

"I thank God to hear that," said I.

"And if it come to a fight," said he, "I had as soon see your pirates yonder sweep the sea as these milords. They did little enough for my Queen while she lived, and they cannot bring her back now she is dead."

"Think you we shall come to blows in the morning?" asked I, anxious to hurry off the sore subject.

"'Tis said so," replied he. "It would not surprise me if yonder sea-dogs did not wait till then."

After that we sat and watched the beacon-fires ashore blaze up one after another and spread the news of our coming far and wide. Presently, too, the moon came up, and by its light looking westward we could discern sails to windward, which fluttered nearer and nearer, till it seemed

MERRY SPORT FOR THE ENGLISH

a shot from one of our pieces could reach them. The news brought many of the *Rata's* men on deck, some of whom doubted what to make of it all, and others cursed the impudence of this English Drake and his low-born salts.

But at daybreak, when we looked out, there hovered some threescore or more English craft, drawn up in an irregular line from south to north, looking at us. Foremost sailed their great flagship called the *Ark Raleigh*, so near that I could plainly discern the royal cross of St. George at the poop. Compared with the mighty *Rata* she was a small craft, yet, beside the light, low ships that followed her, she towered aloft like a castle, and looked the only ship of all that fleet could stand a quarter of an hour of our ordnance.

While we looked, there came a dull boom from the Spaniard who lay nearest her. We could see the shot, pitched high, plough up the water some twenty yards short. And then—as I thought, rather foolishly—we sat glaring across at one another in the still air, waiting for a breeze.

It came at last, freshly from westward.

We could see the English catch it, and come along with it before ever it filled out our great sails. Nay, when it did reach us, there was not enough to give us way. I marvelled to see how like a log the *Rata* lay, while the lively Englishmen slipped through the water.

Then followed the strangest beginning to this great sea-fight.

For the *Ark* and one or two others, having run in towards the end of our line (which lay as near as possible west and east, looking into Plymouth), suddenly put into the wind and ran jauntily down our rear, putting a broadside into each of the Dons as she went by, us included. Nor was that all. When she reached the end of the line, and everyone looked to see her sheer off out of reach, she gaily wore round and came back the way she had gone, giving each Spaniard her other broadside on the road, her consorts behind following suit.

I think I never saw any men so taken aback as were the Spaniards by this performance. For the *Rata* and the rest of them lay almost helpless in the light wind, while these light-timbered Englishmen darted hither and thither at pleasure, almost as fast in the eye of the wind as down it.

SIR LUDAR

The surprise at first was so great that the *Ark* was halfway down the line before any attempt was made to close with her and stop her. But she waited on no man, and even when one great galleon, with a mighty effort, swung round to face her, she swerved not a fathom out of her course, but let off two broadsides instead of one to help the presuming Don back again into his post.

Loud and bitter was the wrath among the noble youths on the *Rata*, as they saw the Invincible Armada of Spain thus flouted by a handful of Englishmen. Bitterer still was the rage of the sailors, when, by no manner of luffing and trimming of sail, could they stand out to chastise these impudent cruisers. But when, after (as I have said) careering down the line, the English admiral put about and came back, the wind freshened and lent some little life to our great hulls, one or two got round far enough to let fly with their culverins and great pieces. But their shot, if it reached the Englishman at all, whizzed over his head and never stopped his course.

Don Alonzo, however, having rather better wind than his unlucky comrades, decided on a bolder stroke to punish the enemy. Ludar and I, as we stood and watched, could see the troops paraded on deck, and grappling irons and chains laid in readiness. The small arms were loaded, and every man stood with his naked knife in his belt.

"He means to come to close quarters and board her," said I.

Ludar laughed. His sportsman's blood was up; and for the first time for many a day the care had vanished from his face, and left there a glow of sheer enjoyment.

"A cow might as well try to board a cat," said he.

And he was right. For as the *Ark* bore down our way, blazing out at every galleon she passed, Don Alonzo, dropping clear of the line, put his nose in her course, and, so to say, bade her stand and answer him.

Then, for the first time that day, the *Ark* swerved on her tack and put out her nose too, so that presently we two lay well astern of the line, closing in on one another's course. Then there was great joy on board the *Rata*. The noble youths shook their lovelocks and gripped their swords. The gunners lay with their eyes on the captain, waiting his signal to fire; and the men on the tops and in the rigging got ready their

A SURPRISE FOR DON ALONZO

grappling tackle, and held their cutlasses betwixt their teeth, ready for a spring.

Ludar and I on the forecastle watched the *Ark*, as, half in the wind, she bore down our way. Her decks, like ours, were cleared for action, and above the gunwales we could spy many a bare head peeping over at us. I marvelled that she had not long since given us a shot ; but, like the Spaniard, she seemed bent on close quarters, and was saving up for a hand-to-hand fight.

So, at least, we and all who watched them thought : when suddenly, scarce a cable's length away, she put about full in the wind, and letting fly at us with every shot in her broadside, slipped gaily under our helm, on her way to regain the course she had left, and finish her career down the line of the Dons. Don Alonzo was so taken by surprise, and unready for this sudden move, that he had not a word to say. His broadside, when it went off, fell wide of the mark in the open sea, at the very moment when the English shot rang about his stern, riddling his sails, and knocking the gilded cross in shivers by the board. Nor did they give us shot only, for a cloud of cloth-yard arrows whistled through the rigging, picking off a dozen or so of the men perched there, and grazing the polished breastplates of not a few of the bewildered grandees on the quarter-deck.

Never shall I forget the howl of Spanish curses which greeted this misadventure. The grandees swore at the sailors, and bade them put about and give chase ; the sailors swore at the grandees, and bade them come and try to turn the ship quicker than they, if they knew how. The gunners blamed the captain for holding them back, and the captain blamed men and crew alike for behaving like spoiled children, and forgetting their honour and dignity. As for Ludar, he was so tickled by the whole business that he laughed outright, and I had much ado to sober him in the presence of the angry foreigners.

But presently a message came for hands to go aft and look to the damage done to the stern ; and we, partly from curiosity, partly from duty, went with them.

'Twas sad to see how the stately poop was battered about. Windows were knocked in, flags tumbled, guns unmounted, and, as I said, the great cross shot in pieces ; while all around

SIR LUDAR

lay bodies of men dead or wounded. I think what troubled the Dons almost as much as the better sailing of the English was to find that these thick wooden walls of theirs were no proof against the enemy's shot, which crashed through the stout timbers, sometimes letting daylight in, and here and there leaving us plenty of work to do to make them good against the inroad of the water.

By the time the *Rata* had put back into line, the *Ark* and her consorts had ended their merry jaunt by tumbling over the mizzen-mast of the Vice-Admiral's ship. And the other English ships having by this time come up, showing their teeth, the Duke sent up a signal to give Plymouth the go-by and sail up Channel. Which was done in a very chapfallen manner; and the great Armada, huddled together, and standing not on the order of its going, turned its heads into the wind, and struggled eastward, the *Rata* being near the rear of the procession.

The Englishmen hung doggedly on our heels; now and then coming up within shot, and then, having let off their broadsides, dropping away before we could put round to engage them. Never once did they come to close quarters, much as the Spaniard longed for it; and never once did they give him time to try conclusions on equal terms.

The rest of that day Ludar and I were so busy at our carpenters' work abaft that we had no clear view of what passed. We heard dropping shot now and then, and now and again a bolt thundered on to our own hull and buried itself deep in our timbers; while, once, a terrible blaze ahead, followed by a rumbling which set the *Rata* shivering in all her planks, told us of disaster and explosion somewhere near among the Spaniards themselves. What it all meant we could only guess. For the night came on us roughly, and, as darkness closed, it was all our helmsman could do, with a sharp look-out, to give his fellow ships a wide berth, without going out of his course to look after them.

As soon as ever it was dark, Ludar and I and some dozen others were ordered over the stern in baskets to patch up the holes made by the English shot, and repair the insulted gilding of his Majesty of Spain. No light work it was; suspended betwixt wind and water, groping with lanthorns at our work, rearing and plunging with the waves, and every

ALMOST QUITS

now and then hearing the boom of a gun behind, which made us wince and wonder whose head was wanted next. Once I thought it was mine; for a great crashing shot came past me out of the darkness, spinning my basket round like a top, and lodging fair in the hole I was mending. Scarce had I time to thank God for my escape, when the man next me uttered a cry and flung up his arms; and there he hung a moment, pinned to the stern by a cloth-yard arrow which pierced his back, before he tumbled over, a dead man, into the sea. One after another of our comrades dropped, till at last it seemed to me Ludar and I alone were left.

"Humphrey," he said, when at last we stood on deck, "I reckon we be almost quits with the King of Spain by now."

"Aye indeed," said I, "and I think further that they who dream of us far away need not despair. For assuredly Heaven wants something more of us before we go under; else we had not been standing here."

But whatever Heaven wanted of us, the ship's master angrily ordered us off to the forecastle, to look to the tackle of the bowsprit. This, but for the plunging of the vessel, was safe work compared with our labour on the poop; for here we were clear of the enemy's shot. But Ludar and I were clumsy with the tackle, not being seamen born; and on that account a trouble arose. For the fellow who overlooked our work chose not only to swear at us by all the saints in the Spaniards' calendar (to which he was welcome), but he pulled out a whip from under his coat and gave Ludar a crack with it, which laid open his cheek-bone, and well-nigh sent him backwards by the board.

Whereupon Ludar, seizing the whip with one hand and the fellow with the other, gave him such a lashing, as the wretch, may be, wished he could give to any man himself; and when he had done that, he threw the whip overboard. But the fellow's howls and yells (for he had a great voice) soon brought a parcel of his mates around him, who, seeing him wallowing on the ground and pointing at Ludar and me, asked no questions, but set on us, with oaths and Spanish cries of " English curs ! "

So we too had a pretty time of it, and, but that we got our backs against a bulk-head and had our splicing tackle

SIR LUDAR

in our hands, we might have seen no more of that great sea-battle. We fought for our lives for five minutes or so, and then, so great became the uproar, that up came some of the soldiers and an officer, who, seeing two men set upon by twenty, ordered every man to stand.

The officer, as fortune would have it, was our old acquaintance Captain Desmond, who demanded what the noise was all about.

Whereupon the fellow whom Ludar had flogged hobbled up in a white heat, and proclaimed his wrongs to heaven and earth, accusing us of being on the *Rata* for treasonable purposes, and vowing, even, he had heard us plot to get at the powder and blow up the ship.

Before we could say a word up came a messenger from the Don himself, who, on hearing the story, ordered us to accompany him forthwith to his Excellency.

I could not help observing, as we marched abaft, the gloom which seemed to have fallen on the ship. Not that the gay young lordlings did not still swagger and laugh; but it seemed to me their mirth was more hollow than it had been, and, when now and again a sullen shot out of the darkness behind whizzed through the rigging or rattled on the hull, they ground their teeth angrily and swore in their grand Spanish style at the fate that kept them beyond arms' length of the foe.

Don Alonzo stood on the quarter-deck, gazing earnestly in the direction of his admiral's lanthorns, and between whiles discussing some grave matter with the lieutenants.

We stood a long time before he had leisure to attend to us. Then he beckoned to the officer to bring us forward. When he saw who we were, he knitted his brows and demanded to know the cause of the uproar in the forecastle.

Whereupon Ludar, his face still streaming with blood, saluted and said:

"Master Don, yonder is one of your lads" (pointing to the smarting Spaniard) "who has mistaken a guest of his Majesty your King for one of his own galley slaves, and struck me. I have chastised him, as he deserves, and thrown his whip overboard. If that be a crime in your country, I pray you hang me at once; for I shall not promise not to do the same thing again to-morrow if he touches me. As

A COURT MARTIAL

for my comrade here, he has done naught but help me defend myself from a score of your brave fellows who thought it not unworthy of their honour to set on us two."

"That I so offended," broke in I, rather foolishly, "is the fault of my being an Englishman, not a Spaniard, Sir Don."

Then the fellow whom Ludar had flogged suddenly found words and broke out in a torrent of rage with his accusations, which grew as he went on, and bade fair—had he but had breath to make an end of them—to picture us as very fiends.

'Twas a fine sight, by the glare of the swinging lanthorns, to see Don Alonzo stand there, calm and grave, with the admirable curl of his lips deepening as the fellow raved himself out.

When the story was done, he turned shortly on him and said something in Spanish, which sent the wretch slinking off with his tail between his legs—a pitiful object to behold, but for the scowl of hate he bestowed on Ludar and me in passing.

"As for you, Señor printer," said Don Alonzo, turning contemptuously to me, "you shall not make me believe all Englishmen are boors. I commend the top of the mainmast to Señor as a spot of Spanish territory where he may learn better manners. Sir Ludar,"—and he turned to Ludar before I could say a word, his bearing changing to that of a gentleman who speaks to a gentleman—"I desire a letter of import to reach the Duke Admiral by an honourable hand. Will you take the cock-boat and deliver it?"

This sudden compliment—for it was nothing short—staggered Ludar for a moment, and he looked quickly up to see if the Don were not trifling with him. But Don Alonzo was grave and serious.

So Ludar said, shortly:

"I will"; and the interview ended.

It went sorely against my stomach then to have to mount to my perch in the main-tops, and I felt a little hurt that Ludar had put in never a word on my behalf. I remember reflecting, as I slowly scrambled to my penance, how strange it was that for so small a difference of demeanour I should be sent aloft, while Ludar was appointed to a task of honour. But I understood not Spaniards—thank Heaven!—nor did I know much about gentlemen.

SIR LUDAR

At the foot of the mast Ludar came up.

"I am sorry for you, Humphrey," said he. "Yet you are like to get a better view of the fight than most. I shall see you soon again if the waves are kind to me, and the Englishman's shot falls wide."

"Think you not, he means you to escape and get clear?" said I. "Would I were with you!"

"Humphrey, you were ever a fool," said he, gravely. "Expect me back soon, and if I come not, 'twill not be my fault or yours. Get aloft, comrade, and keep a good lookout."

So I went up very sadly. And presently from my high perch I heard the running of a cord and the splash of oars. and saw, on the pale water below me, a black shadow glide out from the ship's side, and lose itself in the darkness

CHAPTER XXVI

How Ludar brought back the Duke's Letter

IT may have been near midnight on that Sunday night when I went aloft to the main-tops. The sea was still running high, and it was all I could do, in the drizzling rain and wild wind, to hold on to my perch. Now and then a wild gull, terrified by the invasion of its peace, whirled past me, and shrieked away seaward. Once, with a swish and dull boom behind it, a shot passed below me ; and once or twice a quiver up the tall mast told me the *Rata's* guns were at work.

I could detect nothing in the darkness, save the twinkling of many a dim light ahead, and the glare of the ship's lanthorns on the deck below. But, amid the howling of the squall, I heard the thunder of a battle somewhere near, with now and then a loud shout and a rattling of chains, and knew that King Philip of Spain had not yet muzzled the English sea-dogs.

So the night passed, and when morning dawned, cold and grey, I was stupid with sleep, and hunger, and loneliness. The storm had died away, and the water lay sullen and still, while the sails below me flapped heavily in the wind. The *Rata* had dropped to the rear of the Armada, which spread eastward in a long irregular line, very different from the grand curve with which she had swept on Plymouth.

Behind us, some three miles away, cruised the Englishmen, looking at us ; while, betwixt us and the far distant Portland headland, I could see the vast hull of one of our own galleons (the same which had blown up in the night), surrounded by a swarm of little craft that picked her bones, like crows on a carcase. Nearer still lay a great disabled Spaniard, with bowsprit and top-masts gone, and flag struck, being towed

SIR LUDAR

by her capturers into port. As for the *Rata* herself, 'twas sad to see how dingy the gay gilding had become in one day, and how sails were riddled, tackle flying, and scutcheons toppled over.

Yet, I had but a passing glance for all these. Where was Ludar? Was he returned? Or was he in the Englishmen's hands? Or was the little cock-boat, perchance, floating somewhere bottom uppermost, and he beneath it? I scanned the waters till my eyes ached. Far ahead, miles away, I fancied I could see, towering among the other galleons, the Duke's royal standard. But, amidst these huddled ships, and water littered with many a spar and little boat, with galleys gliding here and there, signals going, with movings in and out, this way and that, who was to find a solitary man in a cock-boat?

Yet, I think, love has keener eyes than most; and so I, looking again towards where a few stout English craft, returning to their line after a cruise up Channel, cracked out their broadside on the nearest Spaniard within reach, I seemed to see between us and them something in the water which made me look twice. It may have been half-a-mile away, a speck on the water, like some floating barrel or spar. Yet, for the stillness of the water, it moved, as I thought, more than an idle log; and once, as the sun flashed out for a moment along the surface, I thought it to be a head and shoulders.

Presently I lost it, for the glare of the rising sun blotted it out like a speck on a shining mirror. I began to think it was but fancy, or, even if it be a swimmer, it could never be Ludar, who would come from the other quarter, where the Duke's ship was; when once again I saw the figure, this time near enough to know it was assuredly a man who, between each few strokes he took, waved a hand above his head.

I was down the mast in a twinkling, caring nought if I were to swing at the yard-arm within an hour, and ran wildly to the quarter-deck.

"Sir Don!" shouted I, breaking in upon him and his lieutenants, "by your leave, yonder comes Sir Ludar, swimming for his life."

The Don rounded on me with knitted brows. But I cared not.

OVERBOARD

"Put out a boat to save him, or he is lost!" I cried.

"Has your night aloft, sirrah, taught you no better manners?" said he. "Go back——"

But here, looking over towards the swimmer, I saw him throw up both arms, and heard a shout which set every vein in me tingling.

I waited not for his Donship, or anyone beside; but flung myself headlong over the tall side into the sea, and struck out with all my might for the place.

A Spanish sentinel on deck, seeing my sudden plunge, and smelling treachery and desertion in it, let fly at me with his musket, grazing my elbow, and sending me ducking a dozen yards or more, before I durst show head again above water. But I had somewhat better to think of than Spanish bullets. For a few minutes I could see nothing of the swimmer, and was beginning to fear I was too late after all, when suddenly a wave brought him close beside me.

Sure enough, it was Ludar, well-nigh spent, keeping himself up with short, breathless strokes, but unable to do more. He was alive enough to know me, and to lay his hand on my arm for support. Hard-pressed as he was, he held betwixt his teeth a paper, which I guessed to be the Duke's despatch, and which, to give him better use for his mouth, I took from him and stuck in my own collar. After that he revived, and together we paddled towards the *Rata*, which lay, with sails flapping, almost motionless in the rapidly calming sea.

The Spaniards on board seemed to have changed their minds as to myself, for, instead of the sentinel with his gun, a sailor with a rope stood waiting at the gunwale to receive us. I think, had we gone down where we were, he would hardly have troubled himself to come after us. But since we held up, and drifted within reach of his line, he honoured us by casting it our way; and so, with some hauling, we got aboard.

Ludar had partly recovered from his fatigue when he stepped once more on the deck and took the letter from my neck.

"You have done me a good turn," said he, with a glow in his face which I prized as much as all the gold pieces in the hold of the *Rata*; "you have made it possible for me to keep my parole with the Don. Thank you, Humphrey."

SIR LUDAR

Then bidding me follow, he led the way to the quarter-deck, and without a word handed his missive to the Don.

"Señor has returned by a strange way," said the commander.

"I have returned the only way open to me. His Majesty your King has lost a cock-boat."

"He has found what will compensate him—a gallant servant."

"Your pardon," said Ludar, shortly, "I am no servant of the King of Spain. I was his debtor, as was my friend. We are quits up to now. What more we accept from him, we shall be bound to repay,—no more."

The Don frowned, and then smiled, and then with a quiet gesture raised his hand to his helmet.

Accepting this salute as a dismissal, Ludar took my arm and walked away.

No more was said about me just then; but I think, after what passed, the Don, however much he disliked me, deemed it not worth his while to separate me from my comrade.

Ludar told me, what he never told the Don, that he had been captured as he returned in the cock-boat by a boat of the enemy's, belonging to the ship *Revenge*. The men of the boat, perceiving him to be of their speech, and suspecting he carried news (though he had hidden his letter in his shoe), resolved to carry him to their Captain Drake, to which he seemed to submit. But waiting till he came somewhere near where he suspected the *Rata* to lie, he had slipped overboard, and hanging quietly under the stern-sheets till they were tired of looking for him, had got off; and after beating about an hour and more, had sighted us in the dawn, and (as he confessed), but for my sight of him, might not have been there to tell the story.

Well, after that, for two days, the weather remained calm; and, as I said, the Spaniard, though now and again he had the better of the breeze, could do little with the enemy which hung doggedly on his skirts, sometimes coming near enough for a broadside, but never, as the impatient gallants on the *Rata* prayed he might do, running in to close quarters.

'Twas pitiful to hear the grinding of noble teeth on board the ship, as day by day the English Admiral plucked his Majesty's feathers one by one, yet never gave a chance of a

A WILD GOOSE CHASE

battle. Even Don Alonzo's grave, mild countenance grew heavy, and as for the sailors forward, where we were, our friend of the whip had a busy time with them to keep them from breaking into open mutiny.

So there was much comfort all round when, on the Thursday, the wind got up and gave us a chance at last of serious business. For, when we looked out at daybreak, there, scarce two gun-shots off, cruised a handful of English craft, gaily hauling after them two great Spaniards, which (so I heard) were full of stores for the fleet, and which the *Rata* had kept an eye on for many a day. How, in the night, they had got separate from the main line and so fallen into the hands of the sleepless Englishmen, I know not; but this I know, that when daylight discovered them being towed at the tail of their captors towards an English port, a cry of rage and fury went up from the *Rata*. All hands were called, guns were manned, arms were served out, and although by so doing he left the Armada without its rear-guard, the Don luffed out into the wind and gave chase.

Then followed merry sport. For no sooner were our backs turned than the main body of the English (who wished nothing better) slipped into our place, and blazed away at the Spanish line right and left, till the whole sea was white with smoke, and you might fancy the thunder of the guns would be heard in Fleet Street itself.

As for us, we had better have stayed where we were. For, while the fight went merrily on ahead, a pretty wild goose chase were we led. For we never got near enough for so much as a broadside. The store ships lay between us and the English, who cunningly used them as a shield, so that from whichever quarter we approached, there were the Dons' own vessels betwixt us and them. Besides that, we could see boats busily taking over the chief of the treasure under our very eyes; while every hour we stayed we dropped further and further astern of the main Armada, so that, had it pleased the Englishmen to spare a ship or two to look after us, I verily believe we might have been cut off for good, and towed into an English port, like these same ill-starred store ships we professed to be rescuing.

Two galeasses, that joined us in our errand, made a gallant attempt, by parting company and coming suddenly upon the enemy, one from either quarter, to compel an action. But the Englishman was ready for this. Keeping the store ships as a shield on the one side, he had a royal salute ready for the galley on the other—so smartly dealt and with such deadly aim, that the wretched slaves at the oars tumbled off their benches and rolled over like so many ninepins; and before others could take their places, a second broadside and a third swept the craft from stem to stern. The Spaniard's shot flew high and harmless, and, for every broadside he let go, the English gave him back two or three.

Thus all that morning and well into the afternoon the *Rata* hung miserably in the wind, watching the sport which the Englishman made of the King of Spain and his galleons, and never once able to get within speaking distance.

At length, amid many a bitter curse and many an angry taunt, the Don gave orders to put about, and, leaving the store ships to their fate, rejoin the fleet, where, at any rate, (now that it seemed a general fight had at last come about), there was some certain consolation in store for the fluttered grandees.

Alas! that I should live to pity her Majesty's enemies! But I did so that afternoon. For when we came upon the scene, the battle was well-nigh at an end, and the Duke Admiral's ship, sorely battered in the bows, was hanging out signals to the fleet to draw off. The sea was strewn with helpless galleons; amidst which the active English craft slipped in and out, giving a broadside here, a shot there, a flight of arrows there, yet never getting within grappling distance, or offering the Don a chance of boarding. Not a single one of their ships could I see in distress; while many a Spanish top-mast and bowsprit draggled shamefully, and many a Spanish corpse could I mark being slipped overboard.

Don Alonzo, wrathful and baffled, affected not to see his Admiral's signal, and made one brave attempt to close with the ships nearest him and so retrieve the honours of the day. But he got more than he gave. For the Englishmen suddenly slipped to the wind of him, despite all his efforts, and lying snugly on his flank, as he yawed over with the breeze, pounded him merrily betwixt wind and water, while his own shot, aimed at the sky, flew yards above the English topsails. The young nobles shouted in vain to the enemy to come

"HANDS BELOW!"

alongside if they dare, and try conclusions. The Englishman laughed back out of every port in his broadside, and bid them catch if they could. Meanwhile, to pass the time, they slid round by our stern and new-blacked the gilding there, and even hovered a few minutes to leeward to pick off a score or so of the crew on the deck with their arrows, before running back to their quarters on the other port.

How long it went on I know not. For a cry suddenly came of "Hands below!" and down we went to patch up with all our might the holes the English shot had made on the water line. And here we worked all night, amongst a swearing, savage gang, who threatened aloud to blow up the ship rather than fight any more, and wished themselves safe back in the drinking-shops of Lisbon.

When, about midnight, half-stifled with the heat, we came on deck, the *Rata* was running before the wind at the rear of the Armada, heading for the French coast; and the lanthorns of the English had dropped a league behind.

Never saw I a company so changed as were the gallants of Spain by that day's fight. They still cursed, and laughed, and shouted. But when they shook their fists it was at the lights ahead, and when they dropped, silent and downcast, their faces were turned to the lights astern.

"Humphrey," said Ludar to me, as we stood a moment looking round before we turned to go to our quarters, "I like not this business."

"Why," said I, "the Spaniard is being beaten, and he knows it. Our English sea-dogs are too many for him."

"Aye," said he, with a curl of his lip, "your English are brave enough when there is no helpless woman's head to be taken. But it is because these Dons are a pack of curs that I like this business less and less."

"It contents me well enough to see them shuffled and routed," said I.

"Yes; but how is it to end? A little more, and instead of sailing up Channel, we shall be sailing down; instead of finding ourselves in London, we may arrive in Lisbon. What then?"

This had never occurred to me. I had calculated so surely on finding myself back in England, that I had

SIR LUDAR

forgotten we were prisoners on the *Rata*, and must even go wherever she took us.

"How can we get away?" I asked. "If we swim to the English they will mistake us for spies or Spaniards. And we are too far from the shore."

"In a day or two," said Ludar, "unless the English stop us, we should be near the French Coast. Wait till then. Perchance your master has a better chance for his type after all than he thinks for."

But any plan of escape was fated to be thwarted then and there, even as we laid it. For as we passed a black corner, turning below towards our bunk, there came a sudden gleam and a Spanish curse out of the darkness, and Ludar, next moment, with the blood rushing from his side, staggered forward and fell to the ground.

In an instant, before the villain could slink away, I had him by the neck. It needed no cudgelling of my brains to guess who it might be; for once and again that day while we worked I had marked the fellow's evil eye on Ludar. Ludar had laughed when I had told him of it, and had not deigned so much as to turn his head to see if I spoke true. And in the bustle that had followed I too had forgot our enemy of the whip. But he had not forgotten us.

Although I caught him in the dark, he was too quick for me. He had his blade still, and though he struck wildly and only scratched my arm, the blow loosed my grip for a moment; and in that moment he dashed past me and up the ladder. I followed madly. As I reached the deck, I saw him before me, running forward, and casting a glance behind to see if I followed. Then, tripping on a rope, he lost his feet, and sprawled forward, as I supposed, my easy prey.

But Heaven had taken his punishment out of my hands. For, at the very spot where he fell, the gunwale of the ship stood open at a place where the refuse of the late battle was being let out from the deck into the water. And here, before a hand could be stirred or a cry raised, the wretch plunged shrieking to the fate he deserved, and there was an end of him.

When I returned below, I found Ludar gasping; but his wound, bad as it was, was not so bad as the villain intended. The blade which had aimed at his heart had turned aside on the rib, leaving, indeed, a hideous flesh-wound in the side, but

A SAD BLOW

not threatening life. He was faint with loss of blood, and I think, with pain; and when I spoke to him, he turned a white face to me and said nothing.

Therefore, in no little panic, I lifted him gently to his bunk, and went in search of help.

By good fortune I met Captain Desmond, to whom I told his fellow-Irishman's plight; and presently he came forward with a leech. This learned grandee seeing the wound not to be desperate, and having plenty of business, I suppose, elsewhere, among his sea-sick lordlings, bade us bandage up the wound as best we could, and find a better place to lay the sufferer in than that foul hole. Saying which, he dawdled away.

Then Captain Desmond questioned me as to how it all happened, and when I told him, he shrugged his shoulders and said:

"Help me carry him abaft. Heaven knows there are plenty of empty cabins on our ship to-night! The Don has enough to think of without this coming to his ears. Therefore, when we have him safely bestowed, do you attend to your duties here, as before, and I will see to him. Come now."

This was a sad blow to me, to be parted from my master and friend in this hour of danger. Yet it seemed better for him to get to the gentlemen's quarters; for in the hole where he was he could scarce have lived. So I was fain to submit. Captain Desmond promised me that once a day I might come to enquire; and further, that if his man—a Spanish clown, who shook in his shoes whenever he heard a gun—should by any chance be killed, I might take his place.

Whereupon, I grieve to say, I prayed devoutly that night that Heaven would speedily relieve the poor fellow of his fears for good.

Next day I was too miserable toiling alone at the rents in the hold to see or care much what passed. But I know that, towards evening, when I looked out, the low cliffs of France were in sight, and that the English sail were a league in our rear, standing out, as it seemed to me, for the white walls of their own land.

CHAPTER XXVII

How Ludar sailed North and I South

THE next day (it was Saturday) I was hovering near Captain Desmond's quarters on some excuse to enquire after my comrade, when there came a summons for hands forward, and a general stir as of something untoward afoot.

So far as I could judge, we were bowling along before a smart westerly breeze with all canvas set, just about where the Channel straitens betwixt Dover on the English side and Calais on the French. Though we were towards the French side, we could clearly see the white cliffs of England to our left, and betwixt us and them, scarcely a mile to rear of us, hovered a certain number of English craft which had not followed their greater ships into Dover. To our right the towers and steeples of Calais town rose up clear and bright, while straight ahead of us the long line of the Armada, of which we closed in the rear, swept forward as though they would dart clean past the Straits and make for the Dutchman's land beyond.

But as I went forward I marked a rapid passing of signals along the line, and a crowding on each ship at the forecastle. The great anchors of the *Rata* were swung in readiness over the prow, and a score of men stood by to pay out the cable. Then, as we strained our eyes eagerly ahead, we could see the tall masts of the Duke's ship, and of all the ships betwixt him and us, suddenly swing round into the wind's eye. There was a great flapping of canvas, a rattle of chains, and a plunging of anchors, and then, as if by magic, the great Armada stood still, at bay.

It was easy to guess the object of this strange movement, and as I looked away towards the English fleet, I felt uneasy. For so suddenly was the Spanish fleet halted, and so near

A WAY I HAVE BEEN BEFORE

upon its heels were the pursuers, that, unless these could halt as suddenly, they would assuredly slip past, and so give the Spaniard—what he so greatly desired and longed for—the wind of them.

Already the young nobles on the *Rata* were laughing at the smart policy of their Admiral, and rejoicing in the near prospect of a turning of the tables—(for could they once get the Englishman betwixt them and the Duke of Parma's fleet, which was waiting on the Dutch coast, they would crumple him up like chaff between two mill-stones)—already, I say, they were counting on seeing the enemy run past them, down the wind; when, lo, with a derisive shot or two into the air, the Englishmen put about quietly, and after hovering a little, and running a little in the teeth of the wind to get a nice distance from us, they dropped anchor too, and turned every one his broad-stern upon us, so that we might all have an eye full of the Queen's ensigns which floated there.

I confess I lifted my hat in joy and loyalty to see how cunningly the Don had been outreached. And the Spanish oaths which hissed out from a hundred lips, as they saw the same thing, sounded to me (Heaven forgive me!) like music.

So overjoyed was I, that without leave I went off, laughing, to tell Ludar the news. But alack! at the very entrance to the officer's quarters, whom should I run against but Don Alonzo himself? So smartly did I come against him, that, had I not caught him roughly by the arm, he might have fallen backwards.

When he saw who it was, his brow darkened (and little wonder!), and he said something in Spanish that I was glad I did not know the meaning of. He recovered himself, however, and drew up coldly a moment after.

"This eternal printer!" said he. "The way to the main-mast you know already, sirrah. Take with you this time to the top three days' rations. If you are found lower than the topmast yard before then, you swing at the bowsprit."

I was sorely tempted to retort then—so put about was I—that there was less chance of my countrymen seeing me if I swung at his bowsprit than if I swung at his stern. But I prudently forebore.

"Sire," said I, "permit me first——"

SIR LUDAR

He turned on me with such a look that I ventured no more parley; and sad at heart, wondering what Ludar would think of me for not coming to him, and wishing this cursed sea-fight was at an end, I went to the hold for biscuits and a bottle of water, and, with no better armour than this, crawled miserably aloft.

Little I guessed what a revenge I was to have on the Dons before my three days were over!

For a while, not a little of my pleasure in seeing her Majesty's ships on the right side of the wind was lost by this untoward accident. And since the wind freshened increasingly during the day, and the Channel in those Straits is wickedly rough, I was soon too ill and out of humour to think of anything at all. I had more than one mind to venture an escape, and perhaps swim to the French coast. Yet, so long as Ludar was on the ship, I could not do it; and he in his grandee's quarters was as close a prisoner from me as if he had still been in the Tower.

I was growing tired of the Invincible Armada, and thought with longing of the snug parlour in the printing house without Temple Bar, where I had sat of old, listening to the music of a certain sweet voice which now seemed all but lost to me in the howling of winds and booming of guns and grinding of Spanish teeth.

Where now was she, and that fair maiden whom Ludar loved? What hope were there of our ever meeting or hearing of one another's fate?

The night passed, and as Sunday dawned, I could see the English ships still hovering not far to rearward; while across, toward the English coasts, shone many white sails, as of the greater Queen's ships returning to join the fleet.

The wind slackened, so that the anchorage of the Armada, which had been sore strained in the night, held good; and with the French town so close on their flank, I thought, despite their loss of the wind, they rode safely enough where they were, and would have leisure to say mass and celebrate their popish rites without fear of disturbance that Sunday.

So it fell out. All day long bells sounded instead of cannons, and instead of powder the smoke of incense rose to where I perched. Moreover, I could guess, by the merry laughter which now and then came the same way, that their

ENGLISH FIREWORKS

Donships were in better heart than yesterday. Perchance the Duke of Parma was already on his way.

As for the English, they lay quietly in their moorings, sparing powder and shot too, and, as it seemed, ready to wait on the Spaniard for the next move.

Towards nightfall, I seemed to detect a stir in their quarters; and presently some seven or eight moderate sized craft fell out of the line, and, with sails set, bore down our way. I marvelled very much that if an attack was to be made, it should be left to ill-armed craft like these to make it, while the greater ships hung idle at a distance. But I supposed it was but a device to take off the Spaniard's notice from something else, and waited curiously to see the result.

They came leisurely towards us, those eight ugly craft, about a cable length apart, steering towards the very centre of our line. As they approached night fell rapidly. But still they held on. I could see their lights hoisted one by one, and strained my ears to catch the first sound of a shot.

Strange to say, they saved their powder. The last I saw of them, as night closed in, they were bearing down full in the wind, each with his cock-boat in tow, within a gunshot's distance of the centre of our line. One of the Spaniards there gave them a disdainful shot, by way of challenge; but they gave never an answer.

Then, all of a sudden, there was a flare, and a roar of flame which leapt up and lit the heavens; and eight blazing vessels drifted full into the middle of the Invincible Armada.

Never shall I forget the scene that followed. There was a moment of bewilderment and doubt; then a hurried random shot or two; then, as the burning masses, spreading before the wind, scattered their fires within the lines, a mighty shout, a rush of footsteps on deck, a hacking of cables and running of chains, a frantic hauling round into the wind; and then, amid panic cries, the galleons of Spain swung round, and, huddled together with tails turned, stood out for sea.

The glare of the English fire-ships lit up the sea like a lake of hell, and amidst the roar of the flames, and the yells of the Spaniards, might be heard the crashing of bowsprits and tumbling of masts, as galleon ran into galleon in the race for safety. A few of them took fire from the English fire-ships; some blew up; others, stove in by their own consorts,

SIR LUDAR

foundered miserably; some went ashore on the shallows; but most got into the wind and fled for their lives out of the Straits.

The *Rata*, being last of the line, escaped with little hurt; for all the vessels ahead of her had cleared off before she got under weigh.

That was a merry night for me up in my perch. I hallooed and cheered, and shouted " God save the Queen ! " till I was hoarse. I jeered the King of Spain, and hooted his men. No one heard me ; but it did me good.

When day broke, there we were, the glorious Armada, like a scared flock of sheep, six miles away from Calais, looking round at one another with white faces, and counting the cost of that night's fireworks. A few charred hulks drifting in the distance were all that were left of the terrible brands which had routed the Don from his beauty sleep ; while many a disabled galleon on our side told of the panic they had caused. Like sheep, at a safe distance, the Spaniards swung round cautiously to face the danger that had passed ; and a cry presently arose, not unmingled with shame, of "Back to Calais!"

But the cunning Englishmen had risen too early in the morning to permit that. Already their sails crowded the western horizon ; and, as we lay in a long crooked line, waiting the Admiral's signal to beat up again for our lost anchorage, down they bore upon us—half of their sail swooping on the right of our line, the other half on the left.

Then followed the biggest battle of all that great sea-fight. For, taking us on either flank, the Englishmen, coming for the first time to close quarters, huddled our ships in towards the centre, sending us one on the top of the other, so that for every ship they sank by their own shot, another went down, stove in by her next neighbour. Where I was, the smoke was soon so dense that I could see but little clearly. More than once, I know, the *Rata* was in the thick of the fight, pounding away at the Englishmen, and receiving broadside after broadside in return, which crashed against the hull and shook me where I hung at the mast-head. The sails round me were riddled with shot, and once or twice I, coming suddenly into view, became a special target for the enemy's marksmen.

Little cared I ! For at every shot that day the banner of Spain tottered lower and lower to its fall, and the flag of old England spread wider and more proudly in the breeze !

I QUIT THE *RATA*

Presently, I remember, an English ship named the *Vanguard*, slipped suddenly in betwixt the *Rata* and another tall Spaniard, so close that we swung there all three together, with our yards entangled, and blazing away at one another, till I wondered if there could be a man left alive below.

As for me, up where I was, I thanked Heaven that the smoke around me rose in clouds and hid me. As it was, many a bullet, shot at random, whizzed through the cords to which I clung, and once a great booming shot tore away the streamer at the mast-head. But so busy were all down below that no one troubled himself to look for the skulker aloft, who sat there, as it seemed, above the clouds, not even knowing, as the day wore on, whether the *Rata* still belonged to the King of Spain or to her glorious Majesty.

Suddenly, hard by, I heard a loud shout, and looking round, saw, on the yardarm of the Englishman's ship, a smoke-bedimmed fellow, with his knife betwixt his lips, crawling towards where, at every lurch, the pole on which I squatted swung across his own. I was in a sore strait when I saw him. For how could I fight against my Queen? Yet, if I let him and the fellows that swarmed up the tackle after him pass, what of my debt of honour to the King of Spain?

The matter was settled for me; for, perceiving me as we swung together, the fellow made a wild grab at me, and, slashing with his knife at the hand by which I clung to the mast, forced me to quit my hold, and clutch at him instead. Then, as I did so, the masts swung asunder, and, lo and behold, I was no longer on the *Rata*, but a prisoner of my own Queen.

I made a dash to spring back to the Spanish ship, but it was too late. The Don was already hauling off, and every moment the gap between him and the English ship became wider. Half-a-dozen stout British hands held me fast, and as many blades at my breast warned me that the game was up.

" Hands off, comrades ! " I shouted ; " I am an Englishman."

At that they laughed, and bade me say my prayers, for my hour was come, and they had other work on hands.

" God save her Majesty Queen Elizabeth, and curse the King of Spain ! " cried I.

Then one or two of them stared round, and cursed me for a Jesuit.

SIR LUDAR

"I am no Jesuit, but a London 'prentice lad," said I, "and have broken heads better than yours for my Queen before now, as I will prove to any two of you that like, even here."

This pleased them better, and they bade me, as I loved my Queen, take a musket and slay them the first Spaniard I could spy on the enemy's deck.

"Give me the gun," said I, with a laugh, "and bullets enough for every dog of them."

At that moment the smoke below me drifted, so that I could just espy, as in a frame of cloud, a little spot on the deck of the *Rata*, where stood a man. He was tall like a giant. The tawny hair waved carelessly in the wind. He carried no weapon, but leaned with both hands heavily on the rail, like a man wounded, and his face, when he turned it, was pale. There was a grim smile on his lips as he watched the panic-stricken sailors hauling off their ship; and once he turned and looked up, not at me, but at where I had been.

"Fire!" shouted the men at my side, "or we strike."

I dropped the gun into the waves below, and with a mighty lump in my throat, whipped out my knife and waited for what should follow.

They fell back amazed at my madness, and, while they consulted what to do with me, I took my chance to grip the first of them by the throat and swing him off his perch.

At that moment a shrill whistle came up from below.

"You are wanted on deck, comrade," said I; "will you go down by the mast, or a shorter way?"

"The mast," he gasped.

So I had my way, and we all went below together.

The English captain—one Admiral Winter—swore roundly when he saw me; and, when he heard my story, said he had bellies enough to fill without a great hulk of a fellow like me to eat more. And he promised me, if he caught me idle at my work, he would trip me by the heels himself. Whereat I thanked him and went forward.

But I was in doleful dumps. For I had lost my friend—perhaps for ever.

"Come, haul away, land lubber that thou art," cried a voice at my side. Looking round, whom should I see but that same Will Peake, the mercer's man of London Bridge, with whom I had had so many a merry bout in times past.

'PRENTICES ALL

He was too busy just then to do aught but grin in my face and bid me haul away. For the other Spanish ship had fared worse than the *Rata*, and was already heeling over on her side.

"Haul away, you hulking lubber," yelled Will, "or she'll be on her beam-ends before we are clear."

So, for five minutes, we and a parcel of other fellows worked might and main to cut away tackle and clear ourselves of the doomed galleon, which settled over farther and farther, showing her whole broadside from gunwale to keel, and blazing despairingly heavenward with her guns.

"Why not give her a broadside to help her over?" asked one who worked near.

"Because," said Will, wisely, "we have no shot left to do it."

"What!" I asked, "are we in such a plight as that?"

"'Tis true," said Will; "I heard it from the gun officer an hour ago. And not only are we at an end, but so is all her Majesty's fleet."

"Then we are lost!" I said.

"No doubt," replied he. "Yet we had merry sport with the Don while it lasted; and methinks he will run a bit without our help, before he find out that we fight him with one arm bound."

So it turned out. The fight dragged on through the afternoon, and ship after ship of the King of Spain went to her doom, or drifted helplessly on the mud banks of Gravelines. But the English fire dropped shorter and shorter; and as evening closed (had the enemy but known it!) we had scarce a broadside left among us.

Yet Heaven remembered us in our extremity. For no sooner had our guns become mute than the south wind came down on us with a burst, catching us in the small of our backs, and sending the Don away in front of us, staggering and reeling seaward, for his very life.

'Twas a sad spectacle for me. I had long since lost sight of the *Rata*. In vain I scanned the smoke-laden horizon for a sight of her. I never saw her more. I could fancy Ludar stalking the deck, or scaling the masts wildly, in search of me; and then, when he found me not, with the cloud deep on his

SIR LUDAR

noble brow, crawling to his berth in the dark to tell himself that I was dead.

I wished that night he could have thought it truly!

Will Peake, when the work of the day was done, was in vast great humour to find me of the ship's company. He had scarce known me at first, so changed was I by the perils of the last weeks. A score or more of swashbuckling 'prentices were on board the ship, he said; and, presently, when I saw them all, and heard their jests, and knocked some of their heads together, I could have believed myself in Cheapside. Having been some two weeks on board, they were mightily proud of their seamanship, and delighted to call me (who had sailed as many seas as they had ponds) landlubber.

However, it mattered not, and we spent a merry night—at least they did—scudding before the wind, and watching the Spanish lanthorns rocking uneasily in the darkness a mile ahead of us.

When daylight came, there they were in a long disorderly line, never looking back, with canvas set, and still running. Some of our ships hung close on their heels, like dogs at a flying ox; but scarce a shot boomed, and never a tack did the Dons slack off their northward course.

As for us, there were two good reasons why we, on the *Vanguard*, should not keep up the chase. We had neither shot to fire nor food to eat. When I came forward that morning to receive my morsel of biscuit with the rest, I understood how ill-pleased Master Winter had been to see another hungry body on board his ship. Even yesterday, as we had helped the bodies of the brave fellows who had fallen for their Queen overboard, it was plain to see that there was something of consolation joined to the pity we all felt for our lost comrades; and the sight of my beggarly rations when I received them made it clear what that consolation was.

So when, after a day's chase, the word was given to put about, and beat up for Margate Roads, scarce a man among us had the stomach to grumble.

'Twas a long, dismal voyage that, in the face of the tempest—with short and tedious tacks that sometimes left us at the day's end little nearer our haven than at the beginning.

NOT WORTH LIFTING ASHORE

And long before Margate was reached half of our company was sick with famine.

I think as brave as any men who fought in that great sea-fight were the few fellows of Will Peake's sort who kept up heart and spirit on that sorry voyage back to Margate. I know I myself had been tempted often enough to give over but for his cheery word in my ear ; and if half the crew remained loyal to their captain till we reached land, Master Winter owed it not a little to his 'prentice-sailors. As for me, I was plague-stricken before we passed the Thames mouth, and when at last we dropped anchor in Margate Roads, Will told me he doubted whether I was worth the lifting ashore.

Yet he did as much for me and more. He nursed me like my own brother, and when, a week or two later, I was able to stand on my feet and set one foot before another Londonwards, I owed it to him that I found myself at last once more in the great city, and had life left in me to look round and know where I stood.

CHAPTER XXVIII

How I enlisted on a New Service

LONDON was merry-making, with bonfires and pealing of bells, when Will Peake and I entered it. Every day that passed, men took in more of the great victory which had been gained against the King of Spain, and rejoiced louder and louder at the deliverance God had vouchsafed the land.

So, when it became known (as it soon did among our old friends) that Will and I had fought in that glorious fight, we lacked neither food nor shelter for our poor bodies. At first Will fared better than I; for he was monstrous little altered from the swaggering lad who tried a bout with me years before at Finsbury Fields. But as for me, men looked once, twice, and thrice at me before they would believe it was Humphrey Dexter. And when one day in a tavern I came upon a mirror I learned the cause. My beard, unkempt now for many weeks, had grown till it made my face look very fierce and manly; and my hair, once close-cropped, now fell heavily below my ears. And the scar I got on the *Rata* gave me so ferocious a look that I had a mind well-nigh to doubt myself, when first I saw it.

" 'Tis little wonder if they know thee not," said Will, " for thou art passably handsome now, whereas once—— "

Here he left me to guess what I had been.

Be that as it may, I was pleased enough with the change for so far, and spared my fee to the barber. And as for my old comrades, I had other signs to make myself known to them, as they soon discovered by the aching of their heads and the soreness of their ribs. For I soon shook off my sickness and was as ready for knocks as ever.

Yet you may guess if, with it all, I was merry!

The printing-house without Temple Bar was as black and

WHICH WAY TO TURN

desolate as a tomb, with a great lock belonging to the Stationers' Company hanging on the door. When I asked the neighbours concerning my master, they pulled long faces and told me he was given over to desperate ventures, and with his family had fled the country; and 'twas well for him, said they, no one knew where he hid.

I knew not which way to turn. My sweet Jeannette was far away amid perils I little dreamed of. Ludar was, perhaps, even now a prisoner in Spain. My occupation was gone, and my pocket and my stomach were both empty.

Could I have lived on naught, I think I should even have tried to make my way to Spain (as if it were no bigger a place than Temple Gardens!), and so find Ludar. Then I changed my mind and thought to set out for Ireland to seek Jeannette. Then, when I saw a fellow enlisting troopers for the Dutch wars, I well-nigh sold myself to him.

I might have done so straight out, had not there come a loud thump on my back as I stood in the crowd, and a voice in my ear that made me start.

"Are you so weary of life, comrade, that you want a leaden pill or two to cure it?"

"Verily, I am," said I, wheeling round and facing Tom Price, Captain Merriman's man.

At first he knew me not, nor when I told him my name would he believe he spake to Humphrey Dexter. But when at last he knew me, he clapped me again on the back and said—

"Thou'rt well met, my little Lord Mayor. By my soul, I might have walked a league and never met thee."

"You might have walked farther than that," said I. "What villainy are you and your master now upon? for I take it you still serve the Captain?"

He laughed. "As for my master, let him be. He's snug enough. I left him—— Look you here, comrade," said he, taking my arm and looking hard at me, "where saw I thee last?"

"Once when you lay as drunk as a dog in Finsbury Fields. And a good turn you did me, comrade, amd more than me, by what you blabbed then."

He gaped rather foolishly at this, and asked did I want my ears slit for a noisy malapert?

Then I told him just what passed, and how I had been

able thereby to save the maiden from the Captain's clutches. When he heard that he laughed, and swore and thwacked me on the back till I nearly dropped.

"By my life, you gallows dog you, if my master only knew what he owed you! Why, my pretty lad, I never saw a man so put about as he was when he came back from Canterbury that time without his prey."

"Where is he now?" I asked.

"Where else, do you suppose, but smacking his lips near the dove's nest? He hath comforted himself for all he hath suffered, ere now, I warrant thee!"

"What!" I shouted. "Has he followed the maiden to Ireland?"

He laughed.

"So, then, you know where the pretty one has flown? I warrant thee, if thou couldst see her at this moment, thou wouldst see my master not a bow-shot away. Ha! ha! I do not say nearer; for when I left, the fair vixen still held him at arm's length. But he is getting on; and now, since the maid's lover is dead——"

"He is not dead," said I; "I parted from him scarce a month ago!" And I told him where and how.

He shrugged his shoulders.

"A fig for his life if that be his case," said he. "At any rate he is believed to be dead; and the Captain, as I say, is getting on, having made himself monstrous civil to Turlogh Luinech O'Neill, who, I think, favours him somewhat for a son-in-law."

"The foul dog!" I exclaimed. "Would I had him standing here, for my friend's sake. Tell me, Tom, what of a little maid who went from London as waiting gentlewoman to the lady. How fares she?"

"Sadly, I hope, since she and I are parted," said he. "For, to tell you the truth, Master Dexter, she is the sweetest wench and hath looked kindly on me. Indeed, 'twas for this reason I think my master sent me off here on this business to get him more men. For he is apt to amuse himself, while he waits for the mistress, with the maid; and I doubt when I return I shall find the little witch hath clean forgotten how to smile on me."

I hope I may be forgiven the words I uttered when I heard

TOM PRICE HAS GREAT NEWS

this. I flew at honest Tom Price like a wolf and cried : " Why, what mean you, hound ? What does he dare to do ? "

Tom shook me off roughly, and pulled out his sword.

" Look 'ee here, Master Humphrey, if that be the way you ask your questions, your ribs shall know the way I answer them."

" I ask your pardon," said I, panting hard. " But for God's mercy say what all this means ? "

" It means," said he, " that you are mightily concerned with this same little waiting lass."

" She is my sweetheart," said I, " and is to be my wife."

It was his turn to look blank now, and catch his breath. He whistled, and stared at me from head to foot, and whistled again. Then he found words, and held out his hand.

" If she be thy sweetheart, she is none of mine. I go halves with no man."

" And this Merriman ? " I asked, scarce heeding what he said.

" This Merriman ! " said he ; " why, take a shame on yourself that you stand skulking here, and leave the defence of those two fair maids to a crack-brained poet and a swashbuckling soldier. I tell you, Humphrey Dexter, those two fellows, little as I love them, are your friends and your master's ; and, if the maids be still safe, they owe it to them, and not to your idle whimpering here."

" Heaven bless them ! " said I. " But, Tom Price, how can I, who have scarce shoes to stand in, or food for one day, go to them ? "

" This way," said he ; " I am here to engage men for my master's troop—join us."

" What ! " I exclaimed ; " serve that villain ? I had as soon serve the devil himself."

" May be you can serve both at one time," said he, with a laugh ; " but join us you must."

" He would hang me at the nearest tree, so soon as he saw me."

" He would never know you. I scarce did."

We stood eyeing one another a minute. Then I held out my hand.

" When do you start ? "

" In two days, if I can find the men by then. Meanwhile,

come with me and put your big carcase in a soldier's trappings, and drink health to her Majesty and Captain Merriman."

A week passed before Tom Price got his company together. I chafed and grumbled at every hour that passed. On the day before we set out, I went to show myself in my soldier's bravery to Will Peake, on London Bridge.

"Every man to his taste," said the latter. "I think thee not as fine as thou thinkest thyself. By the way, thou art like to have knocks enough where thou goest, I hear, for news is come that the Spaniards mean to land on Irish shore, and strike at us from that quarter."

This was great news to me; and on every hand I heard it repeated, till, at nightfall, there was something near a panic in London, and orders were given for all troops possible to set out forthwith. Therefore, Tom Price, though his company still wanted a few of its number, bade us be within call and ready spurred at daybreak.

The road from London to Chester was full of straggling companies of soldiers, hastened forward like us by the alarm of the Spanish attack on Ireland. We, being mounted, distanced most of them. And so eager were the country folk along the march to see our backs, that, had we been minded to tarry long in any place, we should have soon outworn our welcome.

I saw little of Tom Price during the early part of our march. But when, presently, he had leisure to gossip, he told me one piece of news which moved me not a little.

It was that Sorley Boy, being now an old man and broken down in spirit, longed for his lost son, Sir Ludar, as eagerly as he had hated him not long since. He lived a restless life at Dunluce, often and again stalking abroad as of old, and seeming to expect him who was lost. He had even made friends with Turlogh; and the only time that Captain Merriman had hung his head and slunk out of Castleroe, said Tom, was when the Lord of Dunluce came thither to visit his new ally. So long as he stayed, the Captain found business elsewhere.

Sorley Boy, when at Castleroe, saw the maiden, who, after what had passed, scarcely durst meet him. But by degrees her sweet, brave ways took the old man captive, and, ere he left, he knew her whole story, and loved her as if she were indeed already his daughter.

He well-nigh broke his truce with the O'Neill, because he would not permit the maid to visit Dunluce; for Turlogh (dreading, perhaps, the ill graces of the Captain) would not part with her from Castleroe. So Sorley Boy departed discontented, like a man robbed.

All this I heard, and more than ever chafed at the slackness of our laggard steeds. How I wished that, looking round, I might but see Ludar spurring at my side!

Alas! I saw him not. But one day, as we neared Chester, I did see a face in a troop that had joined ours on the road, that made me rub my eyes, and wonder if ghosts truly walked on earth.

If it was not Peter Stoupe, my old fellow 'prentice, it was as like him as one pea is to another. Nay, once, when, to satisfy myself, I made a pretext to ride near him, I could have sworn I heard the humming of a psalm-tune amid the clatter of the hoofs.

Our troops parted company a day after, and I was left marvelling if all this world and the next were marching towards Ireland.

Early next day I had no leisure left me to cogitate more on that; for Tom Price reined his horse in beside mine, and said:

"Humphrey, here is a message come from the Captain in hot haste, to prevent our going north, and ordering us to Dublin."

I let my reins fall with a groan on my steed's neck. Tom heeded it not, but continued:

"The Spaniard, it is said, has been gathering in the northern seas, and is coming down on the western Irish coast, where he counts on the papists of the country to further him. We are ordered to stay in Dublin for orders from my Lord Deputy. Why, how black you look, comrade!"

"Who would not? You know, Tom Price, why I came on this venture. I were better in London, unless our journey lead us to Castleroe."

Tom laughed, and I could have knocked him from his horse, had he not quickly added:

"Gently, my fire-eating jack printer. I came not to tell thee only this. The Captain addeth these words: 'Send me

SIR LUDAR

six trusty men here, for my affairs require such before I am free to join you. Send them forward with all speed. Do you cross leisurely to Dublin, and there await me. I am in hopes it may not be needful for me to return again thither. Send trusty men, and speedily.' What say you, Humphrey? Art thou a trusty lad? Could I trust thee to pick out five honest fellows like thyself and show them the way to a certain pair of black eyes and rosy lips on the banks of the Bann?"

I loved Tom Price like a brother then, and told him as much. In an hour's time I had chosen five stout fellows, all of whom I could trust with my last farthing, and whom I could count on for any service. I had them armed to the teeth, well mounted and provisioned ; and then, without a moment lost, called them to horse.

"Farewell, comrade," said Tom, as he saw me go. "I could even envy thee, though it is like to cost thee somewhat. For the Captain hath twenty men already, and hath eyes and ears in his head. Commend me to thy lass, and let her know she hath had a narrow escape of a sweetheart in Tom Price."

"She shall thank you for your honesty, comrade, with her own sweet lips," said I, and hallooed my men forward.

Next day we were at the sea, and embarked—horses and all—on a barque that was even then weighing anchor with other troops on board for Knockfergus.

To my surprise, among the men that crowded the deck was the fellow I had seen two days ago, who had reminded me of Peter Stoupe. When I saw him now, I knew for certain it was he.

I stood full in front of him, to see if he would know me again, for I cared not if he did. He looked at me meekly without a sign of recognition, and humming ever, passed his eyes to some other place.

"So, so, Peter," thought I, "as you know not your old shopmate, why should I disturb your humming?"

And I carelessly asked a man who stood next him whither his company was bound and on what service.

"Westward," he said, "to look for Spaniards. And you?"

"To join one Captain Merriman in the north."

It tickled me much to see Peter start and change colour at that.

DETAINED AT KNOCKFERGUS

"Ah, 'tis a brave gallant, I'm told," said the man. "'Twas he slew Sorley Boy's son, was it not?"

"Aye, a brave deed that was," said I. "I saw it."

The fellow laughed.

"You know him, then? Ha! ha! You can satisfy Peter here better than I can. He desireth to know the Captain's whereabouts; and when I tell him he is no further off than the nearest pretty face, he turneth up his eyes as if he expected to see him at his own side. Ho! ho! What say you, Peter?"

"I say, alack that such men should wear her Majesty's colours," said he, with a snivel.

"Amen to that," said I, giving him a thwack on the back that made him jump. "'Tis a pity her Majesty hath not more like you, Peter. How do you call your name?"

"Stoupe," said he, looking up at me meekly and rubbing his shoulder.

After that we went to look to our horses, and I saw little more of him that voyage; for from the moment we put out to sea he fell as sick as a dog, and lay on the floor of the ship praying Heaven to put an end to his sorrows, till we reached Knockfergus.

There I suddenly missed him, and heard he had had so sorry a time serving her Majesty thus far, that he had skulked so soon as ever the ship came to land, and made for the hills, where no doubt he meant to lie till he could go back the way he had come.

Whereat I laughed, and ordered my men to horse.

At the town gate, much to my vexation, we were met by a guard, who ordered us to report ourselves to the English governor. I had looked to get a fair start of the other troops going west. But now, so far from that, two days passed idle on my hands before I even got audience of the governor, and by that time many companies had started westward. For the panic of the Spanish invasion was very great among the English soldiery at Knockfergus; and every man that could be had was being hurried across the country.

When I saw the governor and told him my orders, he said, shortly: "Captain Merriman has already had orders to go forward to Tyrone's land, and will have left Castleroe before now. You will join him sooner by sea than by land Be ready to sail three days hence. Till then, leave not the town, but abide at the hostel for further orders."

This was a thunderbolt to me. I knew the Captain well enough to be sure that, if he had indeed left Castleroe, he had either not left it alone or had left worse than desolation behind him. He was too well known to his comrades in these parts to leave much doubt of that ; and when that same night I heard by chance that Turlogh for a month past had been away in Dublin, leaving the protection of his castle to this English champion of his, I made sure, what I had feared all along, that I was come too late.

One thing I was resolved on. Come what would, I would make for Castleroe and learn the worst for myself. 'Twould be better even to be hanged for a deserter than live a day longer in this misery and suspense.

So I bade my men, if they were minded still to serve me, be ready and stand by for the first chance of escape.

It came soon enough. Bands of soldiers were coming in and going out of Knockfergus all the night long ; and while we sat in the hostelry and watched them depart with longing eyes, like prisoners through a dungeon cage, I suddenly found myself calling myself a fool and starting to my feet.

" Follow me," I cried to my men, and led them to where our horses stood, still saddled, in the stable.

" Mount," I said, " and stay under the shadow of this wall, till you see me ride out. Then fall in quietly at my heels."

Presently, as we stood there, came a noise of trumpets and a clatter of hoofs down the steep street. As they passed, we could see by the torches of those that marched beside them that this was a great company of foot and horse, dragging a gun or two with them. 'Twas more of a rabble than a troop ; for the horses, frightened by the glare of the torches and the shouts of the footmen, reared and plunged, and scattered the towns-folk who had turned out to see them pass, right and left.

As they passed the corner where we lurked, some of the horses plunged in among us, and in the darkness all was confusion for a moment.

Then I quietly rode in among them with my five men at my heels, and so, unseen and unheeded, we joined the troop and passed the gate in safety into the black country beyond.

Once outside, 'twas easy enough to get clear. I bade my

POST-HASTE FOR CASTLEROE

men lag behind all they could; till at last we must have dropped fifty yards or so, where, in the darkness, we were quite lost to view. Then I gave the order to gallop; and overtaking the company, as in hot haste, I rode up to the officer and saluted.

"A good journey to you, Captain," said I. " 'Twill be slower than ours, for the troop we are to join is already beyond the Bann, and we ride post-haste to overtake it."

"You are of Merriman's troop then?" said the officer.

"That are we. Good-night to you, Captain. Lay to, my men, and spurs all!" And so we rode forward.

CHAPTER XXIX

How Captain Merriman came and went betwixt me and the Light

OUR speed did not last long; for very soon the hard road turned off to the coast, whereas I, being chary, even of minutes, resolved to strike inland and make direct for the Bann.

I was a fool for my pains, as I presently found; for we were soon crawling and floundering among thickets and morasses like blind men.

Add to that that the weather grew boisterous and stormy, that our provisions were sunk very low, that now and again we were set upon by the clansmen of the Glynns, who, for all the truce, hated England with all their hearts, and you may guess if we made quick progress.

At length we captured a countryman, who, to save his neck, offered to guide us out into the Route country, where Castleroe was. But ten precious days had been lost us in that journey; during which, who was to say what evil might not be befalling those two helpless maids?

'Twas a dark evening when at last we swam the river and rode to the gate of Turlogh's house. Well I remembered the place!

Lights were moving in the courtyard. There was a noise of horses standing, and of men calling to one another. Even the sentry at the gate was not at his post to challenge us, and we rode in almost unobserved.

" Where is your Captain? " demanded I, dismounting, and addressing a fellow who stood busily harnessing his horse.

He looked round, and, seeing a stranger, dropped his saddle and shouted:

" Here they be at last! Tell the Captain."

Presently, as I waited, scarcely knowing what to make of

A FAMILIAR COURTYARD

it, Captain Merriman himself came up. And at sight of him 'twas all I could do to hold my hand from my sword.

He ordered lights to be fetched, and when they came said:

"So you are here at last, sirrah? By my soul, I know not what Tom Price calls nimble men; but I could have walked as far on foot in the time. Come, who is your leader? Let me see your papers."

I stood forth and handed him Tom's letter, whereby the Captain was to know we were the good men and true he was in need of. He eyed me keenly, and said:

"Had you come an hour later, you would have had a longer ride still, for we are even now setting out westward. Nevertheless, laggards as you be, you are come in good time. Harkee, you," said he, beckoning me aside, "a word in your ear."

I was ready to make an end of the villain then and there; for I smelt falsehood and devilry in every word he spoke. But I waited to let him say his say out first. There was little fear in the dark night, and the unsteady flare of the torches, of his guessing to whom he spoke.

"I require you and your men to stay here," said he, "to guard this place. Tom Price tells me you are a trusty fellow, that understands his business and asks no questions, which is well. In this house are two fair maidens, who, when we leave, will have no other protector but you and your men. Now then, I bid you, guard them close. Let no one in to them, and see they go not out. They are my captives, and but for this cursed war I should not be leaving the charge of them thus to a stranger. Hold no talk with them, and, if they be riotous, lock them fast in their chambers. So soon as I have shown myself to the Deputy Lord I shall return; or I may send you word to bring the maids to me. Remember, hands off; and if you serve me well in this, I may, perchance—for they are both fair——"

"Enough!" exclaimed I through my teeth, and digging my fingers into the palms of my hands till the blood came.

"I understand you, Captain. Depend on me,"

"Thanks, good fellow," said he, not heeding my troubled voice. "We shall meet again soon. And, by the way, see specially that a certain hare-brained poetic fool and a swaggering bully, his companion, come not near the place. If you catch them, you will do well to hang them on the gate.

SIR LUDAR

Heaven knows they have marred sport enough! And now, farewell. Your hand on this."

I gave him such a grip that he well-nigh danced with pain, and let him go.

I was in a state of wild tumult. Within those very walls, then, unconscious of all that came and went, lay the two sweet maids, for whose sake I have travelled thus far from London. And this fool of a villain was even now leaving me to guard them, while he, deferring his crime for a more convenient season, went to show himself to my Lord Deputy! 'Twas more like a dream of good fortune than real fact; and I dreaded every moment to find myself awake with all my hopes vanished.

But no. The Captain and his men went to horse, and presently the order was given to march out.

"Farewell," cried he to me as he rode forth; "be trusty and vigilant. Draw up the gate after we be gone, for there be rogues in plenty about. We shall meet again. Meanwhile, when you see my angel, tell her I left in tears, breathing her name. Ha! ha!"

And he spurred off gaily.

I stood stockstill, I know not how long, till the sound of the hoofs had clattered away into silence, and the voices were lost in the gentle moaning of the night-wind among the trees. Then I turned and glanced up at the house. All was dark; not a light flickered, nor was there aught to show behind which of these windows slumbered my sweet Jeannette or her fair mistress.

"Sleep on for to-night, dear hearts," said I. "To-morrow by this time ye shall be safe for ever from the talons of yon cursed hawk."

Then, bidding my men draw up the gate and dispose themselves for the night, I took up my post by the door, and waited patiently for the morning.

My men were soon snoring, for we had travelled hard and long. But sleep was never further from my eyes. As I sat there, listening to the rising wind in the trees, and the rush of the river below, with now and again the wail of a sea-bird crying out seaward, I grew to hate the darkness. Despite the fair innocents who slumbered within and the sturdy rogues who slept without, the loneliness of the place

I MEET PETER STOUPE ONCE MORE

took hold upon me, and made me uneasy and anxious. Once I thought I heard returning footsteps without, and rushed to the gate. But it was only a creaking of the trees. Another time I seemed to hear a calling from within, and sprang wildly to the door. But it was only a hoot-owl. And when the leaves tapped on the window above, I looked up expecting a face to appear there. And when a horse in the stable whinnied, I imagined it the mocking laughter of a troop of traitors left behind to rob me of my trust.

At length I grew so restless and weary of waiting, that I determined to delay no longer, but enter the house.

As I stood a moment at the door, hesitating, the wind suddenly dropped, and there fell a silence on the place which made me shudder, and tempted me after all to await the dawn. But, with a mighty effort, I gathered up my courage, and, laughing at my qualms, pushed the door.

It was not even shut to, so that, giving way unexpectedly under my hand, I stumbled heavily into the hall. As I did so, I struck my face against something icy cold.

In the darkness I could see nothing; but I felt the thing swing away from my touch; and before I could step back, or put out my hand, it returned and struck me once more, harder than before. I clutched at it wildly; then, with a gasp of horror, flung it from me, and rushed, shouting to my men, into the open air.

For what had touched my face was the hand of a dead man!

It seemed an age before, amongst us all, we could strike light enough to kindle a torch. Then, shuddering in every limb, I returned to the house.

There, just within the open door, from a beam in the hall roof, hung a corpse, still swinging slowly to and fro. And when I held up the torch to look at his face, there leered down upon me the eyes of my old fellow 'prentice Peter Stoupe! At the sight the torch fell from my hands, and I reeled back into my comrade's arms, stark and cold, well-nigh as the corpse itself. Then there came upon me, with a rush, an inkling of what all this meant. I seized the light again, and dashed past the hall and up the staircase. Every room was still and empty as death. We searched every nook and corner, and called aloud, till the place rang with our shouts. The only occupant of Turlogh Luinech O'Neill's house was that lonely corpse swinging in the hall.

Now all the truth dawned upon me, as if I had read it in a book. Peter, little as I dreamed it, had both known me and guessed my errand. He had overheard enough to know where the Captain was, and how he might revenge himself on me. He had contrived to slip away at Knockfergus, and, being better guided than we, had reached Castleroe in time to warn the villain of my coming. Whether he lent his hand to the carrying off of the two maids, 'twas hard to say, But it seemed plain that, at the first warning, they had been carried off, and that the Captain that night had ridden away, not to leave them behind, but to make good his possession of them elsewhere. Why Peter should be left hanging thus, 'twas not hard to guess. He never played straight even in villainy, and doubtless had given the Captain reason to desire the shortest way to be rid of him. As for me, thanks to Peter, the villain had known me through my disguise, and, God knows! he had had his revenge on me this night.

While I speculated thus, I wandered to and fro in the house like a man distraught, till presently my footsteps brought me back to a little chamber at the end of the long passage into which I had scarce dared peep before. The dawn had already begun to chase the night away, and was flooding the room with a flush of light that suited its sacredness better than my flaring torch. So I left that without and entered in the twilight.

All was in the sweet confusion of a chamber whose owner expects to return to it anon. The bed had not been disturbed since it was last settled. Raiment lay scattered here and there. On the table lay a book open, and beside it a jewel. What moved me most was a little scarf which lay for a coverlet over the pillow on the bed. For it was the selfsame scarf I had once seen Ludar fasten round the maiden's neck that night she took the helm beside him on board the *Miséricorde*.

I durst touch nothing I saw, yet that single glance roused fires within me which, if it be a sin to hate one's enemy, will assuredly stand to my hurt in the day of reckoning. Yet how could mortal man stand thus and not be stirred?

I passed on softly into the tiny chamber beyond.

AN ALLY

There the air was fragrant with the scent of a sprig of honeysuckle that lay yet unwithered in the window. On the floor lay scattered a few papers, written in a notable poetic hand, and addressed—as I could not but read—" To one who bade the poet give o'er his singing," or " To the fair moon, handmaiden to the glorious sun," or in such wise. On a chair was another paper half written, and beside it a pen : "Humphrey," it said, in Jeannette's loved hand—" Humphrey, come over and help——" Here the pen had hastily ceased its work.

This mute appeal, lying thus to greet me, roused the whole man in every pulse of my body. I seized the dear paper in my hands and kissed it, and then, placing both it and the maiden's scarf in my bosom, I dashed from the room with drawn sword and called my men to horse.

" To horse ! " I cried, " and ride as you never rode before, men ; for I vow to heaven I will not quit this saddle till I find the foul dog who has robbed me of my dearest jewel."

They obeyed quickly and cheerily, for the horror of that night had given them enough and to spare of Castleroe.

A mile through the forest road was a woodman's hut whose master looked out curiously to see us pass. It seemed to me worth while, being the first man we had met, to question him. So I ordered a halt.

" You are an O'Neill ? " said I.

" Who told you so ? " growled he in Irish ; and I guessed from the look of him that he was the man I wanted.

I signalled to two of my men to dismount and seize him.

" Now," said I, fumbling my pistol, " time presses. Tell me which way the O'Neill has gone."

" How do I know ? " said he.

I cocked my pistol and laid it across my saddle.

" He went to Dublin, a month since," said the fellow, quickly.

" And the English Captain ? "

He growled a curse, and said :

" He passed here last night for Tyrone's country."

" And the Lady Rose O'Neill and her maid. Who carried them off, and when ? "

He paused and looked doggedly at me.

I raised my pistol and laid it at his head.

SIR LUDAR

"Two days since they rode hence under escort of three of the Captain's men."

"And whither went they?"

"The Captain knows. Follow him and you shall find them."

"Look you here," said I, "if what you say be true, you shall have your life. If not——"

"I'm no liar," said he, "and I curse the English."

"Then," said I, "help me and my men to save your chief's daughter, and slay yonder Captain."

He pricked up his ears at that.

"'Tis too late, I doubt," said he. "The villain works quickly. 'Twere better to find the maids dead. It took him not many hours to rob this house of all its light."

"'Tis not too late so long as a breath is in this body," said I. "Come, take us to him, as you are a loyal clansman."

"I know no more than I have told you," answered he. "He is gone to Tyrone's country, and the maids have been carried thither before him. I will guide you so far."

Without more words he came, springing at our sides over the heather and along the mountain paths at a pace that put our nags to shame. 'Twas easy to follow the tracks of the soldiers on the wet ground; and once, towards evening, as we mounted a tall ridge, I fancied I could descry on the crest opposite some figures that moved.

At our first halting-place, where we paused but to give our horses and ourselves a hasty meal, we heard that about midday certain English soldiers had passed the place at full gallop. And two days back, as night fell, some travellers, amongst whom rode two women, had likewise hurried by, westward.

With news such as this we could scarce afford our weary horses the rest they needed, before we set forth again. Our guide led us down a steep track into the valley, and then, striking straight across, we toiled up the mountain path which ascended the high ridge opposite.

He checked our pace as we neared the top, advising us to await daylight for the descent.

When at length at our backs rose the glorious sun over the eastern hills, flashing his light past us into the valley

NEWS FROM DYING LIPS

below, we saw, stretched out, a great plain like a map, through which the windings of a river sparkled; while, beyond, rose another ridge of hills higher still than that on which we stood.

Our guide beckoned us to a place whence we could look out without being exposed to the view of any one in the valley. For awhile we searched the plain in vain. Only a few herds drove their cattle afield; and now and then the sharp bark of a dog broke the stillness. At length, on the slope of the hill opposite, we saw a flock of sheep break suddenly into panic flight; and there appeared, crawling up the ascent, a body of horsemen, who, by the occasional glancing of the sun upon steel, we knew to be soldiers.

Whether they were the troops we sought, and whether amongst them they carried the captive maidens, 'twas too far to determine. But at sight of them we plunged with new hope towards the valley.

Half-way down, in a wood, we found a wounded trooper prone on the ground and gasping for breath; while beside him grazed his horse. He was bleeding from his side, and too faint to turn his head as we came up.

Our guide started as he saw him, and whispered:

"This is one of Merriman's men."

I knelt beside him and tried, in my clumsy way, to bind his wound, and help him back to life. But 'twas plain we were all too late for that. He lay gasping in my arms, his eyes, already glazed, looking vacantly skyward, and his arms feebly tossing in his battle for breath. 'Twas no time for questions. I ventured but one:

"Where is O'Neill's daughter?" I asked in his ear.

He turned his head and stopped his panting for a moment.

"I could not save her," he gasped; "Merrim——" and here he fell back in my arms a dead man.

We covered him hastily with the fallen leaves, and, taking his horse for our guide's use, spurred grimly on.

There was no doubt now. The villain's plot had succeeded only too well, and the fair innocents were already delivered over to his clutches!

At a little cluster of houses in the valley we halted a moment longer.

"Has a troop passed this way?" asked our guide of a cow-herd.

SIR LUDAR

"Surely," said he, "they will scarce be over the hill by now."

"Carried they two women in their company?"

He laughed and said no.

"Have not two women been carried this way lately?"

"I'll be hanged if there was a sign of a woman," said he.

We looked blank at one another. The fellow seemed to speak true. Yet his story agreed not with that of the dying man.

There was naught but to spur on, and by all means come level with the villain, wherever he was.

As we commenced the steep ascent, we could discern the moving figures of horsemen on the skyline above—as it seemed to us, in two bands, one of which suddenly disappeared on the other side, while the other, numbering some half-dozen men, made southward along the ridge. As we came higher we saw these last still there, moving hurriedly to and fro, as though seeking what they found not. It could hardly be us they looked for, for their faces were set southward, nor was it till we came within a mile of where they stood that they turned and suddenly perceived us. Then they too vanished below the skyline and we lost them.

By the time we reached the ridge top, the first party was clattering far down the plain, raising a cloud of dust at their heels, and, as it seemed, pushing on with all speed to their journey's end.

Of the other party for a while we saw nothing, till presently our guide pointed to them as they stole from out a wood below us and suddenly broke into a canter in a southward direction.

It seemed to us their desire was, by doubling on their track, to regain once more the ridge on which we had first discovered them. Whereupon, smelling mischief, I called to my men, and, turning after them, gave chase.

'Twas a fool's errand! For, whatever their purpose had been, they abandoned it, and half-an-hour later we spied them striking westward once more, as in haste to overtake their fellows. So near upon them were we by this time, that not only could we count their number, which was seven, but could spy the feather on their leader's hat, by which I knew for certain that this was indeed the man I sought. For an

GETTING NEARER

hour and more we followed close on his heels, sighting him now, missing him now, and neither nearer nor further for all our riding.

At last, towards afternoon, when, after swimming a strong river and skirting a town, we already stood, as our guide told us, in Tyrone's country, we could see the party suddenly halt and hold a hurried parley. The result was that while the leader rode on, his six men stood, and, spreading themselves across the road, waited for us. 'Twas a spot not ill chosen for standing at bay. For, on either side of the steep track, the land fell away in desolate bog, on which we scarce dare venture; so that there was nought to do but either fall back ourselves or come face to face with those who stood in the way.

"Men," said I, "for me there is but one goal, and that is yonder flying villain. I keep my sword for him. Look you well to the others. They must not hinder me."

And before the lurkers had time to prepare for our coming, we charged in upon them full tilt, and I, slashing right and left, cut my way to the far side, while those who followed me held them there in hand-to-hand fight.

How that battle betwixt Englishmen and Englishmen sped I know not, for before it was at an end I was a mile on the road, with my prey little farther beyond. Yet, to my woe, I perceived him to be better mounted than I, and better acquainted with the roads. So that every hour the distance betwixt us widened, till at last, when night fell, I could see him disappear, with a defiant wave of his hand, over a hill well-nigh a league ahead.

I know not how my wearied horse ever carried me that night; but when at sunrise I staggered into the yard of a wayside farm, he sunk dead-beat beneath me. Therefore my vaunted boast not to quit my saddle till I had met my man went the way of other boasts, and came to the ground too.

The lad who came out of the barn to meet me told me that an hour since a soldier had gone through at a hand's pace bound for the coast, where already, it was said, the Spaniard had landed and was devouring the land like locusts. Of women, either to-day or for many a day, he had seen or heard nothing.

SIR LUDAR

My faithful beast was too feeble, even after a halt, to carry me farther, and I had perforce to proceed on foot. My one hope was that ere long the Captain might find himself in a like plight. But that was not to be for many an hour yet.

Towards night the wind, which had been blowing in gusts over the hill-tops and along the valleys, gathered into a gale; and in it I could hear the distant boom of surf on an iron-bound coast. Ever and again I met country folk hurrying inland, with now and then a soldier in their company. And once, as I passed a lonely moor, there slunk past me a fellow who by his swarthy face and black flashing eyes I knew to be a Spaniard.

As hour passed hour through the night the storm raged fiercer, till presently I could scarce make head against it and sank for an hour on the turf, praying only that this weariness might befal mine enemy also.

When at dawn I struggled to the hill-top and looked out, I dreaded to find him vanished. But no. My prayer must surely have been answered, for he staggered on scarce a mile ahead of me down towards the valley.

'Twas a narrow valley, with a swampy tract below, and rising again sharply to the hill opposite. Half-way along that hill, through a narrow gap, I, standing on higher ground, could catch a glimpse of the grey ocean beyond, sending its white horses in on the land, and moaning with a cry that mingled dismally with the rush of the wind. Surely our long journey was near its end now!

Looking again towards the gap, I perceived—what my enemy below must have missed—the form of a man who stood there, motionless, clear cut against the sky, with his back on us as he gazed seaward. He was too far off for me to see if he were a soldier or only a peasant. Yet I remember marking that he was great of stature; and as he stood there, with his hair floating in the wind, he seemed some image of a giant god set there to stand sentinel and brood over the wild landscape.

Then, as the sun broke out from behind the sweeping clouds, it flashed on a sword in his hand, and I concluded this must be an English soldier placed there to keep the road inland against the invading Spaniard.

GONE TO HIS OWN

'Twas a fine post of defence, verily; for, looking round, I perceived that the hills on every hand seemed to close in and stand like the walls of a basin, with no outlet save the crest on which I stood on the one hand, and a gap where he stood on the other; while betwixt us stretched the moist plain, across which the Captain was even now spurring.

So intent had I been on the solitary sentinel, and the strange form of this wild hollow, that I had forgot for a moment my quest. But I remembered it as the sun suddenly fell on the form of my enemy labouring heavily through the swamp below.

A sudden fierceness seized me as I flung myself forward in pursuit; I shouted to him with all my might to stand and face me where he stood.

I can remember seeing the form of the soldier in the gap turn quickly and look my way. Next moment there rose, below me, a yell; and I stood where I was, like a man petrified.

For the Captain, having spurred his jaded steed some way into the bog, reined up suddenly, and tried to turn back. The horse's legs were already sunk to the knees, and in his struggle to get clear plunged yet a yard or two farther towards the middle. Then he sank miserably on his side, throwing his rider to the ground. The man, with a wild effort, managed to fling himself on the flank of the fast sinking beast; but 'twas a short-lived support. With a yell that rings in my ears as I write, he struggled again to his feet and tried to run. But the bog held him and pulled him down inch by inch—so quickly that, before I could understand what was passing, he was struggling waist-deep like a man swimming for his life. Next moment I saw his hands cast wildly upwards. After that, the bog lay mirky and silent, with no record of the dead man that lay in its grip.

Before I could fling off the awful spell that held me and rush to the place, the man on the other side of the valley had uttered a cry and dashed in the same direction.

And, as we stood thus, parted by the fathomless depth of the dead man's grave, we looked up and knew one another.

For this was Ludar.

CHAPTER XXX

How the Sun went down behind Malin

I THINK it was the sudden shock of this great discovery, and naught else, that arrested our feet in time and saved us from madly rushing on the doom of our lost enemy.

At such a time how could we think even of him?

Of all my long fierce journeyings, no part seemed half so long as the few minutes it took me to skirt round the fatal bog and reach the hand of my long-lost friend.

"Humphrey," said he presently, after we had stood silent awhile, "I scarce knew thee. How rose you from the dead?"

"The God who parted us hath brought us together again," said I. "Thanks be to Him."

"Amen," said he. "Therefore, while I lead you to the Don——"

"The Don!" cried I; "is he here then?"

"Why not, since the *Rata* came ashore weeks ago on these coasts?"

"And are the Spaniards all here too?" said I, with my hand feeling round my belt for my sword.

"Nay," said he, smiling. "That is my story. Tell me yours."

So I told him, and he listened, marvelling much. His brow grew black as thunder when I came to speak of the lost maidens. He wheeled round, and, laying his hand with a grip of iron on my arm, pointed to the black bog below us.

"Is it certainly Merriman who lies there?"

"As certain as this is you," said I.

"God forgive him!" said Ludar, and walked on.

Then he told me how, missing me after the battle, and seeing the mast on which I had perched shot away, he had

LUDAR'S STORY

mourned for me as dead, and, for my sake, taken a gun with a good-will against my Queen. How, when after Gravelines the south wind sprang up and the Invincible Armada began to run, the *Rata* sailed as rear-guard and bore the brunt of the few English ships that dogged them. How it was resolved by the Spanish captains, Don Alonzo himself not protesting, that the shortest way back to Spain now lay by way of the Orkneys and the Atlantic. How, thereupon, that glorious fleet trailed in a long draggled line northward, never looking behind them, even when the Englishmen one by one drew off and abandoned the chase. How, after a while, when they looked out one morning they found the *Rata* staggering through the stormy northern seas alone.

"'Twas a sad sight," said Ludar. "You would not have known the queenly vessel we had met scarce a month before off Ushant. Her main-mast clean gone, her tackle dishevelled as a wood-nymph's hair; with flags and sails and pennons blown away, guns rusted in their ports, and the very helm refusing to turn. The bells, all save the dismal storm bell in the prows, were silent; the priests had crawled miserably to their holes. No one read aloud the King's proclamation; and even the gallants of Spain sat limp and listless, looking seaward, never saying a word but to salute and cheer their beloved Don, or talk in whispers of the sunny hills of Spain.

"Captain Desmond, the one man on board who, after you, was my friend, had died in the fight off Gravelines. I had not the heart or the wish to seek new comrades; and, save when the brave Don himself gave me a passing word of cheer, I forgot what it was to speak or listen.

"Well, when off Cape Wrath (just as we sighted a few of our scattered consorts and hoped for food and comfort), a new storm overtook us from the north-east and drove us headlong, under bare poles, southward again. We none of us, I think, cared if the next gust sent us to the bottom. Many a weary young Don did I see fling himself in despair overboard; and but that we daily drew nearer to Ireland, I had been tempted to do the same.

"How long we drove I forget, or what wrecks we passed; but one day we found ourselves flung into a great bay, where, for a while, we held on to our anchors against the storm. But the *Rata* had lost her best thews and muscles at Calais, and, after two days, dragged towards the shore and fell miserably over, a wreck.

"We came to land in boats, or on floating spars, but only to meet worse hardships than on sea ; for the savages on the coast, aided by your gallant Englishmen, fell on us, defenceless as we were, stripped us of all we had, and drove us from the shore in an old crank of a galleon, which, if it carried us thus far, did so only by the grace of God and His saints."

"And where be we now ? " I asked.

"At Killybegs," said he, " and Heaven grant we may get out of it. For a while, Tyrone, the O'Neill in these parts, sheltered and fed us. But since the English came, he has left us to our fate, and the men lie rotting here as in a dungeon."

"Why," said I, " 'twas rumoured in England that the Spaniards had descended on Ireland to take it, and so strike across it at the Queen."

He laughed.

"May your Queen ne'er have sturdier foes, Humphrey. Come and see them."

As we turned the corner of the hill, we came suddenly on three men, standing with their faces seaward and engaged in earnest talk. The oldest of them was white-haired and slight of build. But the nobleman shone through his ragged raiment and battered breastplate, and I knew him in a moment to be Don Alonzo da Leyva himself.

He greeted Ludar kindly, and looked enquiringly at me.

"Do the spirits of English printers walk on earth ? " asked he.

"No, Sir Don, not till their bodies be dead," said I, saluting ; " I am here to warn your Excellency that the English soldiers are drawing a cord around this place, and will fall speedily upon you in force."

" 'Tis well they come only to slay and not to eat us," said he, with a grim smile.

And I perceived that both he and his companions were half-starved.

"Yet they should not delay, for if they haste not, they will find us gone. Sir Ludar, the *Gerona* "—here he pointed to a large galleass that lay at anchor in the bay—" is ready, and sails to-night for the Scotch coast. I claim your services yet, as you claim those of your squire."

A SHARP FIGHT

Ludar looked at me. I knew what passed in his mind, for 'twas in mine also. How could we leave Ireland thus, on a desperate venture, while those two fair maids——

But before we could even exchange our doubts, there sprang out upon us from behind a rock half-a-dozen fellows with a horseman at their head, who waved his sword and called loudly on us, in the name of the Queen, to yield.

I groaned inwardly as I pulled out my sword. Once more I was about wickedly and grievously to wage war on her Majesty, and break my vows of allegiance. Yet, how could I otherwise now?

The Don deigned no reply, but waited calmly for the attack. We were but five to six, and the two Spaniards were so lean and ill-fed as scarce to count as a man betwixt them. At the first onset one of them dropped dead, and the other, after scornfully running his adversary through, fell back himself in a swoon of exhaustion.

Meanwhile, the Don was struggling with the horseman. I can remember, occupied as I was with the sturdy rogue who flew at me, how noble he looked, as, with head erect and visage calm, he parried blow after blow, stepping back slowly towards the rock.

'Twas a sharp fight while it lasted; for, though Ludar made short work of his first man, the other three were stubborn villains, and, being well-fed and well-armed, put us hard to it.

Presently, he on the horse, enraged that, for all his advantage, he got no closer to his foe, pulled out a pistol from his holster and levelled it full at the Don's head.

With a shout like a lion's, Ludar flung away his own assailant, and rushed between the two, dealing the horseman a blow which sent him headlong from his saddle and echoed among the rocks like a crack of thunder.

He was none too soon, for the shot had flashed before ever the blow fell, and, only half diverted, rattled on the Don's breastplate, hard enough to fell and draw blood, though, happily, not hard enough to kill.

After that, Ludar and I had a merry time of it, with our backs against the rock, and four swords hacking at our two. I know not how it was; but as I found myself thus foot to foot again with my dearest friend, listening to his short, sharp battle snort, and seeing ever and anon the flash of his trusty steel at my side, I felt happy, and could have wished the battle to last an hour. I forgot all about my Queen, and, but for sundry knocks and cuts, had half forgotten my adversaries themselves. Nor were they any the better off for my daydream; for the four swords against us presently became but two, and these ere long were in the hands of flying men.

When we had leisure to look at one another and see how we stood, we found we had been playing no child's play. Ludar was pale, his sleeve was bloody, and his sword broken in two. As for me, drops were trickling through my hair and down my cheek, and I needed no astronomer to tell me the earth turned round. But the Don, when we came to him, was in a worse plight yet. For he lay where he had fallen, white as a marble statue, his eyes closed, his breath coming and going in quick, short gasps. As best we could we tore off his breastplate, and looked to the wound beneath. 'Twas but a gash, the ball having grazed the ribs and flattened itself on the steel beyond. But the blood he had lost thereby, and the feebleness of his ill-nourished body, made it more dangerous a wound by far than our vulgar scratches.

We caught the Englishman's riderless horse, which grazed quietly near, and laid the gallant gently on his back; and so, painfully and slowly, brought him off.

Even as we did so, we could see on the crest of the far hills behind the figures of men on foot and horse moving our way; and, nearer at hand, when we stood and halted a moment, the sound of a trumpet broke the air.

There was no time to lose, verily, if these worn-out Dons were to leave the place alive. And as for Ludar and me, wounded and weak as we were, what chance was there for us to break through the lines and wander on foot in search of our lost ones?

"Humphrey," said Ludar, guessing what was in my mind, "we sail with the Don to Scotland. Thence we will cross to the Glynns, and so be where we must be sooner than if we ventured by land."

"So be it," said I.

The sight of the wounded Don completed the panic which had already set in among the Spaniards at the report of the coming of the English.

A HIDEOUS SCENE

"To sea! to sea!" they cried, and followed us as we bore their beloved captain to the bay.

The *Gerona*, Ludar told me, had been found on the coast, a half wreck, some weeks since, and, by dint of great labour and patching, had been made passably seaworthy.

"She will carry but three out of every four of this company," said he. "After the nobles are all on board, there will be but place, I hear, for one hundred beside, and these must work at the oars. Lots have already been drawn, and, unless I mistake, 'twill be a hard parting betwixt those who go and those who stay."

So indeed it was. No sooner had we the Don safely on board, and delivered him to the leech (to whom he opened his eyes, and showed signs of returning life), than a strange turbulent scene ensued on shore. The Don's second in command, fine gentleman as he was, had little power to deal with a rabble that was fighting for dear life. He drew up his men on the beach and bade no man stir for the boats till his name was called, under penalty of death.

While the young nobles (who, of course, were exempt from lot) silently and anxiously took their places in the boats and were rowed out to the ship, all stood gloomily by, mute and obedient. But when, these being safely embarked, the order was given for the hundred who had drawn the lot to follow, a hubbub and tumult began which it was pitiful to witness. Men, desperate with hunger and fear, fought tooth and nail to reach the boats. They that had the right and they that had none were mingled in a fray which strewed the water's edge with corpses. Some flung themselves into the sea after the boats, yelling and cursing till the flash of a sword or the pitiless thud of an oar sent them back into silence. Some, rather than others should go and not they, tore the craft board from board, and fought with the fragments. Some with muskets poured fire on the boats. And some wreaked their vengeance on the haughty Spanish gallant and hurled him from the rock on which he stood into the depths below.

'Twas a hideous scene; and when, after all was done, sixty gasping souls scrambled on board, glaring at one another like beasts of prey, and hissing defiant taunts at the wretches on shore, it boded ill—very—ill for this voyage.

For a while neither Ludar nor I was fit to take our seat

SIR LUDAR

on the thwarts or lend a hand with the oars, much as help was needed.

For two days, indeed, the *Gerona's* sails were of little service owing to the perverse south-wester, which threatened to imprison us in the bay of Killibegs, and well-nigh defied every effort of the crew to bring the galley beyond the great headland of Malinmore.

But once out in the open, where the south-wester would have favoured our course to Scotland, the wind veered to westward and drove us in perilously near the rocks. So that we at the oars (for, by then, Ludar and I perforce had to take our share of the toil) were kept hard at work, and the roar of breakers on our starboard quarter never ceased, day nor night.

The *Gerona*, moreover, had been but indifferently patched, and, in the heavy sea across which she laboured, answered her helm hardly, and could by no means be counted upon to sail more than a point or two out of the wind. So in this hard cross gale her canvas was all but useless, and, had it not been for the oars, she would have been on the rocks about the Bloody Foreland before a week was out.

How we rounded that dreadful head I scarce know. Strong man as I was, I was well-nigh dead with the endless toil of the rowing, broken only by short snatches of repose when I laid my head down in the galley-slaves' reeking hold. Ludar, on the contrary, grew mightier and bolder day by day. He neither wearied nor lost heart; but like a man who has recovered faith in his destiny, he talked as if each stroke brought us nearer, not to Scotland, but to the end of our hopes and the arms of those we loved.

"Courage, Humphrey," said he, "I can row for you and me both. Save your heart, brother, for those who shall welcome you when all this tossing and toil shall be passed."

"You talk of beyond the grave."

"Beyond the grave!" cried he. "I never talked less of it. Come, are you, too, like these Spanish gentles, down in the mouth for a puff of wind and a pailful or two of salt water over the deck? Courage, man. If you be an Englishman, show these Dons how an Englishman can hold up his head and keep a stiff upper lip."

That brought up the courage in me; and though for a day or so the weakness of my thews caused me to rest my

PRAY FOR THOSE AT SEA

hands idly on the oar, while he lugged at it cheerily and mightily, my heart came up from my boots and knocked louder and stronger within me day by day.

So, after ten days out, we came off the black headland called Malin, where, as the wind still held westerly, the welcome order was given to ship oars and spread all canvas for the Scottish coast.

Ludar alone looked grave when the order came, and pointed to the furious, livid swirl of purple clouds that crowded round the setting sun.

"I have seen yon sky before," said he, "often when I was a boy. And they taught us, when we saw it, to pray the saints for those at sea."

"May be there are saints ashore who see it and pray for us to-night," said I.

"There had need be," said he, solemnly.

CHAPTER XXXI

How we came into Calm Water after all

LUDAR'S forecast was destined to a swift and sudden fulfilment. The red glare was scarcely out of the west when the wind began to howl and whistle through our rigging with a presage of the tempest that was to come. What was of worse omen still, the long streamer on the main-mast, which hitherto had spread due eastward, now suddenly flapped to south-east, showing that the gale was coming upon us from the one quarter we had most cause to dread, namely, the north-west.

For, as Ludar well knew by this time, unless we could keep the *Gerona's* head out so as to clear the far Antrim Headlands of Bengore and Benmore, we ran the peril of being driven in on an iron-bound shore, which had short shrift and little mercy for such as fell upon it.

The danger soon became manifest to others beside Ludar, and once again the oars were ordered out and the ship's head put across the wind.

Ludar and I were among the party of cursing and mutinous rowers whose turn it was to be relieved, and we were about to crawl below for a snatch of repose, when a messenger came from Don Alonzo bidding Ludar attend him.

"Come with me," said Ludar, and we followed the man.

Don Alonzo, who, from the moment he could stand upright, had resumed his post of command, stood in his cabin, pale and stern, surrounded by his officers, who, by their uneasy study of the charts before them, were plainly alive to the peril that threatened the ship.

"Sir Ludar," said he, "your presence on board is not without a fortunate meaning for us. The account betwixt us runs high already. I have no means to pay you, but by

THE GALE IN FULL FURY

demanding a further service at your hands. You know this Irish coast well?"

"I have sailed from Malin Head to Cantire in an open galley many a time as a boy," said Ludar.

"And you know specially the coast about your father's castle, and this great causeway of rocks near it?" said he, pointing on the chart to Dunluce and the jagged headlands beyond.

"I know them, every inch," said Ludar.

"Then," said Don Alonzo, "I make a request of you, Sir Ludar, in the name of my master, the King of Spain."

"'Tis more than enough," said he. "Ask me in your own name. I owe you, Sir Don, more than I do the King of Spain."

"Well, then, will you honour me and my company by taking the helm, and, if it be possible, clearing us of the peril which this foul wind threatens?"

"I will do my best," said he. "But I doubt the ship's power to keep a course across the wind. 'Twill need more than one man at the tiller; and, by your leave, I appoint my comrade here to assist me."

"So be it," said Don Alonzo. "And, whatever befal, we thank you, Sir Ludar, for this service."

Thus honourably did Ludar M'Donnell step, where he deserved, to a post of command on board this ship. As for me, 'twas glory enough to stand his second; and, so soon as I saw his hand on the helm, all my doubts of our safe passage round the headlands and on to Scotland, were at an end.

Not so his.

"I have undertaken more than I can perform," said he, "and the Don knows it. If this wind hold, nothing can persuade this lob-sided, ill-trimmed craft out of the bay. Away with sleep, man! and chain down the helm across the wind. Bid them put all their strength on the starboard oars."

An hour after that the gale broke in full fury from the north-west. It must have caught us some two leagues north of Malin Head; for, as we drove down before it, we could hear a thunder of breakers on our right, which Ludar pronounced to be the Tor Rocks, off the island of Instrahull.

"'Tis a mercy to be past them, anyhow," said he. "But see, for all our turning of the helm, we are driving down the wind."

SIR LUDAR

So indeed we were. To our dismay, the *Gerona* sailed almost as far sideways as she did forward; and, had we not been well out to seaward to start with, we might have been hard put to it even to clear the headlands of Innishowen.

About midnight there was nothing for it but to order the sails to be let go, and depend only on the oars for our course. After that, for a while, we went better. But the men, worn out and dispirited, pulled with but half a heart; and hour by hour the vessel drifted in, until it was clear that nothing but a shifting of the wind or standing to at anchor could keep us off the opposite rocks.

Off Innishowen, as we crossed the mouth of the Foyle river, we fell on a shoal of terrible shallows, which spun the *Gerona* round like a top, and washed her in raging foam from stem to stern.

"Go and tell the Don he must either let go his anchors, or double the men at the oars," said Ludar, when presently we had staggered out again into blacker water.

Word was given immediately to try the former, and the only two anchors we had were let over. For a moment or two, as the ship swung round, creaking in every joint, it seemed as if she would ride out the gale thus. But with a report like the crack of a gun, first one, then the other of her cables broke short at the gunwale, and we knew we had only lost time and water in the attempt.

Instantly the Don called upon his nobles to volunteer for the oars. Gallantly they responded; and occupied the after benches, while all the slaves rowed forward. Then, for an hour, the *Gerona* seemed to hold her own, and reeled across the bay on an eastward course.

But, presently, even the lordlings of Spain flagged, and once again we drove in, amid the thunder of surf, on an ever nearing shore.

"We should be near the Bann mouth," said I. "To think of the last time we heard that thunder together!"

"We are clear of that," said Ludar, quietly. "Tell the Don his lordlings must work harder if we are to weather the next point."

I told the Don as much, hat in hand; and once again the gentles gathered themselves together and made a course for the labouring ship.

DRIVING ON TO THE BREAKERS

Ludar was breathing hard when I returned to his side.

"That may put us past Ramore," said he. "In the bay beyond that lies Dunluce. If we be driven in there, Heaven help us indeed!"

"I would as soon perish there as anywhere else."

"Talk not of perishing, fool, while a hope remains! Bid the Don cut away his poles forthwith. They are worse than useless now."

So, one after another the stately masts of the *Gerona* went by the board, and the ease their going gave us, added to the fresh vigour of the rowers, helped us, as Ludar foretold, round the rough little head of Ramore.

No sooner had we passed it than the wind and current together got hold of us again and swept us in betwixt the islands of the Skerries and the mainland. Not even twice the number of rowers could have saved us then.

"Listen!" said Ludar presently.

I listened, and could hear ahead of me a thunder deeper and more awful than any we had yet passed.

"What is it?" I asked.

"My father's castle," said he. "We are going home with a vengeance now!"

Scarce a man remained at the oars. We could hear shouts of praying and cursing intermingled, as all hands crowded to the decks and gazed forward in the direction of that warning sound.

A lanthorn on the quarter-deck showed us the Don, standing there alone, bareheaded, in his steel breastplate, and sword in hand, quietly waiting the end. Beyond was a troubled crowd of doomed men, counting the moments and straining their eyes into the darkness.

Beside me, on the poop, Ludar stood erect and noble, with the half-defiant, half-triumphant gleam on his face, as, with hands still on the tiller, he listened to the fatal music of his old home ahead.

In the darkness we could see nothing but the white waste of breakers on to which we were driving.

Presently, as we were almost upon them, Ludar grasped my arm, and pointed high overhead.

There was a momentary gleam of light, and with it a glimpse of a rugged battlement at the rock's edge.

SIR LUDAR

"Dunluce! Dunluce!" he shouted, and let swing the now useless tiller.

Scarce a minute later the *Gerona* was in her death agony among the lashing breakers.

For a moment or two she held up bravely. Then with a mighty swirl she reared upward and hung quivering an instant in suspense.

Ludar's hand and mine sought one another, and, as we waited thus, we could see above us the noble form of Don Alonzo, cool and impassive as a man on parade, saluting his King's ensign for the last time.

Then all I remember was a great yell from the slaves at the poop, and the dull thunder of a broadside, as the *Gerona* fell crashing to her doom.

* * * * * *

It was broad daylight when I opened my eyes and saw the sun struggling to break through the black clouds overhead. The thunder of waves still dinned in my ear, the salt wind was still on my lips, while a sharp pain at my shoulder, when I turned my head to look about me, told me that I was at least alive.

The pain was so acute that I closed my eyes again, and opened them not till I heard the sound of a harsh voice at my side.

What it said I know not, but some one turned me over with his foot, and brought from me a cry of agony which made him reel a pace or two back in consternation.

Then, just as I heard another voice, in plain English, say, "Great God, he lives!" all was dim again before my eyes. Once more the pain awaked me; and I found myself lying, I suppose, on some stretcher, being slowly borne on men's shoulders up a steep path. I was too weak to do aught but groan, and my groans my bearers heard not. But at last the English voice said; "Halt, and set him down. He may be dead already and so save us the pains of carrying him further."

'Twas a voice I knew; but the agony of my setting down made me forget whose, until once more bending over me, and putting back the hair from my brow, the fellow exclaimed:

"Why, this is—mercy on us!—if it be not him they called Dexter."

"What!" cried another voice, "doth Neptunus yield us

WHAT OF LUDAR?

pearls? and on these inhospitable shores doth Arion indeed discover his lost 'prentice? hath the Hollander wings to carry——"

"A curse on thy tom-fooling tongue!" said the other. "Hath not the poor wretch had drenching enough, that you must spout thus on the top of him? Say, Humphrey Dexter, how fare you?"

"Is that you, Jack Gedge?"

"Sure enough."

"And Ludar?"

The fellow gave a gasp, but said nothing. And, in the horror of that silence, I lost all care of life.

I must have been lying still in the same place when next, with a strange thrill of wonder, I lifted my eyes and saw, bent over me, the sweet face of my own Jeannette.

"Humphrey," whispered she, as she kissed my wet brow, "is it indeed thou?"

"Aye, sweetheart," said I.

And I forgot all else for a while.

Presently they carried me up to the top of the path, Jeannette walking with her hand in mine. And so, till before us rose a grim portal which I knew well to be the gate of Dunluce.

The sight of that familiar entry recalled to my mind the great burden on my heart.

"Jeannette," said I, as she bent beside me. "What of Ludar?"

"We hope, dear Humphrey, thine is not the only life saved from the wreck."

"Is he heard of? And the maiden——?" I asked.

"I know not. Till you named him just now, no one knew he was with you. But now the soldier and the poet have gone to seek news. And my dear mistress, I think, waits here."

"She is here? How come you both in Dunluce?" I asked.

"The old M'Donnell will not allow the maiden out of his sight, so dearly he loves her," said Jeannette.

As soon as I was laid in a bed, and my broken arm set by the castle leech, I revived quickly. And as I did so, the load on my heart concerning Ludar grew so heavy, that not even the presence of Jeannette could banish it.

I begged to see the maiden.

SIR LUDAR

'Twas wonderful to see her as she came in, stately and beautiful as ever, betraying only in the pallor of her cheeks the terrible anguish that possessed her.

She came and kissed me like a sister, and then, laying her hand in Jeannette's, tears came to her eyes as she gave us joy of our happy meeting, after so much peril.

"Maiden," said I, "we know no happiness while you stand thus desolate. But Ludar lives. As sure as I lie here, you shall find him, and we shall all thank Heaven together."

Her face brightened.

"You have said as much before," said she, "and it has come to pass. Yes, I will hope still."

But her voice fell sadly with the words, and her face turned to the window, seaward.

Then she bade me tell her what had passed since we parted in London, and how Ludar and I came on the *Gerona*. And, hearing of all the chances that had befallen us, I think she took a little hope that all this buffetting and peril was not assuredly to end in loss.

But she said nothing. Only she kept her hand in Jeannette's; and when I told her of the horrible scene on the bog by Killybegs, she shuddered, and muttered what, I fear, was a prayer for the soul of a dead man.

"But how come you in Dunluce?" I asked again, presently.

'Twas Jeannette who answered me.

"'Tis easily told, dear Humphrey. After Sir Turlogh departed for Dublin, leaving us in charge of this "—here she shivered—" this Captain Merriman, my mistress and I kept our chambers, and durst not so much as venture beyond the door. Our good protectors—Heaven reward them!—had been banished the place; and but for a few of the O'Neill's men, who stood in the way, we had not been safe where we were for a day.

"At last, one day, there came suddenly a messenger, purporting to be from the O'Neill, bidding the Captain send his daughter to him under an escort to Dublin. On this the Captain rudely broke into our chambers, and bade us there and then set out. What could two weak maids do? We could read treachery in his wicked eye, yet naught we could say or pretend could put him off; and there and then, without

HARD TO LIE STILL

time so much as to speak a word to one another, we were marched forth, like prisoners, and mounted on our steeds.

"Just as we set forth, he came up to the leader of our party, and said in a whisper I could overhear: 'Remember—the mistress to the house by the wood, and the little one to Dublin—and hands off.' Then all the villainy of the thing flashed on me in a moment. 'Mistress,' cried I, 'we are betrayed!' But before the words were out, a rough hand was laid across my mouth, and we were galloping. Nay, Humphrey," said she, laying her hand gently on mine, "if thou start and toss like this, 'tis a sign my story doeth thee harm, and I will cease."

"Would you have me lie still and hear all this?" cried I, in a fever.

"Yes, dear heart," said she, and that so sweetly that I was forced to obey. "We were galloping away from Castleroe. For a whole day we galloped, till we were faint and ready to drop. Then, as we came to a wood, which I guessed to be the place where my mistress and I were to be parted, our leader suddenly reined in and turned to give an order to the man who held me. As he did so, four men sprang out from among the trees and a horrible fight ensued. In the midst of it, one of the new-comers advanced to me and said, 'You are safe!' and I knew it to be no other than the soldier Gedge himself."

"And he who came to my side," put in the maiden, smiling amid her heaviness, "said: 'Let Diana shake off her clouds. Apollo himself hath come to lead her out into the Empyrean.'"

"God reward them both for this!" said I.

"Amen," said Jeannette. "Two of the villains they slew and the other staggered away, as I fear, mortally wounded. 'Twas him you saw.

"As for us, our rescuers brought us here, where the M'Donnell hath welcomed us, and, as you know, loveth my mistress as his own daughter. Yet, little thought we, as we looked out from the turret window at the storm last night, and prayed side by side for those at sea, that you, and—and Sir Ludar were coming to us on the wild waves!"

The day wore on, and still neither soldier nor poet nor any news came to comfort us.

Then I demanded to be taken to Sorley Boy M'Donnell,

and the maiden led my tottering steps to the great hall. There sat the old man, bareheaded and motionless, at the head of the empty table, with his sword laid out before him.

"Is my son come?" demanded he, as we entered.

"Not yet, dear sire," said the maiden, going to him.

"He is not far away, sir," said I; "of that I am sure."

"I know that," said the old chief, half angrily. "The Banshee has been dumb since Alexander M'Donnell fell. Why comes not Ludar? I grow impatient."

Even as he spoke there came a knocking on the door, and a Scot entered hastily.

He brought news that in a hut a mile eastward of the castle a man had been found, who had been brought up from the shore, dead; and that, further east still, the bodies of——

Here Sorley Boy smote his fist on the table, and ordered the fellow to hold his peace.

"I want no news of the dead," said he, wrathfully, "but of the living. Where is my son Ludar?"

The man slunk off chap-fallen.

The maiden knelt beside the old man's chair, and laid her white cheek on his rough sleeve. Jeannette drew me gently to a bench at the far corner of the hall, and bade me rest there beside her.

Thus, while the afternoon slowly wore into evening, and the storm without moaned itself to sleep, we sat there in silence.

About sundown, just as—despite the sweet presence at my side—I was growing drowsy with weariness and pain, Sorley Boy suddenly uttered an exclamation and rose to his feet. The maiden rose too. And as she stood, motionless but for the heaving of her bosom, the slanting rays of the sun caught her and kindled her face into a wondrous glow.

Jeannette's gentle hand restrained me, as the old man, taking a step or two down the room as far as the end of the table, stood there facing the door. Then there fell on my ears a voice and the ring of a footstep in the courtyard without. Next moment, the door swung open and Ludar walked quietly in.

Jeannette led me softly from the place, and kept me cruelly pacing in the outer darkness for half-an-hour before she said:

"Art thou not going in to welcome thy friend, Humphrey?"

SAFE IN PORT

Need I say what passed, when at last we stood all four together in that great hall?

The old chief had taken his seat again at the table, and sat there solemn and impassive, as if all that had passed had been but the ordinary event of an afternoon. But the fire in his eye betrayed him, as now and again he half turned his head to the window where Ludar and the maiden stood gazing out across the waves.

"Humphrey, my brother," said Ludar, when at last Jeannette and I drew near, "'tis worth a little storm to be thus in port at last, and to find you there too."

"Aye, indeed," said I. "And, as you see, there are more than I here to greet you."

Then he stepped up to Jeannette and gazed in her face a moment, and kissed her on the brow.

"Thou art welcome to Dunluce, sister Jeannette," said he.

Jeannette told me afterwards that she never felt so proud in her life as when Ludar's lips touched her forehead, and she heard him call her sister.

'Twas not in me to complain that it should be so; for the ways of women are beyond my understanding.

Presently the old man rose from his seat, and without a word left us to ourselves. Ludar then narrated how, when the *Gerona* broke up, he had fallen near a broken oar, which held him up and enabled him to reach land almost without a bruise. For a long while he lay in the darkness, not knowing where he was; but when day broke, he found himself in the deep cave that goes under the castle, a prisoner there by the rising tide, and with no means of escape. For to stem the waves at the mouth was hopeless, and by no manner of shouting and calling could he make his presence known to anyone outside.

So all day, faint with hunger, he had perched on a ledge just beyond reach of the tide, and not till evening, when the wind, and with it the water, subsided, was he able to swim out and come to land at the foot of the very path up which, long months ago, he had led the party who recovered Dunluce for the M'Donnells.

His story was scarce ended when a cheering without called us to the courtyard, where the news of the return of Sir Ludar

SIR LUDAR

had gathered the M'Donnells, eager with shouts and music to welcome him.

But Ludar would by no means go out till his father arrived to command it. Then it did us, who loved him, good to see him stand there, with the maiden's hand in his, receiving the homage of his clansmen.

While thus we stood, there was an uproar at the gate, as two men fought their way through the throng and approached us.

"Jove and the Muses grant their beloved son a soul to celebrate so notable a festival in the strains which it deserves!" cried the poet, shaking all over with emotion, and his eyes dim with tears. "Achilles hath his Briseïs; Odysseus his lost Penelope, and all four have to their hand an Orpheus (woe's me! without his Eurydice) to chant their fortunes. Oh! my noble son of a wolf, and thou, my Hollander, how I rejoice to see you, and to hand to your arms the nymphs of whom one day, perhaps, it shall be accounted to their honour that they were nourished on the dews of Parnassus by the Muses' most unworthy disciple."

"A nice dry nurse you be!" said Jack Gedge. "'Tis a mercy the fair ladies have their ear-drums sound after half-a-year of your noisy buzzing in them. Sir Ludar, by your leave, captain, you hold in your hand what you gave me in charge to keep for you; so I owe you nought but my farewell."

"Nay," said Ludar. "By heaven, we are all debtors to you both, and shall compel you to own it. And since you both and my comrade here be Englishmen, let me tell you that, for your sakes, I shall salute your Queen's ensign when I next see it."

That night the poet related to me with much embellishment and flourish all that had passed since the maids left London, most of which I already knew, yet was not loth to hear again from his lips.

"Thank me no thanks, my Hollander," said he, when once more I blessed him for the serivce he had done. "The poet's glory cometh not from earth. I have, while I waited here, written an excellent and notable epic on the wars of the illustrious house of the M'Donnells, the which I will even now rehearse thee for thy delectation. And when once more thou art returned to thy press, I reserve for thee the glory of

LITTLE MORE TO BE TOLD

imprinting three noble copies of the same on paper of vellum, to be bound after the manner of the Venetians, in white, with clasps of gold, to be given, one to my lord Sorley Boy, one to Sir Ludar, and one to thee, for thy private and particular delectation."

Again I thanked him, and begged he would reserve the reading till to-morrow, when I should be more wakeful.

To which, marvelling much at my patience, he agreed.

"As for me," said he, "naught falleth ill to the favourites of the Immortals. I owe no grudge to the day I took thee into my protection. As a printer, count on me as thy patron. As a man, call me thy friend. And if some day, at thy frugal fireside (for the which thou art already provided with the chiefest ornament), thou shouldst have a spare chair and platter, I will even deign to fill the one and empty the other now and again, in memory of this, our time of fellowship. Therefore count on me, my Hollander ; and so, good night."

. . . .

There is little more to be told. Of the crew of the doomed *Gerona*, the tide washed some hundreds, before many weeks were past, into a bay near the Causeway Headlands, east of Dunluce. Amongst them, Ludar and I discovered the body of Don Alonzo, calm and gentle in death, and buried him with what honour we could in holy ground near the tomb of the M'Donnells. A few cannon and guns we helped haul up and set on the walls of Dunluce, where they are to this day, much to the wrath of my Lord Deputy and his English Councillors.

Jack Gedge remains body servant to Sir Ludar M'Donnell ; where, if his trust be not so great as it was (now that his master and mistress are one), he is none the less faithful or joyous in his service.

As for the poet, he was true to his promise of visiting Jeannette and me at our frugal fireside. But this was not for many years after the promise was given.

As soon as my arm was healed and I could persuade Ludar to release me, I returned to London, to find the house without Temple Bar still empty, and Master Walgrave's name still a caution to evil-doers. Despairing of seeing me and his type from Rochelle, he had sold himself to those firebrands Masters Udal and Penry ; and by means of his secret press had given utterance to certain scandalous and seditious libels on the

SIR LUDAR

bishops and clergy of the Church, known by the name of Marprelate, his books. A merry chase he gave the beadle and pursuivants all over the country, dropping libels wherever he went, till at last he suddenly vanished and left them to whistle.

For Jeannette's sake as well as my own I wandered far for news of him, and heard of him at last from Mistress Crane as having fled to Rochelle with all his family. Thither I wrote him of my welfare, and had a letter back bidding me, if I was still minded to serve him, meet him in Edinburgh. Thither, then, I took sail, and presently found him; and should you meet with any books imprinted by Robert Walgrave, Printer to the King's Most Excellent Majesty in Edinburgh, know that the hand that set them in type was the same which now writes this true history.

In due season Mistress Walgrave and the little ones came northward too; and one glad day I wandered to the western coast, and there met Ludar and his fair bride, and with them my own sweet Jeannette, from whom I never parted more.

Ere this happy meeting took place, Sorley Boy M'Donnell had ended his stormy days and was gathered to his fathers, and Sir James M'Donnell, his son, became Lord of Dunluce.

Ludar dwelt quietly on his lands in Cantire, refusing allegiance to any crowned monarch, but loyal to the end to his wife, his clan, his comrade, and to the memory of those perils and chances which had made him and me brothers.

THE END

www.ingramcontent.com/pod-product-compliance
Lightning Source LLC
Chambersburg PA
CBHW022025240426
43667CB00042B/1178